Right to Information and the Grievance Redressal System in India

Right to Information and the Grievance Redressal System in India

Dr. Bibhuti Bhusan Nayak

LEXINGTON BOOKS
Lanham • Boulder • New York • London

Published by Lexington Books
An imprint of The Rowman & Littlefield Publishing Group, Inc.
4501 Forbes Boulevard, Suite 200, Lanham, Maryland 20706
www.rowman.com

86-90 Paul Street, London, EC2A 4NE

British Library Cataloguing in Publication Information Available

Library of Congress Cataloging-in-Publication Data Available

ISBN 9781666925647 (cloth)
ISBN 9781666925654 (e-book)

Dedicated
To
My Parents

Contents

List of Figures

List of Tables

Acknowledgments

To me every journey is an adventure. Working on this book has been one of the most challenging and learning experiences of my life. I feel that this work would be incomplete without expressing my gratitude and obligation to those who have provided me the valuable cooperation in completing this book. I find myself overwhelmed by the limitless, unflinching, and untiring generosity of not just family, friends, and academicians but also of people that I interacted with at different stages of my journey. While it is impossible to individually document the contribution of each of these individuals, I can only hope to indicate the depth of my gratitude by mentioning their names here. Those who have wished to remain anonymous must remain unacknowledged in name, and I hope that this book has done at least some measure of justice to their contributions.

I take this opportunity to tender my heartfelt love and regard to my elder brother Prof. Bhabani Sankar Nayak for strength, support, encouragement, and valuable suggestion in spite of his heavy academic pressure at Coventry University, UK. He never forgot to call even a single day and ask me about the progress of this work which made it possible for me to complete this challenging work in time.

I tender my deep sense of gratitude and indebtedness to my father for his constant moral support that made it possible to me to undertake this work.

Further good wishes to my brothers Sibani and Sidharth for their constant source of motivation and emotional support which stimulated me to keep on working on this book.

I take this opportunity to tender my heartfelt gratitude and reverence to all my esteemed teachers especially Dr. Susama Mohanty, Prof. Swarnamayee Tripathy, Dr. Padmalaya Mahapatra, Prof. Brahmananda Satpathy, Prof.

Bijayani Mohanty, Prof. Suryanaryana Mishra, Prof. S. P. Guru, Prof Johani Xaxa, Dr. R. K. Kujur, and Mrs. S. Mishra for their constant inspiration and meaningful suggestions.

I tender my deep sense of gratitude and indebtedness to Mr. Vishal K. Dev (IAS), Dr. Prasanta Pradhan (IAS), Mr. Pradeep Jena (IAS), Mr. Tarunkanti Mishra (IAS), Mr. Sunil Kumar Mishara (IAS), and Mrs. Sashiprava Bindhani (IAS) for their encouragement and cooperation from the primary to the final stage of this work.

I extend my heartfelt thanks to Geeta didi for her love, encouragement, and support.

I am thankful to all my friends especially Smita and Subhalaxmi and Babita and Baijayanti for their cooperation and encouragement.

I am thankful to Carter Moran and Joseph Parry of Lexington Books, an imprint of the Rowman and Littlefield Publishing Group for their timely editorial support in the making of this book.

In the end, after giving all sincere attention, I, however, have to admit that this list is still incomplete and I, therefore, apologize to anyone I might have omitted.

Dr. Bibhuti Bhusan Nayak
Odisha, August 12, 2022

Introduction

The right to information (RTI) was provided in the form of legislation to the people of India on October 12, 2005. India's Right to Information (RTI) Act 2005 has been described as a revolution and acclaimed as even the most radical legislation since the introduction of Constitution of India. The RTI has been a fundamental right of every Indian citizen, being part of the freedom of speech and expression enshrined in Article 19(1)A of the Constitution of India. The struggle for transparency and accountability at the grassroots level has created a social revolution of sorts in India as far as enforcement of the freedom of speech and expression is concerned. The promulgation of this RTI Act has been able to touch the lives of the common man despite stiff resistance from the government and the bureaucracy.

It is important to consider that the quality of individual life in a civilized society depends upon the quality of exchange of information about the governance and other related aspects. It is not possible for any democratic government to survive without accountability and transparency, which can be realized only when the people have information about the functioning of the government. Thus, the RTI of an individual is one of the important democratic privileges and one of the essential requirements of good governance. However, the numerous debates and controversies that have arisen after the implementation of the Act and thereafter the frictions created between the affected parties, that is, the government, bureaucracy, and judiciary, on one hand, and the general public, on the other hand. The governmental and institutional support for the RTI is important to develop effective mechanisms and procedures for the redressal of the employee's grievances. It is important to analyze whether this act has been able to actually result in citizens' empowerment by ensuring accountability. While a lot has been said in praise and appreciation of the act, it is important to examine whether the act has actually been able to deliver all that is promised. It is a common critique of this act that it has led to an additional burden on a bureaucracy that is already crumbling under pressure. Also, this book initiates analysis into the debate of whether the act leads to an actual redressal of grievances or is it merely an attempt to gather innocuous information that may not have further use, which leads this book into the third most important question, that is, whether the absence of an in-built redressal mechanism defeats the core purpose for which the act was promulgated. A quasi-judicial system of addressing complaints regarding the denial of information has sprung up from the genesis of this act. However, it seems that instead of reducing the burden on the judicial system of India, the act has resulted in increasing the cases related to denial of information from public offices that have reached the courts of law.

First, this book is an effort on exploring many legal lacunas which the new legislation works with and henceforth weakens the objectives prescribed to justify the need for such an act for governance reforms. Second, this book is trying to explore how the RTI Act redresses the grievances of the common people. Third, this book focuses on administrative procedures of bureaucracy and working of Public Information officer and appellate authorities in the different departments of the Odisha Secretariat. Finally, this research is an attempt toward accountability and how the grievance redressal mechanism related to work culture in India.

Since this book deeply engages into the practical application of law at the operational level, it is very significant in the present times.

Dr. Bibhuti Bhusan Nayak

Chapter 1

Right to Information and Public Accountability

BACKDROP

The global movement toward a knowledge-based information society as a prelude to institutional reform has led to many state-led initiatives toward achieving this objective. Information as a plea for knowledge-based governance and as a condition for accountable governance has in recent times become a challenging objective for democracy and citizen's rights all over the world. Indian governance has also witnessed this rights-based approach to access information. Max Weber (Blau 1956)[1] attributes the concept of "official secret" as the specific invention of bureaucracy which is also defended strongly by the bureaucracy and official or government documents are kept secret by the bureaucracy. The greatest blow to the Indian democracy is diminishing credibility of the government and its machinery due to ever-rising corruption, wasteful expenditure, and other malpractices under the cover of the Official Secret Act 1923. The RTI Act was introduced into public departments to enhance institutional accountability and citizens' access to seeking information from an otherwise secretive and closed bureaucracy.

Information to citizens about administrative action is undoubtedly a vital component for fair democracy. The down fall of existing society is due to lack of information as well as the development of existing society is through the help of information. Information is a powerful tool that provides people with the knowledge to demand political, economic, and social right from their governments. Sharing that information with the people at large, we promote decentralization and participatory governance.[2]

The RTI Act in Odisha which aims at a transparent, proactive good governance is regarded as a historic enactment, whereas the preamble of the Act aims at an informed citizenry and transparency of information for containing corruption in the system. The third president of the USA Thomas Jefferson remarked rightly—"We must realise seriously that information is the currency of the democracy whenever the people are well informed they can be trusted with their own government." It reflects that the RTI Act is one of the strongest pillars of democracy in the era of globalization. An informed citizenry and transparency in governance are vital to the functioning of a vibrant democracy in which corruption is minimal and the government and its instrumentalities are transparent and accountable to its people. The RTI is a unique and unprecedented effort in strengthening grassroots democracy in India. The genesis of RTI may be located exactly in this liberal democratic paradigm (Messick 1993; Tarlo 2003).[3]

As Madison said in 1982, "Popular government without popular information with means of acquiring it is but a prologue to a farce or tragedy or perhaps both." A democratic society has given liberty and equality to its citizens to realize the goals of life. This goal can be realized with the help and proper functioning of the administrative machinery called as state government (Ferguson 1994).[4] Democracy can be successful only when the people take an active interest and participation in the political activities. People cannot remain silent spectators to all that the government does, nor can they remain quiet once they elect their representatives. In the course of the last 60 years, a lot of development has taken place. Yet, the government has not done much to provide basic amenities like drinking water, health services, sanitation, and education. People have waited for a long time and their patience is exhausted.

It is important to analyze whether this Act has been able to actually result in citizen's empowerment by ensuring accountability. While a lot has been said in praise and appreciation of the Act, it is important to examine whether the Act has actually been able to deliver all that it promised. It is a common critique of this Act that it has led to an additional burden on a bureaucracy that is already crumbling under pressure (Harvey, David, 2005).[5] Also, this book initiates analysis into the debate of whether the Act leads to an actual redressal of grievances or is it merely an attempt to gather innocuous information which may not have further use, which leads this book into the third most important question, that is, whether the absence of an in-built redressal mechanism defeats the core purpose with which the Act was promulgated.

Even after 70 years of parliamentary rule, we saw that people were denied of information in the name of "official secrecy." No doubt, the governments carried out so -called development programs and projects. However, in most of these cases, there was no accountability on the part of the government. But, after passing the RTI Act, people are empowered with a strong weapon to monitor the government activities. After nearly 70 years of independence, the citizens of India have a real opportunity to exercise this very important right and the RTI is redefining the relationship between the government and citizens. The Supreme Court of India has on more than one occasion declared that the RTI is a fundamental right under the Indian Constitution (see Swamy Raju Naryana 2011).[6]

The RTI is a part of the fundamental rights under Article 19 (1) of the Constitution. Article 19 (1) says that every citizen has freedom of speech and expression. As early in 1976, the Supreme Court said in the case of *Raj Narain v. State of U.P.* that people cannot speak or express themselves unless they know (Godbole Madhab 2003).[7] Therefore RTI is embedded in Article 19, in the same case, Supreme Court further said that India is a democratic country. People are the masters. Therefore the masters have a right to know how the government meant to serve them and is functioning further, and also every citizen pays taxes. Even a beggar on the street pays taxes (in the form of sale tax, excise duty, etc.) when he buys a piece of soap from the market; the citizens therefore have the right to know how their money is being spent and these three principles (freedom of speech and expression, the right to know about the functioning of the government, and citizens paying taxes) were laid down by Supreme Court while saying that RTI is a part of our fundamental right (Noorani. AG, 2006).[8]

The RTI bill, 2005, in the summer session, introduced by the Union Ministry of Personnel, Public Grievances and Pensions, was passed by the Lok Sabha on May 11, 2005, and the Rajya Sabha on May 12, 2005, and received the presidential assent on June 15, 2005. It comes on the statute book as "RTI Act—2005" (Act 22 of 2005). It came into full force on the October 12th, 2005, except the State of Jammu and Kashmir as an improvement over its earlier version Freedom of the Information Act (FOIA), 2002, is a significant constructive approach and a welcome step toward a more transparent and informed social order in the democratic republic of India (Madabhushi. Sridhar, 2007).[9]

At this juncture, moving the bill the then-prime minister Dr. Manmohan Singh said that "the bill would usher in a new era of performance and transparency to benefit the common man in the complex modern world and empower the people to judge if the government was functioning in public interest." RTI will give public-spirited people an instrument to prevent the misuse of public power and funds. He said that the intention of the bill is to enlarge the interface between people and government and not to paralyze the administration. RTI Act would not only provide open surgery to the administration but also make efforts to improve the health of administrative system (Das Bhabesh and Bhattacharyya Rajiv. K 2007).[10] Amartya Sen argued that, "You don't have famines in a country that has a free press." He has further demonstrated that inequality of access of information is a type of poverty. The RTI Act aims at removing this inequality of access to information and empowering the citizen (Sen Amartya 1982).[11]

The freedom fighters had dreamed of a free India as "Ram Rajya." But soon after independence, all the moral and ethical values were thrown to winds. People in general and politicians in particular became selfish and self-centered. As a result, rampant corruption made its way in all walks of life. By hook or crook grab the power and make the hay when the sun shines became the mantra for our politicians. People had no choice but silently watch the politicians' tamasha because people had no knowledge of the politicians' doings and dealings and their underhand dealings (Chalfin, Brenda. 2010).[12] However, RTI Act brought a great change.

CONCEPTUAL FRAMEWORK

RTI is the basic ingredient of democracy. It is an instrument to hold the government and the state machinery accountable. The core subject of this study is the RTI Act which was promulgated in India on October 12, 2005, and its relation with the increasing demand and necessity for accountability in the bureaucracy. The RTI Act was introduced into public departments to enhance institutional accountability and citizens' access to seeking information from an otherwise secretive and closed bureaucracy. The RTI Act has been a phenomenal boost to an otherwise closed and alienated state structure, which over the years had reduced democracy to conducting elections and forming a representative government. The Act makes disclosure of information mandatory to a citizen requesting for unless the information sought is specifically exempt under the Act. The Act has been enacted in India after much public debate, civil society movements, and much resistance from the bureaucracy and reluctance from the political class (Patricia, Radolph. 2010).[13] Accountability in a democracy should entail answerability for actions taken on behalf of the citizens. It is arguably the right of citizens in a democracy, both as voters and as taxpayers, to hold accountable anyone who handles public resources or holds public office. This is also a necessary prerequisite for responsive governance, such that a democratic political system becomes capable of formulating policies that reflect the preferences of citizens. Accountability has two dimensions: horizontal and vertical. The horizontal dimension is largely concerned with the effective operation of the system of checks and balances and with due process in governmental decision-making (Jenkins, Rub. & Marie Anne. 1999).[14] The vertical dimension focuses instead on elections and other mechanisms that citizens use to control their government. This book is based on the premise that the process of democracy is strengthened by the presumption of openness which is a prerequisite in a situation where rules are developed prior to their publication or implementation and accountability is the motive.

The relevant dimension of accountability—horizontal or vertical—may be different depending upon whether our focus is on elected or nonelected holders of public office. It is generally assumed that the accountability of nonelected officials, such as civil servants, is adequately ensured by the presence of mechanisms of horizontal accountability. There is also the further assumption that members of the permanent executive are not directly accountable to citizens. That relationship of accountability is seen to apply only to the political executive because they are elected by citizens.

Hence, vertical accountability mechanisms—such as five-yearly elections—are the preeminent instruments of holding elected officials to account. Contemporary discussions of accountability seek to be more encompassing in their coverage of both elected and nonelected holders of public office, as of the vertical and horizontal dimensions of accountability. However, it is the accountability of the nonelected government officials, that is, administrative officials of the state which is intriguing for this research since there does not seem to exist any extant mechanism that ensures direct accountability of this section of public representatives to citizens. The concept of horizontal accountability is an area that has not been given due weightage but there is increasing consensus arising that the nonelected representatives of the public must not only be accountable to each other but also that they must be made responsible and accountable for the actions that they take on behalf of the public at large. There are many ways in which the nonelected representatives can be made accountable to the citizens they serve. An important mechanism that can give an impetus to ensuring the accountability of the nonelected representatives is access to information that is held by such elected representatives in their official capacity.

The implementation of the right to freedom of expression and the RTI is established to be prerequisites for ensuring the voice and participation necessary for an open democratic society (Frank, Webster 2006).[15] This implies that the promotion and protection of both access to information itself and flows of information that exist between constituents—both men and women, government, Parliament, community groups, civil society organizations, and private sector—are of equal importance. Moreover, modern reform processes which stress on the need for institutional building require a sustained democratization process in which the flow of information plays a very important role. It is important to research on this issue because it is increasingly becoming clear that the problem of governance is intrinsically linked to the issue of systemic accountability.

For the purpose of this book, if the viewpoint of some eminent scholars is taken and taking forth the argument that if the information is considered to be a commodity that is to be used by the public, then in many ways it can be argued that providing information to the public is a public service that the government and those who serve the public while working in the government must perform. The argument in this book influenced by the sayings of ancient philosophers such as Pilates (Dreze, Jean. & Sen, Amartya 1995)[16] who prodded into the meaning of truth and the same question is being asked again and again, over a period of time. In the year 1954, for the celebration of its Bicentennial, Columbia University decided that freedom of inquiry and expression was the most appropriate subject which a free , university in a free country should choose and therefore the theme that was chosen was Man's Right to Knowledge and the Free Use Thereof. Not only is knowledge important but also freedom is necessary in every field of opinion and inquiry. However, with freedom comes the responsibility and privilege to exercise the freedom.

PUBLIC ACCOUNTABILITY AND GLOBAL MOVEMENT

The global movement toward a knowledge-based information society as a prelude to institutional reform has led to many state-led initiatives toward achieving this objective. Information as a plea for knowledge-based governance and information as a condition for accountable governance has in recent times become a challenging objective for democracy and citizen's rights all over the world. Indian governance has also witnessed this rights-based approach to access information.

Democracy is accepted as the best form of the government, but it can only thrive with the support of enlightened citizens and through transparent, proactive, people-centric good governance and strong mechanism to oversee the operation of the system. A democratic society has given liberty and equality to all its citizens to realize the goals of life. This goal can be realized with the help and proper functioning of administrative machinery called state government. India's RTI Act 2005 has been described as a revolution and acclaimed as even the most radical legislation since the introduction of the Constitution of India. RTI has been a fundamental right of every Indian citizen, being part of the freedom of speech and expression enshrined in the Article 19 (1) A of the Indian Constitution. RTI in Odisha significantly sought to expand the democratic space and empower the citizens to exercise more control over the corrupt practices under the power of the state. It is as crucial as freedom of expression in any democracy. An ingrained mindset of the denial of information is coming to surface time and again and jeopardizing the implementation of RTI Act.

At this juncture, review of existing legislation on RTI is hopefully relevant because information is vital not only for life of society and state but also for the life of an individual. In a democratic state, each government official is accountable to the citizens. In Indian democracy, however, we have a convoluted system of accountability, which is not only very little to understand but also almost impossible to put to use. The system of accountability has rendered all the government servants completely unaccountable to the public but accountable to their bureaucratic or political bosses, who exert a corrupting influence on them. RTI is an important tool in such a democratic set-up to fill this gap and to make the officials directly accountable to the citizens.

Over the last two decades, the world has seen a sharp rise in the number of countries which have some sort of a law pertaining to public access to government documents. Until 1989, only eight countries in the world had any such legislation. In 2011, this number stood at 88. Unsurprisingly, a number of publications that address the issue of transparency, accountability, and access to information have also emerged concomitantly. Curiously, only limited academic literature has specifically addressed the RTI Act in India. In addition, within this literature that has appeared intermittently over the last decade or so, a few consistently repeated tropes can be discerned.[17]

This section highlights the theoretical gap in the existing literature on accountability and gray area of the RTI Act. Public accountability has been defined by economic development agencies such as United Nations Development Programme (UNDP) in terms of rationalized and transparent systems of bureaucratic control. On the other hand, the legal perspective focuses on checks and balances. One of the important links to this process has also been turning to bureaucracy to examine accountability problems of electoral democracy.

Conventional practices of accountability have relied heavily on the idea of judicial checks and judicial review. In this context, Dicey's (1959:240)[18] idea of rule of law becomes pertinent. Dicey argued for a strong judicial check on the growing administrative state. What consequently came to be established was a symbiotic relationship between judicial review, procedural visibility, and public faith in government. Also the Constitution is the embodiment of the rule of law and as described by Dicey, in a country where the right to freedom is part of the Constitution because it is inherent in the law of the land, the right cannot be negated or subverted. It becomes embedded and inherent to such an extent that it can only be destroyed through a revolutionary change in the various institutions and manners of the state.

This idea assumes importance for the proposed research. Roberts, A. (2006)[19] indicates that the progress toward linear process of the market and management efficiency has increased administrative orthodoxy, which is further leading to isomorphic and global trends which shrink aspects of accountability. This is exacerbated by the fact that history is seldom linear and may require less orthodox arrangements for citizens which the new situation may not be in a position to provide.

Accountability in the form of judicial review would constitute horizontal accountability as delineated by Guillermo O'Donnell (1998),[20] who makes a distinction between two key dimensions of accountability: horizontal and vertical. The horizontal dimension is largely concerned with the effective operation of the system of checks and balances and with due process in governmental decision-making. As such, it pertains to checks placed by institutions on each other and does not involve citizens. The vertical dimension focuses instead on relationships between citizen and state and therefore includes elections and other mechanisms that citizens use to control their government. There is widespread consensus in most scholarly literature on Latin American democracies that governmental accountability in both dimensions is sadly lacking.

The difficulty of securing vertical accountability has been remarked by many—from democratic theorists like Larry Diamond to scholars of law such as A. G. Noorani. Diamond has argued that the governing elite must be made accountable to one another and to the people, not only in theory but in fact. Moreover, institutions must be constructed or reformed to ensure that this will happen. A. G. Noorani (2002)[21] in his work highlights the problems in the enforcement of the Rights and Civil liberties of accountability.

Fox, Jonathan (2007)[22] argues for the need to understand the concept of accountability through the lens of accountability regimes. He delineates three types of regimes: those associated with public governance, marketplace, and nongovernmental and social realm. What assumes importance for this study is his idea of public governance where the author also examines the processes of accountability of nonelected officials within the legal administrative and political framework. Jonathan explores the relationship between the solution for various challenges faced by the public functionaries while carrying on their duty or the fit between the various normative commitments that various accountability regimes support and the normative commitments of a particular program. For example to protect democratic values and the rule of law the fit would be to strengthen public governance accountability regimes. However, such solutions or fits may not be the best answer and might lead to a set of rules of thumb for institutional design. This study attempts to analyze whether the RTI Act has been successful in addressing the normative issues that surround an accountability system.

Mulgan, Richard (2000)[23] emphasizes the idea of public accountability and links the meaning of accountability to the electorate, to the taxpayers, or to the citizenry, either directly or through their representatives. The key argument of his work is that accountability is a relational mode of responsibility but at the same time it is also a specialized social goal. His work also critically examines the question about what accountability is for.

Richard states that the threat-based mode of accountability to which public officials are routinely subjected is counterproductive. The focus on accountability has created an era of suspicion because the system constantly accuses officials of being up to something. Therefore, institutionalized mechanisms may have made public services cheaper but also may erode their value. This study proposes to analyze whether the mechanism of ensuring accountability that has been provided through the RTI Act has resulted in the erosion of the surplus unpaid cooperation known as public service ethos. Also it may have also made people disinclined to explain themselves honestly and openly for fear that every little slip they make will be punished. Therefore, the threat-based mode of accountability may be counterproductive even from the point of view of accountability.

Transparency and accountability in governance "have a direct impact on issues of survival in the poorest communities including their right to food, shelter, health, environment and livelihood"[24] Accountability is referred as "cornerstone of public governance and management" and "the heart of governance within democratic societies." But what purpose does it serve? Aucoin and Heintzman argue that the answer is threefold: the first is to control the abuse and misuse of public authority. The second is to provide assurance in respect to the use of public resources and adherence to the law and public service values. The third is to encourage and promote learning in pursuit of continuous improvement in governance and public management.[25]

Newell and Joanna (2006)[26] provide an interesting insight into the critique of the process of accountability and do reiterate that while it is a critical element in any government system, it is also not just pure good.

Keohane and Held (2003)[27] have also raised the issue of organizational entropy due to asymmetric accountability which shrinks people's participation and weakens political power.

Goetz and Jenkins (2001)[28] in their work argue that "accountability can take place through paths different from the ones usually acknowledged by democratic theory." This work provides a window to reexamine alternative paths to theory and praxis.

Accountability implies not only to majority aspirations but also answerability of those in power. It postulates performance guided by integrity. It further implies that important decisions should be explained to the people to allow them an opportunity to appraise how well those in power have handled their responsibilities. Nirmala Lakshman says that, "A common definition of accountability is 'answerability for performance or the process of holding someone answerable for performance.' In a democracy it means, among other things, that every citizen must have a right to answers." It presupposes transparency in the public functioning of those who hold the reins of power either it is at the village and township level or at the state and national level.

RTI has both inherent and instrumental values. Its inherent value comes from the fact that citizens have a right to know. It is a crucial step toward a deeper, more meaningful democracy. More tangibly, in a country like India, it can promote action for development and therefore has considerable instrumental value. The information enables people to make enlightened choices and keep tabs on elected representatives and officials who claim to act on their collective behalf.

Abhimanyu Ghosh (2006)[29] discuss the concept of information as a product and it also attempts to examine the key legal structure that is evolving to deal with this concept of information as a commodity. "Open government is not always easy government but it is good government" (Thomas 2007).[30] Open government gives rise to a lot of debate and criticism which increases the work of the bureaucracy, that is why it is said that open government is not necessarily easy government.

The work of Goetz and Jenkins resonates with the Indian experience, where the RTI Act was substantially the result of a civil society initiative by the Mazdoor Kisan Shakti Sangathan (MKSS). Other civil society organizations such as Parivartan and National Campaign for People's Right to Information (NCPRI) have also played an important role in making possible the enactment of this path-breaking legislation.

The work and writings of Arvind Kejriwal[31] and Parivartan also assume importance in the context of current debates on RTI. The UNDP report on *Civil Society and Right to Information: A Perspective on India's Experience*[32] by Pradeep Sharma delineates how the role of the civil society has helped bring about a paradigmatic shift in the debates on RTI. The author particularly examines the concepts of public hearing, social audit, and public networking.

The RTI is expected to improve the quality of decision-making by public authorities, in both policy and administrative matters, by removing unnecessary secrecy surrounding the decision-making process. It would enable groups and individuals to be kept informed about the functioning of the decision-making process as it affects them and to know the kinds of criteria that are to be applied by government agencies in making these decisions. It is hoped that this would enhance the quality of participatory political democracy by giving all citizens further opportunity to participate in a more full and informed way in the political process. By securing access to relevant information and knowledge,[33] the citizens would be enabled to assess government performance and to participate in and influence the process of government decision-making and policy formulation on any issue of concern to them.

With the growth of competition among various countries through free market, globalization, and liberalization, there seems to be immense growth of corruption level too. Many international bodies like the IMF, World Bank, and so on grant aids to various countries but how accountable are these bodies themselves? A general debate has come up with these bodies opening up for public accountability.[34]

India's rank is among the top most in the corruption level. Being a poor country with enormous diversity in terms of culture, language, region, and religion, it has remarkably been successful in maintaining democracy and has given a preamble to the citizens which grants fundamental rights to one and all. The Directive Principles enshrined in Chapter IV of the Constitution ordain that the state shall strive to promote the welfare of the people and in particular strive to minimize the inequalities in income and endeavor to eliminate inequalities in status, facilities, and opportunities.

While debating on democracy and accountability,[35] many experts felt that for a country of India's size and complexity and particularly taking into account its problems of illiteracy and economic democracy, parliamentary democracy might prove to be unworkable. Parliamentary democracy had never been tried in any large country until India decided to adopt it. The United Kingdom, where it has been a great success, the population is 58 million, which is much less than that of Maharashtra. Experts believe that India should opt for a relatively simpler system like the presidential one in the United States. But the framers of the Constitution not once had doubt on the suitability of parliamentary system. They believed that people in spite of their handicaps will prove themselves equal to the demands of the system and will be able to work the system smoothly and effectively.

Accountability in parliamentary democracy has two aspects: one is the accountability of the elected legislators to the people who elect them and the other is the accountability of the executive to the legislature but unlike the established practice in Western democracies, the legislators in India do not seem to be keen on keeping their constituencies informed of their work in the legislatures or in ascertaining their views on the issues which come up for consideration of the legislatures. They may be vigilant about looking after the interests of their constituencies. Accountability involves reflecting the views of the electors on major issues which come for discussion in the legislature, informing the electors on the pros and cons of different issues, and explaining to them the reasons for the stand taken by them on the important issues in the legislature. This requires close contact with the voters and the fact that India is such a large country is the biggest excuse given by these legislators, who do not seem to believe that they are accountable to the citizens to those who elect them. The second aspect of accountability is that of the ministers to the legislatures. When the ministers are made accountable to the legislature, they become accountable to the people as a whole because the legislative instruments like questions, short-notice questions, adjournment motions, and so on are intended to ensure accountability of the executive on a continuing basis to the legislature and ultimately to the people. Unfortunately, the time available to every legislator for discussion over the performance of individual ministers and their department is very limited. Very often the demands of only a few ministers are heard and voted and others are devoted without any discussion because of shortage of time. This practice has also contributed to the erosion of accountability in civil servants.[36]

In colonial America, there was the issue of "no taxation without representation." So at the heart of the problem, the question of accountability is the question of the control of purse, raising and spending of public resources or the exercise of authority, or the control of power.[37] Thus, in a democracy, it is related to empowerment, participation, and control of authority by the people. Negatively, the concept of accountability aims to prevent the misuse or abuse of power and authority, while positively, it seeks to ensure the satisfaction of the people's demands and a better order of things.[38]

The work *Right to Information: Law and Practice* (Sridhar, Madabhusi 2007)[39] refers to a vast content regarding the new law, state laws on RTI, and the then international perspective by which the people at large empower themselves the demanded and obtained information.

The work *The Information Age: Economy, Society and Culture* (Castells, Manuel 2010)[40] is a brilliant effort in the field of information society. The book studies empirically the collapse of the Soviet Union tracing it back to the incapacity of industrial system to manage the transition of the information age. Castells documents how inequality, poverty, and social exclusion nationally and globally an inherent feature of the type of network society emerge from the domination of global capitalism.

A dynamic effort in the field of information revolution *The Theories of Information Society* (Frank, Webster 2006)[41] examines the major postwar theories of the information society and approaches to the informational development. At the same time, the author highlights rapid growth of internet and accelerated globalization.

Another excellent academic work in the scenario of RTI *Neoliberalization: States, Networks and Peoples* (Kim, England, & Kevin, Ward 2007)[42] discusses the origin rise and consequences of neoliberalism in different parts of the world and trying it into a wider discussion of globalization, American imperialism, and current phase of capitalism and at the same time emphasizes on global networks and people's involvement with the reconstruction of the state.

Another pioneering work in the field of information *International Exploration of Technology Equity and the Digital Divide* (Patricia, Randolph Leigh. 2012)[43] explores the historical, political, sociological, and economic factors that engender global inequities related to digital technologies. The contributing authors present the phenomenon of digital equity from various critical social theory perspectives. These critical perspectives, together with the histories of domination and oppression on different continents, provide contexts for understanding the fertile grounds made available for the international growth and expansion of digital inequity.

Another pioneering work *Right to Information and Good Governance*" (Rajvir S, Dhake 2010)[44] analyzes the RTI in international and national scenarios. The book presents a comprehensive appraisal of the needs of the RTI Act 2005. It covers the salient features, FAQs, and important judgments of central and state information commissions and points out the gray areas of the Act as well. The book also highlights the role and responsibility of the assistant public information officers, public information officers, and first appellate authorities and information commissions. In addition, the book delineates the practical aspect of its implementation as well as charting the road map for the bright future in the days to come.

Another brilliant work *Citizens Rights Judges and State Accountability* (Noorani AG, 2002)[45] highlights the process of accountability in these institutions, the citizens' right to know, and correspondingly the state's accountability to the people. It analyzes the working of commissions of inquiry and the decline in the quality of political process in the recent years. This volume demonstrates how the citizens can assert their rights and bring to accent those who wield power.

The mega work in this field *The Rights and Wrongs of It: The Right to Information* (Das, Bhabesh & Bhattacharyya, Rajiv K. 2004)[46] gave importance to various aspects of RTI and inherent limitation of such right on certain occasions in the greater interest of body polity has been highlighted in the article compiled in the book.

An important work in the field of RTI *Media and Sovereignty: The Global Information Revolution and Its Challenge to State Power* (Monroe, Price, 2002)[47] explores how the state controls the information society and media in the process of social transformation. At the same time, the book discusses about the global information revolution in the developing and developed society.

The work *Constitutional Questions and Citizen Rights* (Noorani, A.G. 2006)[48] explores the Indian Constitution and its basic structure, Parliament and making of foreign policy, the issue of lobbying and needs for appropriate legislation, and also the ethical codes for parliamentarians and ministers. Further the omnibus includes a discussion of courts and their power of competence, journalist right, and freedom of information. In addition, this volume deals with the issues concerning the president, the state, the judiciary, the civil services, the election commission the armed forces, and the process of accountability on which the constitutional machinery is based. It highlights the citizen rights judges and state accountability. It supplemented with insights into the freedom of information and citizens' right to know.

The Changing Times (Godbole, Madhav 2003)[49] explained and suggested the recent development in the contemporary era on socioeconomic-political bases as well as the administrative reforms in a democratic state which includes passing of a law on freedom of information, adoption of a code of ethics, Declaration of Citizen Charters, and generally make the administration accountable and transparent.

The Network Society A Cross Cultural Perspective (Castells, Manuel 2004)[50] is a brilliant effort in this field. The volume explores the pattern and dynamics of the network society in its cultural and institutional diversity. By network society, we refer to the social structure that results from the interaction between social organization, social change, and technological paradigm constituted around digital information and communication technologies and examine the complex interaction between technology and society in our world. The perspective of this volume is cross cultural.

The work *The Power of Identity* Volume II (Castells, Manuel 2010)[51] explores the construction of collective identities as they relate to social movements and power struggles in the network society. It also deals with the transformation of the state, politics, and democracy under the conditions of globalization and new communication technologies.

The article entitled "Information Right: A Jurisprudential Audit" (Amitabh, Ranjan 2009)[52] opens with a discussion on jurisprudential perspectives of RTI; information rights are a tactical subset of human rights. He finds them to be procedural means to realize human emancipation. His article displays the interplay between the spurts of social awakening and sheer inertia of history which determine their instrumental efficacy. Without the proper information about the entitlements available to the citizens under the various schemes, the intended beneficiaries remain bereft of their benefits. The article "The Official Secret Act to Right to Information Act Down of 'Glasnost'" (U.G., Agrawal 2009)[53] says why most of the government business and work are shrouded in secrecy and confidentiality which breeds corruption, waste, inefficiency, abuse of power, and many other acts of maladministration.

The RTI is a critical factor that is needed for moving from a representative to a participatory democracy. In spite of an entrenched mindset inefficient process and organizational factor, "RTI Implementation at the District Level: Issues and Challenges" (Jain, Abhishek 2009)[54] analyzes there is enough reason to be optimistic about the efficacy of the RTI Act. He enumerates positive outcomes from the emerging information regime and argues the whole issue in a demand-supply perspective.

In the context of RTI Act, the judiciary and judicial functioning have become issues of public concern. The article "Right to Information: Some Emerging Issues of Public Concern" (Roy, Jaytilak Guha 2009)[55] discusses the intriguing role of judiciary in ensuring transparency which is expected of all the public authorities.

The role of government functionaries and those who are working at other public authorities is extremely important for the successful implementation of the RTI Act. The article "The RTI Act and Training – Brief Comments on Capacity Building at the State Level" (Hooja, Rakesh 2009)[56] discusses the areas where training on the various facts of the Act is required.

The article "A Comparative Study of Freedom of Right to Information in India, United States and England" (Bhava, Noorjahan 2009)[57] has undertaken a comparative analysis of similarities and differences and scope and effectiveness of information laws of India, United States, and the United Kingdom.

In spite of people, empowerment to available information, the basic problem that remains, is what to do with information and the information received. The article "The Role of RTI in Reforming the Indian Administration" (Kataria, S.K. 2009)[58] recounts various options that have been thrown open to a common citizen, yet laments that accountability in the functioning of public authorities will not prevail till such time internal working and machinery of public administration do not change.

RTI and decentralized governance are interrelated in the sense that accountability is the basic prerequisite for decentralized governance. The article "Right to Information and Decentralized Governance" (Mishra, Sweta 2009)[59] discusses RTI in the context of decentralized governance and how it can be made effective and meaningful.

Ten years of experience in implementation has revealed that there are several anticipated and unanticipated consequences of RTI Act, the article "The Dynamics of Right to Information Act" (Singh, Shivraj and Jain, Aarushi 2009)[60] evaluates the implementation of the Act in its procedural aspect and human aspect with the help of data and information gathered at the field level in Himachal Pradesh.

In order to make RTI Act effective and purposeful, it is essential to introduce the consequential changes in the provisions of certain laws having negative information on the free flow of the information. The article "Implementing RTI: A Practical Approach" (Chadah, Sapna 2009)[61] analyzes the major concerns expressed so far regarding implementation of its working and touches upon the major impediments in the way of its operationalization.

Upholding of transparency, accountability, and participation requires government to break bureaucratic resistance and generate political will to create a culture of information sharing. The article "RTI Act. 2005: A Critique with Governance and Administrative Reform Perspective" (Raj, Triranjan & Sharma, Sanjeev Kumar 2009)[62] recommends removal of restrictive laws, steps to ensure free flow of information, and more importantly create a culture of openness. Good governance has four elements: transparency, accountability, predictability, and participation. RTI is a basic necessity of good governance.

As Madison said in 1982, "Popular government without popular information with means of acquiring it, is but a prologue to a farce or a tragedy or perhaps both." The article "Organisation Other than the Government and RTI Act" (Swamy, Raju Narayana 2009)[63] discusses how information is empowering the citizens of our country through the effective operationalization of this Act.

The article "Accounts and Accountability: Theoretical Implications of the Right to Information Movement in India" (Jenkins, Rob & Marie, Anne 1999)[64] examines the process by which this campaign emerged and the means by which it pursues its goals. It then analyzes the implications of the MKSS experience and the larger movement it has spawned for contemporary debates in three areas: human rights, participatory development, and, of course, anti-corruption.

The broad trend which appears in the literature is of placing this narrative within the conceptual framework of accountability of public institutions. Another brilliant work on RTI *The Conceits of Civil Society* (Neera, Chandhoke 2003)[65] points out in the context of the discourse on civil society, flattening of the RTI narrative in India is intriguing and needs deeper examination, especially given the fact that obvious silences exist in this literature. For example, the existing literature does not address the issue of the arrangement of formal political forces or the political context within which the "people's struggle" was carried out and how these might have impacted the process. While the literature celebrates the RTI Act as a very successful outcome of a movement, very little has been written about possible causal factors behind the lack of effective resistance from a powerful adversary, the bureaucracy, to the RTI Act.

ARGUMENT AND RATIONALE FOR ACCOUNTABILITY

The foundation of this book is the assumption that the concept of democracy requires accessible governments which are accountable to its citizens and that the RTI Act has made only a feeble attempt to strengthen accountability of the bureaucracy. Though, it must be said that the potential of this Act is tremendous and manifold, it is a basic tenet of liberal democracies such as India to have a government and bureaucracy that functions according to the rule of law and the creation and maintenance of representatives who are accountable to the people. This also implies by corollary that these representatives are also removable by the people. It is of utmost importance for citizens to understand the basic nature of these factors of governance since it is the citizens who are being governed through various mechanisms of the government. For gaining an insight into the workings of the government and to enforce accountability of these factors, all citizens need access to information from the government about government documents and records. The World Bank document titled "Governance and Development" (World Bank, 1992)[66] states accountability and transparency as the most important prerequisite for good governance out of the seven aspects that have been outlined by it. This research tries to ascertain whether the RTI Act has really been able to make visible an invisible bureaucracy or has it just created another form of an invisible government which only appears to be accessible but is actually as distant from the common public as the previous one.

It has been mentioned by Roy, Jaytilak Guha (2006:559)[67] that an invisible government is no longer the norm of the day. All the players in the field of democracy, be it the citizens, civil society, business, and commercial houses, as on date, demand accountability and transparency from the government. It is common knowledge that everywhere government officials maintain secrecy in public functioning, which serves as a means for avoiding criticism, hindering opposition, and maintaining power over citizens and their elected representatives. All of these parties demand information legitimately from the public authorities. According to Guha (2006:561),[68] dissemination of public information is possible only if the government is legally responsible for providing the public with information. The importance of having such legislation in place that ensures accountability from the bureaucracy is reflected in the fact that the Second Administrative Reforms Commission has focused its first report on the RTI, which it defines as the Master Key to Good Governance.

Thus, even though the mandate of the Second Administrative Reforms Commission is to suggest various methods to be adopted for a complete revamp of the public administrative system and its terms of reference have been given a wide scope that covers all aspects of public governance, it chose to analyze the RTI in it first report since it views this legislation as one that would be instrumental in bringing about a paradigm shift in public administration. The Second Administrative Reforms Commission has highlighted the importance of the RTI Act in a maturing democracy such as India's. It has emphasized the need for such an Act as essential for a democracy to emerge as an accountable and transparent entity that shares information freely with the citizens and leads to a more vibrant, open, and accountable form of government. Anne Marie Goetz and Rob Jenkins (2005:1)[69] have defined accountability as a perpetual struggle when power is delegated in the interest of governability from the many to the few. The question of accountability is a deep and intertwining question.

Once the power has been delegated, the power to hold accountable those to whom the power is delegated is itself delegated. And this delegation is usually to a handful such as judges, auditors, public accounts committees, tribunals, and so on. "The question of who will watch the watchdog is as old as it is unavoidable." Taking this argument of Goetz and Jenkins[70] forward, this research shall also examine the accountability of the judiciary in India with a special focus on the aftermath of this Act and the mixed reaction of the judiciary to demands from the people for access to information from the judiciary. In the form of its most common usage, accountability refers to democratic accountability.

GOVERNANCE AND TRANSPARENCY

A transparent government is needed to fulfill the goal of transparency and accountability, which in turn leads to a strong democracy. For transparency to prevail in government functioning, access to information and access to knowledge is needed which would then create the solid foundation of information access which leads to transparency, accountability, good governance, and so on. Thus one factor is a prerequisite for the other and each factor both supplements and complements the other.

This book discusses RTI Act grievance and redressal system in India on bureaucracy. It is now widely recognized that the principle of "discretionary secrecy" is no longer relevant in a modern democracy. This principle implied that the government had the discretion to curtail the information that it wished to curtail from the public.

It is easier to draw a critique of the current stipulations and practices than it is to move on to specific constructive proposals for improvements. Most administrative reforms across the world are based on this approach, Chapman and Hunt (2010)[71] have termed this approach as the piecemeal or incremental approach. According to them, the democratic form of government not only requires continuous attention but also the willingness of individuals to participate as citizens. The rationale proposed by Chapman and Hunt, which is a rationale that this work proposes to adopt is that the elements in a democracy need to be continuously monitored to ensure that actual changes are consistent with the intended values and principles; otherwise even the best intentions may be threatened. Carrying this proposition into the present work, one may state that it is important to assess the implementation of the RTI Act to see if the Act is being implemented in the right direction and if its implementation remains true to its intended purpose. The RTI has to be studied within the framework of accountability in the changing nature of the state. It has attempted to redefine traditional accountability and contours of a rational-legal state held by parliamentary accountability. Thus accountability has become more instrumental than a design for articulating collective interests. Thomas rightly points out the unfortunate replacement of ministerial responsibility by contract-based accountability.[72]

Also the RTI Act becomes important in a regime where only the rich and powerful have access to resources and a very important component of these resources is information. The balance between secrecy and openness is indeed very delicate and fine. Stuart Corbridge, et al. (2005),[73] has studied the process of hollowing out and concluded that this process has been gradually eroding political responsibility. Newell. and Bellour (2002)[74] highlights the asymmetry of accountability when a few operating and regulatory agencies control and hold enormous power. Robert O. Keohane (2003)[75] indicates that the progress toward linear process of the market and management efficiency has increased administrative orthodoxy, which is further leading to isomorphic and global trends which shrink aspects of accountability. This is exacerbated by the fact that history is seldom linear and may require less orthodox arrangements for citizens which the new situation may not be in a position to provide. Held, David (2005)[76] has also raised the issue of "organizational entropy" due to asymmetric accountability which shrinks people's participation and weakens political power.

Accountability has three main problems:

- Institutional: because the organizational links between political responsibility and managerial accountability are loose and disjointed.
- Political Processes: Managers have no clear norms for neutrality and value-free decision-making.
- Organizational Structure: Managers are not allowed to answer for the direct action or performance of a service provider to people or stakeholders.

Thus Peters (1998)[77] warn about the ambiguity in the processes of accountability which is more than what it was in a traditional rational-legal model of state. Pollit and Bouckaert (2000)[78] sum up the three pillars of accountability which strongly recommend the need for information as a right of citizens.

These are:

- Authorization: An identifiable superior.
- Support: Those who support the political leadership have to claim rights and hold rulers accountable.

- Impact: Those who are choice determining for some people should be accountable for their action.

Access to information is a pivotal empowerment tool that underpins effective interventions in the area of democratic governance, which is central to any democratic structure. Accessible and understandable information and the means and ability to communicate are important for enabling people to participate in policy-making processes and the decisions that affect their lives. The implementation of the right to freedom of expression and the RTI are prerequisites for ensuring the voice and participation necessary for an open democratic society.

The study would draw from the work of John Ackerman (2006),[79] who argues that information in fact is a first step to strengthen democracy. It is further stated that an informed citizenry will lead to dialogue, deliberation, and creation of community. However, the intended purpose and the meaning of the Act have not been implemented in practice. The proposed work would specifically attempt to critically examine the RTI Act 2005 and focus on the key lacunae such as interpretation of the exemption clause of the RTI Act 2005, applicability of Act only on public authorities, overriding effect of the Act, bar on the jurisdiction of courts and lack of employees grievance redressal in Odisha Secretariat after receiving information under the Act. This would be located in the theoretical framework incorporating the key concepts of horizontal accountability and public accountability regimes. The study would draw on the key arguments by O'Donnell on mechanisms of vertical accountability.[80]

In the context of RTI what is particularly relevant is the thrust on the system of checks and balances and due processes in government decision-making. A step further in the work would be an attempt to locate why in practice this has not been achieved. The key variable for examination would be a redressal mechanism which is absent in the current legislation that has been promulgated by the Parliament. Here Dicey's (1959)[81] emphasis on the idea of rule of law becomes pertinent particularly the need for a strong judicial check on the state. One of the most important features of the rule of law is the redress afforded by courts for the damage caused by illegal interference in any person's personal freedom. The right to receive information from the state has been established to be a valuable personal freedom. To bar the jurisdiction of courts seems against the basic tenets of rule of law to say the least. A second key variable for examination would be the need for extension and applicability of the RTI Act 2005 on private entities and not limiting its scope only upon public authorities. Further the study would also examine the role of the quasi-judicial bodies, that is, the Central Information Commission (CIC) which functions through the Information

Commissioners, and whether it would result in a parallel body of judicial activism which may or may not be justified. This would be located in the current debates on judicial activism.

OBSTACLE IN ACCOUNTABILITY—INFORMATION DEFICIT

Even though accountability has been established to form an integral part of good governance and it is vital for a democratic discourse between the state and the public, the lack of complete information to the general public creates a situation of information deficit which undermines the purpose of a democracy. It is well-known that bureaucracies everywhere tend to be less than open, preferring to confuse practices of rule. Colonial bureaucracies are particularly immune to norms of transparency, as the Official Secrets Act of 1923 in India shows. This Act was carried over into the postindependence period, by the bureaucracy, and served to hinder the free flow of information. The bureaucracy functioned under the auspices of the Official Secrets Act 1923 along with provisions of the Civil Service Conduct Rules, 1964, which prohibit communication of an official document to anyone without authorization. This was further augmented by Section 123 of the Indian Evidence Act 1872 which prohibits the giving of evidence from unpublished official records without the permission of the Heads of the Department.

In the colonial era, the Official Secrets Act 1923 had been enacted to deal with matters of security and integrity of the nation. However, it created an all pervasive culture of mistrust and thickly guarded information. Confidentiality was the norm and disclosure the exception among the bureaucracy. The Law Commission in its 43rd Report (1971) summarized the difficulties encountered with the all-inclusive nature of Section 5 of the Official Secrets Act, in the absence of a clear and concise definition of official secret. The rationale behind Section 5 of the Official Secrets Act 1923 was to deal with the potential breach of national security, however, the wording of the law and the colonial times in which it was implemented made it a catch-all legal provision converting practically every issue of governance into a confidential/classified matter. Moreover, the closed and secretive nature of the Official Secrets Act was complemented by the Civil Service Conduct Rules 1964 which prohibit communication of an official document to anyone without authorization. The Supreme Court in *Sama Alana Abdulla v. State of Gujarat* [(1996) 1 SCC427] has held (1) that the word "secret" in clause (c) of sub-section (1) of Section 3 qualified official code or password and not any sketch, plan, model, article or note, or other document or information and (2) when the accused was found in conscious possession of the material (map in that case) and no plausible explanation has been given for its possession, it has to be presumed as required by Section 3(2) of the Act that the same was obtained or collected by the appellant for a purpose prejudicial to the safety or interests of the state. Therefore, a sketch, plan, model, article, note, or document need not necessarily be secret in order to be covered by the Act, provided it is classified as an official secret (Barowalia, 2006).[82]

India's democratic functioning witnessed a drastic change in the post-emergency period wherein a number of political activists along with many social activists and public-spirited professionals decided to opt against and out of party and electoral politics and instead to work from the grassroots on the micro-level process of social mobilization. Therefore, from sometime during the mid-eighties there has been a consistent effort by many political reformers and civil society groups to define and rearticulate the rights of people.

A very effective set of proponents of transparent governance has been grassroot action groups like the MKSS in Rajasthan, an advocacy organization that sought governmental accountability as part of the citizen's right to know and the right to participate in governance. Moreover, The NCPRI formed in the late 1990s became a broad-based platform for action. Therefore, with the collective efforts of various civil society groups and momentum built at the grassroot level of democracy, legislation in the form of the RTI Act 2005 was promulgated in India and it came into force in India in totality with effect from October 12, 2005. There was an attempt to make this law very comprehensive and it covers almost all matters of governance and has the widest possible reach, being applicable to government at all levels—Union, state, and local as well as recipients of government grants. (Barowalia, 2006).[83]

TRANSPARENCY AS A PREREQUISITE FOR ACCOUNTABILITY

The concept of "Accountability" cannot be studied in isolation from the concept of transparency. It is imperative for a democratic bureaucracy to be open and unambiguous in its functioning. It has been argued by Roberts (2006)[84] that it is well-nigh impossible to hold governors to account if their governance is invisible to constituents. If regulatory operations are to be subject to effective public scrutiny, then they must be open to public view. Citizens need to be aware who is governing them, toward what objective, with what decisions, by what processes, and using what resources. Only then can people have adequate grounds to judge the performance of the rules and the rules that govern them.

Public transparency is, therefore, a crucial precondition for effective democratic accountability. Thus, it can be safely assumed for the purpose of this work that public transparency is an indispensable part of governance which is essential to run an accountable government. In the broader framework of a fully effective and efficient democracy, it helps in achieving capacity building. According to Birchall (2011)[85] openness is measurable and consists of the motive of access to information whereas transparency involves the description of the decisions made in government departments and the ways and means by which such decisions have been reached. Banisar (2006)[86] gives a broader definition of transparency in the context of complete information that is required by an individual for the fulfillment of a specific function in any given context. Heywood (2009)[87] has classified the three dimensions that are vital for transparency to exist, that is, access to information, the reasoning behind the decision, and an understanding that the decision-making process is open for public debate and participation. According to Roberts (2006),[88] the RTI is a basic human right and a derivative right since it arises as a consequence of the human rights commitment. Jonathan Fox (2007)[89] view transparency as a policy and useful management tool in public and private sectors. Transparency has emerged as a leadership style and many organizations have made transparency their goal which has led to a high level of access to information. With changing times, there is no room for secrecy in public functioning anymore considering which (Haque, M.S. 2008)[90] has analyzed that public functionaries need to win the trust of the common public by providing more transparency, accountability, and openness. It is this notion of trust and openness that this research fundamentally attempts to address.

This work is important to understand whether the genesis of the right to know for the people of India provides in the form of a formal legislation and its implementations by the legislature and judiciary in its true spirit. Record-keeping is important in today's information society and it has acquired wide-reaching implications as far as maintaining the balance of power in an information society's structure is concerned. The power balance is also reflected in relationships between individuals and government, on one hand, and individuals and private/corporate organizations, on the other hand. These relationships are in some way dependent on the information about public functioning that is available with these variables.

Most of the information that is available with these authorities is obtained from records that are maintained by public authorities. The power balance in a country is bound to be affected with a growth or change in a society's record-keeping capabilities and in some cases, it may even upset the power balance in a society.

CONCLUSION

The first chapter of this book highlights the crucial relationship between public accountability and the RTI movement and the challenges that arise while implementing the RTI legislation. Out of these challenges are the basic questions that are raised and tackled in this work. The reason for the secrecy maintained by the nonelected officials of the government, that is, the bureaucrats, is explored in this chapter. The factors that have led to the promulgation of the RTI Act 2005 have also been elaborated in this chapter. The difficulties in the promulgation of the Act and thereafter the implementation of the Act are two different realities which have been explored in this chapter.

NOTES

1. Blau, Peter. (1956), *Bureaucracy in Modern Society*. New York: Crown Publishing Group/Random House.
2. Castells, Manuel (ed.). (2004), *The Network Society: A Cross Cultural Perspective*. United Kingdom: Edward Elgar Publishing Limited.
3. See Missick, Brinkley. (1993), *The Crlligraphic State: Textual Domination and History in a Muslim Society*. Berkeley: University of California Press. Also See Tarlo, Emma. (2003), *Unsettling Memories: Narratives of Emergency in Delhi*. Delhi Permanent Black.
4. Ferguson, Jemes. (1994), *The Anti-Politics Machine: Development Depoliticization and Bureaucratic Power in Lesotho*. Minneapolis: University of Minnesota Press.
5. Harvey, David. (2005), *A Brief History of Neoliberalism*. Oxford: Oxford University Press.
6. Swamy, Raju Naryana. (2011), "Organisation's Other than the Government and RTI Act", *University News,* 49(2).
7. Godbole, Madhab. (2003), *Public Accountability and Transparency*. New Delhi: Orient Longman Private Limited.
8. Noorani, A.G. (2006), *Constitutional Question's and Citizens Rights*. New Delhi: Oxford University Press.
9. Madabhushi, Sridhar. (2007), *Right to Information Law and Practice*. Nagpur: Wadhwa.
10. Das, Bhabesh, and Rajiv K. Bhattacharyya. (2007), *The Right and Wrongs of It: The Right to Information*. Kolkata: Gangchil Publication Matir Bari.

11. Sen, Amarty. (1982), *Poverty and Famines: An Essay of Entitlement and Deprivation*. Oxford, UK: Oxford University Press.

12. Chalfin, Brenda. (2010), *Neoliberal Frontiers: Ethnography of Sovereignty in West Africa*. Chicago: University of Chicago Press.

13. Patricia, Radolph. (2010), *International Exploration of Technology Equality and Digital Divide: Critical Historical and Social perspective*. New York: Information Science Reference.

14. Jenkins, Rub and Marie Anne. (1999), "Account and Accountability theoretical information of Right to Information Movement and India", *Third Journal Quarterly*, 20(3): 603–622.

15. Frank, Webster. (2006), *Theories of Information Society* (3rd Edition). Canada: Taylor & Francies Group Library.

16. See Dreze, Jean and Amartya Sen. (1995), *India: Economic Development and Social Opportunity*. New Delhi: Oxford University Press.

17. Baviskar (2007), Goetz and Jenkins (1999), Roberts (2010), Roy and Dey (2002) and Singh (2007, 2011) are key publications which develop and reinforce the dominant narrative.

18. Dicey, A.V. (1959), *An Introduction to the Study of the Law of the Constitution* (10th Edition). London: Macmillan and Company Ltd.

19. Roberts, A. (2006), *Blacked Out: Government Secrecy in the Information Age*. New York: Cambridge University Press.

20. O'Donnell, Guillermo. (1998), "Horizontal Accountability in New Democracies", *Journal of Democracy*.

21. Noorani, A.G. (2002), *Citizens Rights, Judges and State Accountability*. Oxford University Press.

22. Fox, Jonathan (2007), "The Uncertain Relationship between Transparency and Accountability", *Development in Practice*, 17(4): 663–671.

23. Mulgan, Richard. (2000), "'Accountability': An Ever Expanding Concept", *Public Administration*, 78(3): 555–573.

24. Lakshman Nirmala, "Information: An Inviolable Right", *The Hindu,* Tuesday, Jan. 04, 2005.

25. Aucoin, Peter and Ralph Heintzman. (1998), "The Dialectics of Accountability for Performance in Public Management Reform", *International Review of Administrative Sciences,* 66(1): 45–56.

26. Newell, P. and Joanna Wheeler (eds.). (2006), *Taking Accountability into Account: The Debate So Far*. London: Zed Books.

27. Keohane, Robert and David Held. (2003), *Global Governance and Democratic Accountability in Taming Globalization (Ed)*, frontiers of governance.

28. Goetz, A.M. and R. Jenkins (2001), "Hybrid Forms of Accountability: Citizen Engagement in Institutions of Public Sector Oversight in India", *Public Management Review*, 3(3): 363–383.

29. Ghosh, Abhimanyu. (2006), *Open Government and the Right to Information*, www.legalservicesindia.com

30. Blanton, Thomas. (2002), "The Openness Revolution: The Rise of Global Movement for Freedom of Information", *Development Dialogue*, 1: 7–21.

31. Kejriwal, Arvind. (2005), "Right to Information Act: Loopholes and Road Ahead", *Economic and Political Weekly*, 41(11): 941–942.

32. Sharma, Pradeep. (2004), "Civil Society and Right to Information: A Perspective on India's Experience", UNDP, August 2004, www.undp.org/oslocentre/docs05

33. See Rajya Sabha Secretariat (2005), "Third Report on the Right to Information Bill, 2004 (Presented to the Rajya Sabha on 21 March, 2005)", Department Related Parliamentary Standing Committee on Personnel, Public Grievances, Law and Justice, New Delhi: Parliament of India, Rajya Sabha Secretariat.

34. Woods, Ngaire (2000), "The Challenge of Good Governance for the IMF and the World Bank Themselves", *World Development*, 28(5): 823–841.

35. Kohli, Atul. (1991), *Democracy and Discontent: India's Growing Crisis of Governability.* Cambridge University Press.

36. Alexander, P.C. (1998), "Accountability in Parliamentary Democracy", in Nigam Raj K. (ed.), *Public Accountability in Indian Polity.* New Delhi: Blackwell Publications.

Also See Wood, E.M. (1990), "The Uses and Abuses of 'Civil Society'", *The Socialist Register*, 26: 60–84.

37. Whitton, J.B. (1949), "The United Nations Conference on Freedom of Information and the Movement against International Propaganda", *The American Journal of International Law*, 43: 73–87.

38. Also See Chaturvedi, T.N., "Accountability: The Concept and Its Significance", Ibid.

39. Madabhushi, Sridhar. (2007), *Right to Information Law and Practice.* Nagpur: Wadhwa.

40. Castells, Manuel. (2010), *The Information Age : Economy, Society & Culture*, Vol – III, end of the New Millennium (2nd Edition). West Sussex, UK: Wiley Blackwell, A John Wiley & Sons, Ltd.

41. Frank, Webster. (2006), *Theories of Information Society* (3rd edition). Canada: Taylor & Francies Group Library.

42. Neo, Kim England and Ward Kevin. (2007), *Liberalization: States Networks and Peoples.* UK: Black Well publishing Ltd.

43. Patricia, Randolph Leigh. (2012), *The International Exploration of Technology Equality & Digital Devide*, Information Science Reference USA.

44. Dhaka, Rajvir S. (2010), *Right to information and Good Governance.* New Delhi: Concept Publishing Company Pvt. Ltd.

45. Noorani, A.G. (2002), *Citizen Rights Judges and State Accountability.* New Delhi: Oxford University Press.

46. Das, Bhabesh and Rajiv K. Bhattacharyya (eds.) (2007), *The Right and Wrongs of it: The Right to Information.* India: Gangchil Publication Kolkatta.

47. Monroe E, Price. (2002), *Media and Sovereignty, The Global Information Revolution & Its Challenge to State Power.* Crambridge, MA, London: The MIT Press.

48. Noorani, A.G. (2006), *Constitutional Question's and Citizens Rights.* New Delhi: Oxford University Press.

49. Godbole, Madhab. (2003), *Public Accountability and Transparency*. New Delhi: Orient Longman Private Limited.

50. Castells, Manuel (ed.). (2004), *The Network Society: A Cross Cultural Perspective*. Edward Elgar Publishing Limited.

51. Castells, Manuel (2010), *The Power of Identity* (2nd Edition). West Sussex, UK: Wiley & Sons Publication.

52. Rajan, Amitabh. (2009), "Information Right: A jurisprudential Audit", *The Indian Journal of Public Administration*, LV (3): 325.

53. Agarwal, U.C. (2009), "The Official Secret Act to the Right to Information Act Down of "Glasnost"", *The Journal of Public Administration*, LV(3): 336–346.

54. Jain, Abhisshek. (2009), "RTI Implementation at the District Level: Issues and Challenges", *The Indian Journal of public Administration*, LV(3): 346–364.

55. Roy, Jaytilak Guha (2009), "The Right to Information Some Emerging Issues of Public Concern", *The Indian Journal of Public Administration*, LV(3): 406–413.

56. Hooja, Rakesh. (2009), "The RTI Act and Training Brief Comments on Capacity Building at the State Level", *The Indian Journal of Public Administration*, LV(3): 413–422.

57. Bhava, Noorjahan. (2009), "Comparative Study of Freedom (Right) of Rights of Information Act in India, United States and England", *The Indian Journal of Public Administration*, LV(3): 619–644.

58. Kataria, S.K. (2009), "The Role of RTI in Reforming Indian Administration", *The Indian Journal of Public Administration*, LV(3): 660–672.

59. Mishra, Sweta. (2009), "Right to Information and Decentralised Governance", *The Indian Journal of Public Administration*, LV(3): 689–702.

60. Singh, Raj Shiv and Aarushi Jain. (2009), "The Dynamics of Right to Information Act and Its Implementation in Himachal Pradesh", *The Indian Journal of Public Administration*, LV(3): 722–734.

61. Chadah, Sapna. (2009), "Implementing Right to Information: A Practical Approach", *The Indian Journal of public Administration*, LV(3): 455–481.

62. Raj, Triranjan and Sanjeev Kumar Sharma. (2009), "Right to Information Act 2005: A Critique with Governance and Administrative Reforms Perspective", *The Indian Journal of Public Administration*, LV(3): 481–504.

63. Swamy, Raju Naryana. (2011), "Organisation's Other than the Government and RTI Act", *University News* 49(2).

64. Jenkins, Rub and Marie Anne. (1999), "Account and Accountability Theoretical Information of Right to Information Movement and India", *Third Journal Quarterly*, 20(3): 603–622.

65. Chandhoke, Neera. (2003), *The Conceits of Civil Society*. Oxford University Press. ISBN-0195661958, 9780195661958.

66. World Bank. (1992), *Governance and Development*. Washington, DC: The World Bank.

67. Guha Roy, Jaytilak. (2006), "Administrative Reform Initiatives for Excellence in Public Services", *Indian Journal of Public Administration*. Special Number on Excellence in Public Service, LII (3).

68. Ibid.

69. Jenkins, Rub and Marie Anne. (1999), "Account and Accountability theoretical information of Right to Information Movement and India", *Third Journal Quarterly*, 20(3): 603–622.

70. Ibid.

71. See Chapman, Richard A. and Michael Hunt. (2010), *Freedom of Information. Local Government and Accountability*. Surrey, UK: Ashgate Publishing Ltd.

72. Weiss, Thomas G. (2000), "Governance, Good Governance and Global Governance: Conceptual and Actual Challenges", *Third World Quarterly*, 21(5): 795–814.

73. Corbridge, Stuart, et al. (2005), *Seeing the State: Governance and Governmentality in India*. Cambridge; New York: Cambridge University Press.

74. Newell, P. and S. Bellour (2002), "Mapping Accountability: Origins, Contexts and Implications for Development", IDS Working Paper 168. Institute of Development Studies, Brighton.

75. Keohane, Robert. (2003), *Global Governance and Democratic Accountability in Taming Globalization, Frontiers of Governance*, eds. Held, David, Mathias Koenig-Archibugi, Polity.

76. Held David and Koenig-Archibugi Mathais. (2005), *Global Governance and Public Accountability*. Blackwell Publishers.

77. Aucoin, Peter and Ralph Heintzman. (1998), "The Dialectics of Accountability for Performance in Public Management Reform", *International Review of Administrative Sciences*, 66(1).

78. Pollit and Bouckaert, (2000), *Public Management Reform*. Oxford University Press.

79. See Ackerman, John M. and Irma E. Sandoval-Ballesteros (2006), "The Global Explosion of Freedom of Information Laws", *Administrative Law Review*.

80. O'Donnell, Guillermo. (1998), "Horizontal Accountability in New Democracies", *Journal of Democracy*.

81. Dicey, A.V. (1959), *An Introduction to the Study of the Law of the Constitution* (10th Edition). London: Macmillan and Company Ltd.

82. Barowalia, J.N. (2006), *Commentary on the Right to Information Act*. India: Universal Law Publishing Co.

83. Ibid.

84. Roberts, A. (2006), *Blacked Out: Government Secrecy in the Information Age*. New York: Cambridge University Press.

85. Birchall, C. (2011), "Introduction to 'Secrecy and Transparency': The Politics of Opacity and Openness", *Theory, Culture and Society*, 28: 7–25.

86. Banisar, D. (2006), *Freedom of Information around the World 2006: A Global Survey of Access to Government Information Laws*. London: Privacy International.

87. Andersson, S. and Heywood, P.M. (2009), "The Politics of Perception: Use and Abuse of Transparency International's Approach to Measuring Corruption", *Political Studies*, 57(4): 746–767.

88. Roberts, A. (2006), *Blacked Out: Government Secrecy in the Information Age*. New York: Cambridge University Press.

89. Fox, Jonathan (2007), "The Uncertain Relationship between Transparency and Accountability", *Development in Practice*, 17(4): 663–671.

90. Haque, M.S. (2008), "Global Rise of Neoliberal State and its Impact on Citizenship: Experiences in Developing Nations", *Asian Journal of Social Science*, 36: 11–34.

Chapter 2

Theories of Right to Information in India

INTRODUCTION

This chapter is a detailed description of the various theories on the subject and helps in forming a basis for the arguments that I want to explore during the course of this work and the most relevant research methodology which will be adopted for this book. Over the last two decades, the world has seen a sharp rise in the number of countries which have some sort of a law pertaining to public access to government documents. Until 1989, only eight countries in the world had any such legislation. In 2011, this number stood at 88.[1] Unsurprisingly, a number of publications that address the issue of transparency, accountability, and access to information have also emerged concomitantly.

Rajni Kothari is of the view that a democratic system must give rise to an open and flexible society where individual freedom has the maximum scope to flourish.[2] A responsible democracy is one which guarantees openness and transparency to its citizens and where the judiciary, the legislature, and the executive are continuously accountable to the people. The RTI is the main instrument for moving toward this goal, the role of the state in granting the right is vital. Curiously, only limited academic literature has specifically addressed the RTI Act in India. To understand the concept of "Right" and "Access," it is important to analyze the concept and universe of research, through relevant theory and empirical work that is available. The foundation of the chapter is based on the theoretical framework of RTI in India.

THEORIES OF RIGHT TO INFORMATION IN INDIA

The argument given by Tocqueville is that "censorship prevents us from correcting errors through critical discussion" and "public sector is by nature internalized, closed and censures information under the pretext of confidentiality of government" (Tocqueville, 1835:10-12).[3] Tocqueville believed that the society had gradually moved from aristocracy to more equality, which he described as an irresistible revolution.

However, true democracy and along with it, political liberty is achieved in a democracy primarily when the citizens are totally free to make informed decisions through information about the state machinery.

> The first duty which is at this time imposed upon those who direct our affairs is to educate the democracy; to reanimate its faith, if that be possible, to purify its morals; to regulate its energies; to substitute for its inexperience a knowledge of business, and for its blind instincts an acquaintance with its true interests; to adapt its government to time and place, and to modify it in compliance with circumstances and characters. The consequence of this has been that the democratic revolution has been affected only in the material parts of society, without that concomitant change in laws, ideas, habits and manners which was necessary to render such a revolution beneficial. We have gotten a democracy, severed from whatever would lessen its vices and render its natural advantages more prominent; and although we already perceive the evils it brings, we are yet ignorant of the benefits it might confer.[4] (Gujaral, I. K, 2007)

For an evolving democracy, the right to access public information is indispensable for democratic sustenance and safety of public life. This chapter would first explain the nature of the transition from government to governance. Primary reliance is placed on the writings of Kuldeep Mathur. Mathur (2009)[5] has explained how the nature of the state, which is the central theme in his discourse, affects the relationship between government and its various institutions and citizens. The government functions through administration and creates a relationship between institutions and citizens which undergo a change with the changing nature and form of the state such as autocratic state, military state, or democratic state. With the advent of globalization, there is a greater role of market forces and less of the state; the welfare state is giving way to the market which involves new relationships between the state and the private citizens, corporations, civil society, international aid providing agencies, and so on. This has led to the redefinition and reconceptualization of the term "governance." The United Nations Development Programme (UNDP)[6] has defined governance as

> the exercise of economic, political and administrative authority to manage a country's affairs at all levels and the means by which states promote social cohesion and integration and ensure the well-being of their population. It embraces all methods used to distribute power and manage public resources, and the organizations that shape government and the execution of policy. It encompasses the mechanisms, processes and institutions, through which citizens and groups articulate their interests, exercise their legal rights, meet their obligations and resolve their differences. (UNDP policy document, 1997: Glossary)

Over a period of time, the term "governance" has become inclusive of elements such as accountability and transparency. Amartya Sen argues that public action has the potential of making a government really accountable and transparent (Dreze and Sen, 1997).[7] Public action is the action that is originated by the people themselves rather than by the government. The government was earlier pyramidical, internalized, and concerned only about itself. However, now it is forced to look outward and form alliances and partnerships with nongovernment organizations, resident welfare associations, companies, and so on. The government usually does not have the expertise to handle so many different relationships, and the change from a single hierarchical model to multiple players and partners can be monitored only by informed citizens. Thus, to ensure that a mature democracy such as that in India moves from government to governance, it is necessary for the citizens to monitor the interplay between various state actors for which an informed citizenry is most important. The transition from government to governance brings in more partners, collaborators, and investors from national and international domains. Developmental activities, budget allocations, and personnel decisions within bureaucracy become matters larger than the established framework of rules which could monitor them. Thus there is a greater chance of misuse, arbitrariness, and hurried decisions to benefit a party at the cost of public money. There is a big gap and a disjunction between established norms of public accountability and the role which the bureaucracy is expected to deliver to the satisfaction of partner agencies. The RTI bridges this gap in a most effective manner.

The concept of democratic government has changed a lot over the centuries with the rise of complex systems and state structures which have completely changed the older democratic notion of direct participation of the citizenry in policy making such as that which existed in Greek city-states or American town meetings of the eighteenth century. The citizens of the modern states are not so directly connected with the policy makers and feel a kind of missing link between themselves and the political and bureaucratic policy makers. This sense of alienation has resulted in the alienation of the electorate. The way to overcome this sense of alienation among the public is by providing free information about government functioning to the public. As in the opinion of Pierre Elliot Trudeau (1997),[8] complete and factual information is necessary for a healthy democracy to exist and develop. Openness in government functioning will lead to the evaluation of government policies by the common public in a better manner. Karl Brandt (1965:629)[9] has stressed upon the need for vigilance in a democracy by socially conscious citizens, "Eternal Vigilance is the price of liberty," he said that "the most effective way to conserve and protect freedom and human dignity is by way of eternal vigilance." According to Brant, eternal vigilance should be carried out in a democracy by those citizens who have an incorruptible conscience and the courage to put their lives at stake for basic rights bestowed by the Constitution. Eternal vigilance, as propounded by Brant, can be carried out through informed citizens. Information is increasingly important in a thriving democracy such as India because the right of the people to gain information from public authorities is used as a tool of vigilance.

The chapter discusses the relationship between bureaucracy and accountability. P. M. Blau (1956)[10] has defined bureaucracy in terms of an organization that coordinates and puts together the work of a large number of individuals. The motive of such an organization is to accomplish large-scale administrative tasks. All literature on bureaucracy is replete with the need for accountability. While some bureaucracies may become humongous and large and thereafter sluggish, there are many bureaucracies that may be more inclined to become arrogant toward their masters, that is, the people. It is for this reason that they are required to be subject to questioning and under constant vigilance by the citizens. Even though many administrative reforms have been suggested time and again as a remedy for the failings of administrative bodies yet democracies run the constant risk of being autocratic and unanswerable to the demands of the common public. It is for these reasons that Mc Turner (1952)[11] advocates for democracy in administration. She states that it may be simpler to run a monarchy form of government rather than a democracy because the shift from a monarchy to a democracy becomes more complex. Education is required to bring more and more people into the electorate and when the government demands education, it must also give education. The idea of a democracy should be that of maintaining contacts between administrators and the people. Not only should there be control and regulation from the bureaucracy but also regular audits of the bureaucracy by the people, which is the crux of vigilance by the common public of the administration which governs them. It may sound like a very simple idea of dissemination of information; however, democracy in administration is easily said than done. It is much easier for the bureaucracy to hastily issue an order in the dark suddenly and then cover up itself when the criticism from all quarters begins. However, it is much more difficult, however definitely much more needed, to have continuous vigilance from the public over the functioning of the bureaucracy. This may take place through direct discussions with the public, involving the public in every decision that the government needs to take, and invitation to the public to engage in constant dialogue with the decision-makers. For the public to be able to perform such kind of an interactive role, it is important that such public is well educated and informed. The bureaucracy has to also accept the role of the common public as an intelligent and argumentative entity which enters into constant interaction with the decision-makers.

Such an interaction would result in a vigilant citizenry and a truly participatory democracy. Moreover, for such vigilance on the part of the people to take place, there needs to be information about the functioning of the government that should be available to the public. It is said by Milton Friedman that eternal vigilance is required and there have to be people who step up to the plate, who believe in liberty, and who are willing to fight for it. The basic characteristics of bureaucratic organization are specialization, a hierarchy of authority, a system of rules, and impersonality. P. M. Blau (1956)[12] has stressed upon the need for finding democratic ways of controlling bureaucracies otherwise such uncontrolled bureaucracies will become overpowering and shall master over the common public. Peter and Charles (1984)[13] have opined that the bureaucratic model is a closed and self-contained model. The RTI is necessary for a healthy democracy such that bureaucratic red-tapism, corruption, and sluggishness can be intercepted.

VARIOUS THEORIES AND THE PHILOSOPHY OF RTI

The thrust of classical model of governance patterned on Weberian model of bureaucracy is to promote the culture of secrecy and discourage sharing of information. It creates information asymmetry between administration and citizens. During the last five decades, the social science work and especially public administration, political science, economics, and management works have provided alternative models of governance. Literature on New Rights School of Thoughts including Public Choice Theory and the Chicago School, a Competitive Public Administration and Reinventing Government has documented both theory and practices of emerging models of public administration (Ghuman. 2012).[14]

These alternative models comprise New Public Management and Entrepreneurial Government. These models not only promote efficiency and economy in administration but also intend to make governance transparent, responsive, accountable, and citizen-friendly. In this context, a host of citizen-centric administrative innovations have been introduced. These innovations include the RTI; Citizens' Charters; e-governance; simplification of procedures to reduce time and cost in the delivery of services; decentralization; establishing regulatory, authorities/commissions; and recently Right to Service Acts in the states. RTI 2005 is one of such initiatives intending to promote citizen-centric and good governance more explicitly in the form of promotion of transparency, accountability, and curbing corruption (Ghuman, 2012).[15]

The underlying philosophy of RTI Act, 2005, which ought to make the working of public authorities transparent, is rooted in the modern liberal democratic theory. The political theorists and the supporters of modern liberal democratic theory perceive transparency (openness) along with accessible government as well as informed citizenry as the indispensable parts of democracy and also view transparency as an essential ingredient of functional liberal democracy (Fenster, 2006, 2015).[16] According to Fenster, political theorists, economists, and philosophers such as John Locke, John Stuart Mill, Jean-Jacques Rousseau, Jeremy Bentham, Immanuel Kant, John Rawls, and Fredrick Hayek through their works have explicitly and implicitly advocated transparency in government functioning as an essential ingredient of liberal democratic theory which is in tune with modern Western political values. The proponents of transparency advance two merits of transparency. First, transparency makes the government more democratic, and second, transparent governments operate in an effective and efficient manner and hence serve the citizens better (Fenster, 2006).[17] These theorists have opined that publicity of government laws and actions facilitates citizens in making informed rational choices and informed citizens initiating and participating in public debates. Among these thinkers, the liberal philosophers who discern a kind of contractual relationship between citizens and government express that openness in the government leads to informed citizenry resulting in informed consent issued by them to the government (Fenster, 2006).[18]

The works of two thinkers, namely, John Rawls and Friedrick Hayek, deserve special mention in regard to role of transparency in the working of the government. Rawls's proposition of "Original Position" in his *A Theory of Justice* (1971) acknowledges publicity as one of the pillars of a just society due to its importance in helping citizens make a rational choice in an informed manner (Fenster, 2006).[19] "Original Position" is one of the revealing features of Rawls's concept of "Justice as Fairness" in his work. The "Original Position" describes a situation, where people are free, equal, and rational and are concerned to decide upon the nature of principles through which they will be governed. While quoting Rawls, Fenster opines,

> The individual's choice must be informed for the thought experiment of the original position to be meaningful. Similarly, Rawls's political liberalism requires that free and equal citizens fully understand and scrutinize society's institutions rather than misconceive the political order due to 'accidental or established delusions, or other mistaken beliefs resting on the deceptive appearances of institutions that mislead us as to how they work. (Fenster, 2015)[20]

Thus, Rawls's advocacy for transparency in the government constitutes one of the major arguments under liberal democratic theory.

Fredrick Hayek, a political economist and philosopher, viewed the use of existing knowledge as a political important aspect of constructing a rational economic order (Hayek, 1945).[21] While endorsing the significance of utilizing accessible and requisite knowledge, Hayek opines, "If we possess all the relevant information, if we can start out from a given system of preferences and if we command complete knowledge of available means, the problem which remains is purely of logic." Gillespie, while embarking on Hayek's views expressed in his work *The Road to Serfdom*, has highlighted the importance of transparent rules in making people able to plan. Gillespie opines,

> A government in all its actions is bound by rules fixed and announced beforehand—the rules which make it possible to see with a fair degree of certainty how the authorities will use its coercive powers in given circumstances, and to plan one's individual affairs on the basis of this knowledge. (Gillespie, 2006)[22]

Thus, transparency also helps in prediction while planning. Hayek has also opined that economics of information does affect market and accountability (Hildreth, 2005).[23]

Fenster (2006),[24] while highlighting the aspect of transparency in the works of Rawls and Hayek, succinctly sums up,

> Indeed, formal notions of the rule of law, whether they emphasise a Rawlsian just state or a Hayekian minimalist, one requires self-enacting, publicly accessible, and comprehensible legislation that limits and confines all exercise of public authority, and that facilitates the private ordering of individual behavior as a result.

The rights-based legislation (RTI) which promotes transparency in the functioning of public authorities also derives its theoretical strength from rights-based approach (RBA) to development. The RBA emerged as a new development paradigm in the late 1990s (Kindornay, Ron & Carpenter, 2012).[25] According to Kapoor and Duvvury, RBA to development has five major features. First, it is based on a framework of rights and obligations. Second, it takes into consideration the whole range of civil, cultural, economic, political, and social rights. Third, it establishes a healthy relationship between a transparency and RBA as it locates transparency and account ability in the framework of RBA because of its emphasis on raising the level of transparency and accountability in the development process. RBA identifies rights-holders and their claims and corresponding duty-bearers and their obligations. For ensuring accountability and transparency, the RBA also promotes the creation of such laws, policies, institutions, administrative procedures, practices, and mechanisms which are necessary for realization of entitlements and responds to the violation of rights (Kapur & Duvvury, 2008).[26] Thus, the RTI Act 2005 is also considered as an outcome of RBA to development. The other two features of RBA are a high degree of participation and focus on problems of discrimination, equality, equity, and vulnerability.

The procedure for seeking information under the RTI Act is simple and easy. The applicant only needs to write an application with details pertaining to the information being sought. The process of getting information under the RTI Act is shown in figure 2.1

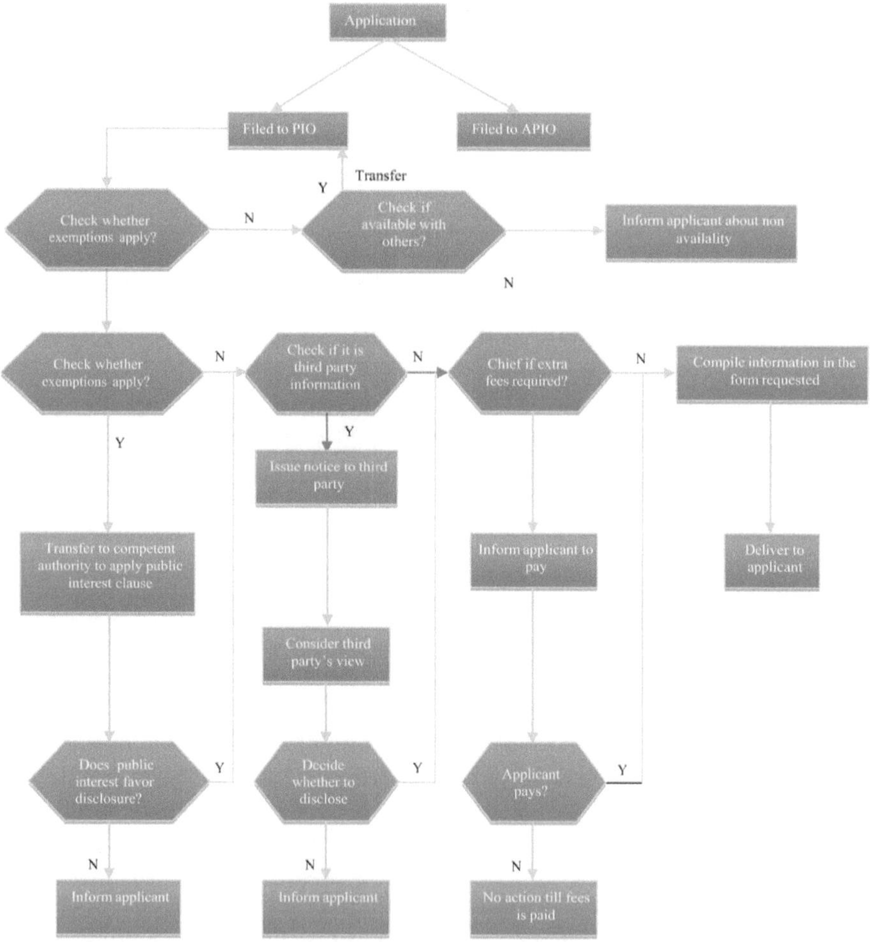

Figure 2.1 Flowchart of the Process Involved in Getting Information under the Act.
Source: Government of India (2006).

PERFORMANCE OF RTI IN INDIA

The RTI Act is a watershed legislation (Public Affairs Centre, 2009),[27] which has the potential to revolutionize the working of public organizations. The RTI Act is a powerful tool in the hands of citizens to make public organizations transparent, accountable, and corruption-free as the Act places records and performance of public authorities open to public scrutiny (Centre for Good Governance, 2009; Government of India, 2006; Kejriwal, 2006; Kulkarni, 2008; Roberts, 2010; Shreyaskar, 2013, 2014; Singh, 2011).[28]

While assessing the performance of the Act, the major focus is on (1) growth parameters of RTI; (2) analyzing the role of RTI in promotion of transparency, accountability, and taming corruption in the functioning of public authorities; and (3) compliance by public authorities and Information Commission to various obligations envisaged in the Act. The Act places certain obligations on public authorities and information commissions, compliance of which is important for the successful implementation of the Act

GROWTH PARAMETERS OF RTI

RTI has been experiencing phenomenal growth overtime. The number of public authorities listed/registered with CIC's database has increased from 938 in the year 2005–2006 to 2,030 in the year 2014–2015 with the number falling from 2012 to 2013 onwards. The number of public authorities, which submitted annual returns relating to RTI, has increased from 837 in 2005–2006 to 1,651 in 2013–2014 but their percentage has come down from 89.23% in 2005–2006 to 72.54% in 2013–2014 and further improved to 75.27% in 2014–2015. The number of RTI applications has experienced a phenomenal increase between 2005–2006 and 2014–2015. The number of applications was 24,436 in 2005–2006 and rose to 845,032 in the year 2014–2015 thus registering 35 times increase. Another positive development in the field of RTI is that the rejection rate of the application has come down from 13.9% in 2005–2006 to 8.39% in 2014–2015. Disciplinary action taken against officers in respect of the administration of RTI Act has followed an erratic trend. The number of cases was 2 in 2005–2006 which increased to 432 in the year 2010–2011, came down to 28 in the year 2011–2012, again rose to 502 in the year 2012–2013, and drastically fell to just 8 and 4 in the years 2013–2014 and 2014–2015, respectively. The total amount of fees, additional charges, and penalty levied have shown a continuous increase over the period. For example, the amount was 509,000 in the year 2005–2006 which increased to 10.5 million in 2014–2015 (table 2.1)

Table 2.1 Growth Parameters of RTI

Year	*2005–2006*	*2006–2007*	*2007–2008*	*2008–2009*	*2009–2010*	*2010–2011*	*2011–2012*	*2012–2013*	*2013–2014*	*2014–2015*
Total Number of Public Authorities Listed/ Registered	938	1,412	1,597	1,770	1,847	2,149	2,314	2,333	2,276	2,030
Number of Public Authorities Who Submitted Annual Return (%)	837 (89.23)	1,168 (82.72)	1,382 (86.54)	1,528 (86.33)	1,427 (77.26)	1,452 (67.5)	1,593 (68.8)	1,864 (79.9)	1,651 (72.54)	1,528 (75,27)
Total Number of Requests Received	24,436	183,424	284,187	362,520	626,748	437,744	705,976	886,681	962,630	845,232
Total Number of Rejected Requests (%)	3,387 (13.9)	15,388 (9)	18,966 (7.20)	23,954 (7.26)	34,057 (6.43)	21,413 (5.1)	52,313 (8.3)	62,231 (7.7)	60,127 (7.21)	63,351 (8.39)
Total Number of Cases Where Disciplinary Action Was Taken	2	7	20	9	35	432	28	502	8	4
Total Amount of Fees, Additional Charges and Penalty Levied (in)	508,749	3,071,167	4,356,782	5,539,162	8,548,568	8,086,216	10,059,199	12.030,964	11,406,379	10,507,823

Source: Data compiled from Annual Reports of the years from 2007–2008 to 2014–2015 of CIC.

SURVEY OF LEGISLATION

The entire effort today is made toward keeping everything secret, away from the general public. The statutes such as IPC, Criminal Procedure Code, Evidence Act, and Commissions of Inquiry Act 1952 "have all been pressed in the name of security and sovereignty to hide the misdeeds of the government and to prevent its collapse" Even a newly elected minister who is a people's representative instead of being open to its people the first thing that he does on entering the cabinet is to take the "oath of secrecy."

There have been many failures of the Parliament that have contributed to the erosion of the confidence of the people in its capacity to deliver good governance.[29] These are the failures, which cast serious doubts on the capacity of the Parliament to deal with important national issues. It further highlights the weakness of the mechanisms provided by the Constitution. Another case like this when the Parliament has failed to function appropriately is in the case of removal of justice V. Ramaswamy.[30] It was shocking to see the Congress party then in power to refrain from voting though the charges against him were established. These all actually show how transparent our Parliament proceedings are. It is very much necessary for the present work to theorize the term information in the present context.

WHAT IS INFORMATION?

It becomes very important for the purpose of this research to theorize the meaning of the term "information" that is the basis for this research. While it is true that the term information may have different connotations in different contexts, it is pertinent to draw a functional and operational definition for the term.

Information means any material in any form including records, documents, memos, e-mails, opinions, advices, press releases, circulars, orders, logbooks, contracts, reports, papers, samples, models, data material held in any electronic form, and information relating to any private body which can be accessed by a public authority under any other law for the time being in force but does not include file noting.[31]

It includes the right to

(i) inspect works, documents, and records;
(ii) take notes, extracts, or certified copies of documents or records;
(iii) take certified samples of material; and
(iv) obtain in form of printouts diskettes floppies, tapes videos, cassettes, or in any other electronic mode or through printouts. Where such information is stored in a computer or any other device.

Webster's New Collegiate Dictionary defines information as "knowledge obtained from investigation, study or instruction." Many scholars have attempted to define the term "information" and all of them have defined it in different ways and from different perspectives. For the benefit of this study, information within the perspective of the information held by public authorities thereby meaning, information that is in the custody of government offices, bureaucrats, and public officials is to be considered. Moreover, since we live in a knowledge economy and the world is increasingly becoming knowledge driven, it is also important for the purpose of this research to understand the relationship between information and knowledge. Fritz Machlup (1962)[32] has interpreted that all information is knowledge since the Act of informing creates a state of knowing in someone's mind. Also important in this context is the concept of public sphere that has been elucidated by Juergen Habermas[33] in his theorization on the subject in 1996. He relies on the importance of discussion, debate, and political discourse that takes place in the common gatherings of people, which he defines as a public sphere. In his initial writings, Habermas sketched out the various forms of democracy beginning with traditional Greek democracy. Thereafter, he detailed the nuances of bourgeois democracy and the modern welfare state. Habermas takes the course of the kind of democracy that is associated with Marx, Rousseau, and Dewey wherein the people's sovereignty was supreme and political discourse among the people against parliamentary form of democracy was common.

He further tries to differentiate between the vibrant liberal democracy in the bourgeois era wherein public discourse by the common people was the norm of the day, with the modern spectator form of democracy in which the public debate is orchestrated by the media and the elite. In the bourgeois era, public sphere was constituted by political discourse and consensus whereas, with the decline in the public sphere, citizens became more involved in debates about private concerns rather than the larger democratic good. However, the crux of his argument is that free and fair public discourse is important in a thriving participatory democracy and for this purpose information is very important. Until the citizenry is informed about the workings of the government, it cannot engage in a discussion that helps shape public policy and the concept of democracy in such a scenario is then incomplete.

The three distinct terms, that is, "open government," "transparency," and "freedom of information" are often used interchangeably. Each of these has been given a specific meaning by some authors (e.g., Hazel 1999, Hood and Herald 2006),[34] however, according to Hunt and Chapman (2010),[35] precise distinctions may sometimes obscure overall meanings. The value of information in today's knowledge economy is evident from the fact that many authors have analyzed and evolved at the conclusion that while information may be a cognitive process, in many instances, it is undoubtedly a marketable product. The amount of information is also on the rise. More information is now being generated and printed or stored than has ever before been done in the history of mankind. Since there is a phenomenal rise in the amount of information that is available with government departments, the result can be a lot of confusion that is generated among the members of the public because of various government orders that are contradictory in nature and come one after the other such that the efficacy of one order gets diminished or wiped by the next order. In such cases, the public has the right to demand details of such orders from the government.

In many cases, the public is fed with information of unreliable nature by middlemen and vested interests. To avoid this eyewash, it is important that the public receives the clarifications from the government itself in the form of information received after the filing of a RTI application. Harry M. Kibirige (1983)[36] mentions in his book that there is a constant tension between the information user (i.e., the citizen in this case) and the provider (i.e., the government).

These six dilemmas can be juxtaposed for the purpose of this research to mean the dilemmas that are faced as far as the transfer of information between the government and the citizen is concerned. The first dilemma pertains to the puzzle and complexities that the citizen has to face while getting the right information from the myriad of potential sources. Therefore, the citizen while making a request under the RTI Act has to first ascertain the right authority to which he can make the request or else it will lead to the application being forwarded to the concerned authority which in effect means a loss of time for the applicant. Information experts in the form of Public Information Officers (PIOs) are usually designated with the task of solving this puzzle. However, seldom they are themselves not equipped and do not understand the nuances of the Act and many times this leads to duplication of work as the application is forwarded from one department to the other. A good system of dissemination is much needed to make the system of dissemination of information effective because the effectiveness of the user's decision may depend on how efficient was the information source (PIO) in tracking, processing, and presenting to him the appropriate information. This dilemma emphasizes the need for an efficient system of information delivery. The second dilemma can be read with the third dilemma that is faced by the users that whether to charge the public for information that is being supplied under the Act because the information that is generated in public offices is also costing money. This puzzle is even more crucial when the level of public funding is progressively shrinking and the demand for online services is rising and accentuating due to more and more applicants using information technology to access information under the RTI Act. (Very recently, the Municipal Corporation of Delhi (MCD) has started accepting RTIs online.) The fourth dilemma that constitutes the problem of information dissemination is the information problems that require instant solutions wherein the citizens approach the information officers seeking instant answers. The life and liberty clause in the RTI Act 2005 tries to provide instant answers to the applicants; however, the efficacy of the same is yet to be determined. The development of new technologies has given a new dimension to this research since the development of new technologies has necessitated the restructuring of the administrative setup. Many applications are received online. Suo moto disclosure of information on the websites of the government offices has become mandatory. In the State of Bihar, the PIOs have started receiving RTI applications over the telephone. Finally, the last problem that is analyzed by this research is the international dilemma of UN Conventions that require the governments of all countries to be open and transparent with overlapping areas of privacy and national sovereignty that sometimes prevent the free flow of such information.

HOW DOES INFORMATION BRING ACCOUNTABILITY?

A thematic engagement into the past and present theories relating to accountability, transparency, grievance redressal, and its relation to freedom of information would help understand the various dimensions of the RTI in contemporary models and discourses. This is significantly important to understand the nature and substance of the RTI as it fundamentally revolves around the concept of strengthening democracy by promoting accountability and one of the tools for doing the same is by providing access to knowledge to the citizens. Therefore, there is an apparent reason to make a threadbare analysis of the current theories and literary and scholarly work on the subject of accountability and access to knowledge.

The RTI has to be studied within the framework of accountability in the changing nature of the state. It has attempted to redefine traditional accountability and contours of a rational-legal state held by parliamentary accountability. The new reforms toward marketization and contractualism have brought new institutional actors in mobilizing and articulating interests of society. This change has replaced the rationality-bound state held accountable through parliamentary channels by a supermarket state model providing services to citizens. Thus accountability has become more instrumental than a design for articulating collective interests and the RTI of the citizens is used as a means toward this end. Thomas (1995)[37] rightly points out that ministerial responsibility has been replaced by contract-based accountability. Further D.F. Thompson (1980)[38] expresses the concern regarding the replacement of the political power of elected officials by an indirect model of political leadership. Keohane (1984)[39] and Held (1999) have also raised the issue of organizational entropy due to asymmetric accountability which shrinks people's participation and weakens political power. Davis, G. et al. (1999)[40] highlights the asymmetry of accountability when a few operating and regulatory agencies control and hold enormous power and are accountable to none. Robert O. Keohane (2003)[41] indicates that the progress toward linear process of the market and management efficiency has increased administrative orthodoxy, which is further leading to isomorphic and global trends which shrink aspects of accountability. This is exacerbated by the fact that history is seldom linear and may require less orthodox arrangements for citizens which the new situation may not be in a position to provide.

The RTI is regarded by many scholars to be the master key to good governance since it helps to

- Promote openness, transparency, and accountability in public administration;
- Empower people to combat state corruption;
- Prevent administrative high-handedness or arbitration;
- Bridge the gap between the provider and recipient of public services;
- Make citizens' part of the decision-making process in the government;
- Provide responsive administration;
- Strengthen the foundations of grassroots democracy through people's participation in local governance and development activities; and
- Empower people to have access to other rights. (Roy and Dey, 2002)[42]

The implementation of the right to freedom of expression and the RTI are prerequisites for ensuring the voice and participation necessary for an open democratic society. This implies that the promotion and protection of both access to information itself and flows of information that exist between constituents—both men and women, government, Parliament, community groups, civil society organizations, and private sector—are of equal importance. The first report of the Administrative Reforms Committee recommended that the "oath of secrecy" should be replaced with "oath of transparency."This underlines the importance that is placed on the transparency and accountability in the functioning of the government.

The third aspect in this chapter is the concept of "right" and "information" within the pro-poor governance framework. As the name of the Act itself suggests, there exist two very important ingredients herein, one being the concept of "right" and the other being that of "information." In the first scenario, the focus is on the right of the people to be informed by those in power such that they become an informed citizenry. In the second concept, the onus is on the bureaucracy to provide information to the public such that the idea of a participatory democracy is complete and evolving.

The right to seek information has been recognized as a human right and goes beyond the right to life and liberty. Article19 of the Universal Declaration of Human Rights[43] adopted in 1948 states that

> everyone has the right to freedom of opinion and expression: this right includes freedom to hold opinions without interferences and to seek, receive and impart information and ideas without interference and to seek, receive and impart information and ideas through any media and regardless of frontiers.

In today's time, freedom of speech and expression is recognized in international and regional human rights law. The right is enshrined in Article 19 of the International Covenant on Civil and Political Rights, Article 10 of the European Convention on Human Rights, Article 13 of the American Convention on Human Rights, and Article 9 of the African Charter on Human and People's Rights. Based on John Milton's arguments, freedom of speech is understood as a multifaceted right that includes not only the right to express or disseminate information and ideas but three further distinct aspects, that is, the right to seek information and ideas, the right to receive information and ideas, and the right to impart information and ideas.

The RTI is a very important part of a bundle of civil rights. Dicey (1959:207-8,240)[44] characterized the right to personal liberty as "in substance a person's right not to be subjected to imprisonment, arrest, or other physical coercion in any manner that does not admit of legal justification." Similarly, the right to freedom of discussion is defined by Dicey as "any man may . . . say or write whatever he likes, subject to the risk of, it may be, severe punishment if he publishes any statement (either by word of mouth, in writing, or in print) which he is not legally entitled to make." This research critically examines the present form of the RTI Act 2005 since there is a need to analyze whether the legislation has been able to fulfill its intended purpose of facilitating the process of accountability and transparency in the Indian democratic framework.

The RTI Act 2005 is an attempt to codify this right to receive information from public functionaries which is in fact an important pillar of democracy where all citizens have the right to freedom of speech and expression which is slated to include the RTI. This helps in making the democratic framework of a country stronger, more dynamic, and truly representative of the people. The study draws from the work of Bruce Ackerman and James S. Fishkin, R. C. Luskin (2005),[45] who argue that information in fact is a first step to strengthen democracy and that an informed citizenry will lead to dialogue, deliberation, and creation of community.

Olson, J. P. has already pointed out in the case of Latin America (2008)[46] that the failure of political society to effectively embed itself in civil society and to make it accountable to citizens, and not just interests, can severely undermine the legitimacy of democratic rule. The RTI tries to address the problem of absence of accountability, lack of transparency in government functioning, and quote one example from the area which definitely requires increased transparency is the long overdue thorough analysis and amendment of the Commissions of Enquiry Act, 1952, so as to make it obligatory for the Union and state governments to provide for the publication of the inquiry reports, once they have been presented before the legislatures in time. Such publication may include a reasonable exemption clause if deemed necessary in the interests of the state, national security, or foreign relations.

In this context, the eminent jurist Justice V. Krishna Iyer (1985:14) has stated that

> when Commissions prolong their enquiries and produce reports which are shelved for long in government pigeon-holes, matters of public importance suffer, fade out and the people are stultified by denial of information.[47] . . . In most such legislations Governments enjoy the option to accept or reject the report which means that a cunning Administration may use Enquiry Commissions as crisis tactics, the end product being conveniently discarded if unfavourable. Thus, unless meaningful mutations are made from the angle of freedom of information, Commission strategy may prove to informational treachery.

James Boyle (2003)[48] has discussed in his article, "The Second Enclosure Movement and the Construction of the Public Domain," the information that is held by public officials in government offices can be considered to be the commons, however, this has been taken over as private property of the government officials in many senses, for various reasons. The tragedy of the commons is that it is no longer common and has been privatized to every end possible. The same seemed to be the situation with the public documents and information held by public officials prior to the promulgation of the RTI Act 2005. Public records were not treated as public property but as private property and these were held very closely by government officials. They were guarded as if they were private property and access to such documents was restricted and to some extent denied by the government. Just as James Boyle makes the case for more property rights slowing down innovation, putting multiple roadblocks, multiple necessary licenses, in the way of subsequent innovation, similarly one can make the case for the bureaucracy placing multiple roadblocks and in many cases censoring the information accessible to the general public thereby creating a veil of secrecy that restricts an effective democracy by lessening the effect of participatory democracy. Using a novel version of the idea of the tragedy of the commons, Kale and Murray (2005)[49] referred to these effects the transaction costs caused by myriad property rights over the necessary components of some subsequent innovation—as The Tragedy of the Anti-commons. This would imply that the information about government functioning that is available with the bureaucracy is covered up under so many different barriers to its free flow that it becomes virtually impossible for the common man to gain access to information. These barriers to open dissemination of information may be in the form of legislation (such as the Official Secrets Act (OSA) 1923) or internal code of conduct framed by the bureaucracy itself or narrow and limited interpretation of the rules and legislation.

James Boyle (2003)[50] further explains that what is true of property is also true of public domain. Borrowing his argument for the matter at hand that relates to information that is available in public domain, it can be said that the information that is available in the public domain should also be protected for rational reasons that are enumerated in the exemption clause of the Act, such as national security, intellectual property concerns, personal information, and so on. Just as in the case of intellectual property, a patent pool kind of structure needs to be created wherein all public information is freely available to all the citizens of the country. It is an irony that in a country like India, which boasts of being a vibrant democracy, access to information is being guarded by the keepers of public records. The bureaucrats are acting opposite to the principles of accountability if they are not sharing information with the public and are not disclosing information that should be publicly known because it is information about the public. This is the concept of taking away from the commons what is of the commons and then turning it into private property on which the common public is viewed as a trespasser. This situation existed in India prior to the promulgation of the RTI Act and in some ways, it can be said that the RTI is an attempt to rectify the problem of almost zero accountability that exists in government functioning in India.

The importance of the Act in bringing about the much-required changes in the Indian bureaucracy is evident from the fact that the first report of the Second Administrative Reforms Commission is dedicated to the RTI. The current trend is to move away from the traditional form of invisible government which has become obsolete in this age of globalization and liberalization (Roy: 2007).[51] The current trends toward the shift from a strict bureaucracy to a minimalist government control era can be traced to the advent of globalization and economic liberalization that took place in the late twentieth century, which according to Guha Roy[52] brought about a paradigm shift in the nature and character of the state and public administration from "the traditional welfare administration state to a corporate welfare state" (Roy, 2006: 396-411).[53]

ACCOUNTABILITY AND GOVERNANCE IN INDIA

Currently, the developing countries are facing a wave of reforms that are being called for in the area of public administration. Some of these concepts are fairly new such as good governance, new public management, citizen's charter, reinventing government, ethical governance, contracting out public services, e-governance, and so on. Some of these concepts are carried over from developed countries and are no doubt targeted toward reforms of various kinds such as social and economic reforms.

In the case of India, the economic liberalization of the country that took place in 1991 brought in a new era of administrative reforms. There was a paradigm shift from the Nehruvian model of socialist welfare to a Westernized model of development through globalization, liberalization, free-market economy, and good governance. As a result of this shift in the economic policy of the government, there was a need felt to haul up the bureaucracy to make it more contemporary with changing times, such that it is more conducive to the changes that were taking place in the economic front of the country and to make the bureaucracy more conducive to growth and to make it a function of growth and not as a roadblock to growth. To this end, a number of reforms were initiated such as the efficiency enhancement in public service delivery, simplification of administrative rules and procedures, capacity building of public functionaries for good governance, downsizing of public bureaucracy, expenditure reforms in governments, civil service reforms and ensuring accountable, sustainable, responsive, transparent, and citizen-friendly administration. "A nation without the means of reform is without means of surviva." was famously said by Sir Edmund Burke (1729–1797).[54] In general, most of these reforms aim at common initiatives such as improving customer service, decentralization, market mechanisms, cross-functional collaboration, and accountability for results which have the overarching theme of improving governmental performance (Page, 205). The current Wikileaks saga wherein the founder of Wikileaks is making public, classified public records is in fact a reminder that the voice of an individual and the common public against the government is becoming popular and vociferous.

There is a new business approach that is now being taken in determining the relation between the citizens and the government, and the citizens are now viewed as citizens. Therefore, providing information is seen as a service that needs to be provided to citizens. Every government has to be aware of information in its related fields such as freedom of information, citizens' access to information, and the administration of information. Accessibility has to be a keyword. Woodrow Wilson has said that "liberty has never come from the government. . . . The history of liberty is the history of the limitation of government power, not the increase of it" (Simon, 1978).[55] The Canadian

Commission Report of 1979 focuses on role of the public institutions and different procedures of the grievance redressal system. For example, the belief of Canadian citizens that government employees do not go out of their way to meet 'citizens' needs. However, in reality, it is completely different in theory and practice. An important characteristic of a modern bureaucracy is that Indian civil servants are recruited and promoted based on their skills and merits rather than on the basis of political or other connections. Also in this report is the quotation cited in the context of the merit principle which states that

> it may appear to some a formidable, if not impossible task, to achieve the state where almost every contact made by a member of the public with a federal employee leaves that person proud of, or atleast satisfied with, the caliber of the public service. The task may well be formidable, which is all the more reason why it must be tackled. Good public relations must be addressed with the skill and vigour that has produced the high standards that exist not only in many parts of the private sector but to a more limited degree in parts of the public services as well. (Stated by Canadian Minister of Supply and Services, 1979)[56]

RIGHT TO INFORMATION: A GENERAL PERSPECTIVE

Berlin-based Transparency International ranks India as one of the most corrupt countries in the world at 90th, out of 145 countries, in 2004. It said bureaucrats in India regularly take kickbacks in awarding government contracts and ask for bribes in return for services, which citizens are fully entitled to and they are hardly aware of it.[57]

When the Freedom of Information Bill, 2000, was introduced in the Parliament there was a great hue and cry about the title of the Bill itself. Many local activists and legal experts prefer to use the term "right to information" instead of "freedom of information" as they see "freedom" as signifying mere prohibition of government interference, whereas applying the term "right" imposes a positive duty on government to disseminate information to the people. In the Indian Constitution, most of the freedoms enumerated in Article 19, which guarantees freedom of expression, require the state to refrain from interfering. A "right," on the other hand, is understood in India as placing a positive duty on the state to take steps to ensure its fulfillment. Madhav Godbole, erstwhile Union Home Secretary and RTI activist, says in his critique of the Freedom of Information Bill, 2000, "Since the Bill makes it a point to talk only about freedom of information as opposed to right to information, it has lent itself to some clumsy construction . . . all citizens have a right to information."[58]

Ever since the UPA government had come up, recommendations had been made up for the Freedom of Information Bill, 2000. The name of the Bill had been changed to Right to Information Bill, 2005, which is a Bill

> to provide for setting out the practical regime of right to information for people to secure access to its formation under the control of public authorities. in order to promote transparency and accountability in the working of every public authority, the constitution of a Central information Commission and for matters connected therewith or incidental thereto.[59]

Information as a term that has been derived from the Latin words "formation" and "forma" which means giving shape to something and forming a pattern, respectively. In general, information adds something new to our awareness and removes the vagueness of our ideas. Two aspects of the RTI are particularly important to the current debate:

- Information to which access must be given upon request and
- Information which must be published and disseminated *suo motu* (proactively) by public authorities, including information which would affect fundamental rights such as food, environment, and civil liberties.

Particular emphasis is paid to *suo motu* publication, given the background of illiteracy and poverty that prevails in most parts of the country. Bulent Yilmaz[60] talks about the need for RTI in a developing country in contrast to the developed country. He says that literacy and RTI are correlated and in a country where the literacy rate is low it is difficult to achieve RTI. He says,

> Information is power for development. For this reason, the right to information is an important human right. However, as many other rights, there are many pre- conditions, which are related to economical, social, cultural and political development for realizing the right to information. While developed countries seem to have important opportunities for the right to information, least developed countries and developing countries are far away from this right. There is a strong relationship between intellectual freedom and the right to information. In other words, the concept of the right to information is based on the concept of the freedom of information. Freedom of information means intellectual freedom. Both intellectual freedom and the right to information are human rights which protect the human life and human development. However, human rights which protect our lives need to be protected by a full democracy in the country. If there is not a full democracy, all members of the society can participate in the decision making process and for this reason they need the right to information. Unless there is a true democracy in a country, the problem of the right to information cannot be solved, fully.

As Koren[61] said, human development can be described as a comprehensive economical, social, cultural, and political process, which aims at the constant improvement of the well-being of the entire population and of all individuals. The RTI as a human right is a result and/or product of the human development. The phrase of the RTI for a person who is hungry, who does not have enough money to live, who is not educated, and who does not have freedom does not have any meaning in either. In the same way, a country which has the problem of hunger, education, economic, and political freedom cannot give the priority to the RTI. Of course, information is a power that plays important role in solving these problems. But governments and individuals generally are not aware of this power and say first comes the right to eat, the right to work, the right to have a shelter, the right to have social security, in short the right to live, and then the RTI. We cannot realize the RTI unless we realize other rights we mentioned earlier and the other rights cannot be recognized unless we are informed of them.

The RTI is important for the protection of other rights. Saras Jagwanth calls it a "leverage right." She argues that the RTI plays a crucial role in the realization of socioeconomic rights. It is linked to other rights in a number of ways. There is a link between a just administration and the right to access information not only textually but also in relation to the goals of transparent, efficient, and accountable administration that they both seek to uphold and protect. The right of being arrested, detained, and accused people also contains frequent references to information. She makes an interdisciplinary approach between RTI and other rights. It imposes a positive duty on the government to provide information especially in countries like India where the literacy rate is low. A component of the obligation on the state to "promote" constitutional rights must include the obligation to provide information and educate people on their rights and how they can be accessed.[62]

PROBLEMS IN THE ACCESS OF THE RTI UNDER THE OFFICIAL SECRETS ACT

Since the ancient times, human beings have tried to exercise control over each other by controlling access to information and knowledge. Starting with the ancient monarchies where official secrecy was more or less identified with the personal intrigues of the royals and in case of oligarchies to affairs between smaller groups of men. Where Plato limited the study or information only to a certain section of society, especially to those who could afford it, in Hindu society, knowledge was restricted to again a certain caste, that is, the higher class (Brahmins). Kautilya believed that knowledge should be restrained only within the boundaries of the King's palace. The vaids (medicine man) kept the knowledge about various herbs only to themselves or within the family. The priests claimed conversation with gods and confined it to themselves, thereby ruling the mindsets of the people.

The practice of implementing official secrecy in governance has been instrumental in providing an implicit sense of security and immunity to political establishments the world over. The onset of democracy saw a more refined justification for secrecy in the name of wider national security. Today everything is a secret official. Restrictive legislations like the OSA was operative in almost all the countries under the British colonial rule. These laws brought into force by the British to suit their own agenda of preserving about oppressive regime have been adopted by the independent nations for promoting vested political interests. Though these countries have become independent, no concrete steps have been taken to repeal these laws. Even India is a signatory to it.

The system of governance in India has traditionally been opaque, with the state retaining the colonial era OSA) and continuing to operate in secrecy at the administrative level. This has been exacerbated by the traditional feudal mindset, which presupposes a distance between the "rulers" and the "ruled," with the former being a privileged class. Openness in government was neither consciously promoted as a culture nor reflected in major legal changes until a few years ago, when laws like the Environment Protection Act started to impose requirements of public hearings and mandatory disclosures.

The country yet seems to follow the old colonial legacy and the OSA is yet used as the means to impose the government's authoritative attitude over the citizens. Of late, if Tikhar Gilani's arrest under this controversial Act which kept him in jail for a long seven months until the Central Government withdrew the cases against him on pressure of various quarters has again shown how the OSA can be misused by the Government. Gilani, Chief of Bureau of *The Kashmir Times*, had been charged under the OSA for possessing "sensitive" documents relating to troop deployment in Jammu and Kashmir. The documents, which he possessed, were obtained from The Institute of Strategic Studies, Islamabad. It was Gilani who in fact brought it to the knowledge of the Central Government that Pakistan knew the movement of the Indian troops along the border of Jammu and Kashmir. The Kargil war caught Military Intelligence of India napping which enabled the Pakistani soldiers to intrude into Indian Territory long before the Indian army caught the scent of them.

In this era of information flooding, no law, however stringent, can stop the flow of information. The info highway has made even geographical barriers totally irrelevant. One does not have to carry incriminatory documents physically. Just a click of a mouse can do it for him. Therefore, the OSA can best serve the government in concealing the documents that reveal the irregularities and irresponsible activities in the administration and the government itself. The OSA cannot effectively check persons who intend to harm the nation. Therefore there should be serious steps taken to repeal this Act.

At Delhi University in his lecture on "Militarism, Democracy and the Right to Information," Chomsky spoke about the concentration of power centers. He said that the United States was a uniquely free country with regard to the RTI and that the task of suppressing the RTI was not undertaken by the state. Chomsky observed in his trademark sarcasm that it was the solemn duty of the intellectuals, the educated class, and the free press to ensure that the RTI was denied to the people. The mass of the population was unaware of what was really happening in Afghanistan and the government did whatever it wanted in the name of "national security."

THE NEED FOR RIGHT TO INFORMATION

In the recent years, there has been an almost unstoppable global trend toward recognition of the RTI by countries' intergovernmental organization, civil society, and the people. The RTI has been recognized as a fundamental human right, which upholds the inherent dignity of all the human beings. It forms the crucial underpinning of participatory democracy; it is essential to ensure accountability and good governance. The greater the access of citizens to information, the greater the responsiveness of the government to community needs. Alternatively, the greater the restrictions that are placed on access, the greater the feeling of powerlessness and alienation. Without information, people cannot adequately exercise their rights as citizens or make informed choices. In the words of Soli Sorabjee, "Lack of transparency was one of the main causes for all pervading corruption and right to information would lead to openness, accountability and integrity."

Although "Information" in the current debate refers primarily to information held by public authorities, strong arguments can be made to extend the scope of the term to certain kinds of information held by private parties. The RTI would then become a right to seek and receive information from public authorities, as well as a right to access certain kinds of information from private actors.

The RTI derives from the democratic framework established by the Constitution and rests on the basic premise that since government is "for the people", it should be open and accountable and should have nothing to conceal from the people it purports to represent. In this context, the following observation seems to sum up the philosophical basis of the RTI (*State of U.P. v. Raj Narain* (1975) 3 SCR 333 at page 360 (AIR 1975 SC 865 at page 884). In a democracy:

> In a government of responsibility like ours, where all the agents of the public must be responsible for their conduct, there can be but few secrets. The people of this country have a right to know every public act, everything that is done in a public way, by their public functionaries. They are entitled to know the particulars of every public transaction in all its bearing.

To cover with veil of secrecy the common routine business is not in the interest of the public. Such secrecy can seldom be legitimately desired. It is generally desired for the purpose of parties and politics or personal self-interest or bureaucratic routine. "The responsibility of officials to explain or to justify their acts is the chief safeguard against oppression and corruption." Harsh Mander, an advocate of RTI movement, has described the importance of this right as follows:

> Information is the currency that every citizen requires to participate in the life and governance of society. The greater the access of the citizen to information, the greater would be the responsiveness of government to community needs. Alternatively, the greater the restrictions that are placed on access, the greater the feelings of "powerlessness" and "alienation." Without information, people cannot adequately exercise their rights and responsibilities as citizens or make informed choices. Government information is a national resource. Neither the particular government of the day nor public officials create information for their own benefit. This information is generated for purposes related to the legitimate discharge of their duties of office, and for the service of the public for whose benefit the institutions of government exist, and who ultimately (through one kind of import or another) fund the institutions of government and the salaries of officials. It follows that government and officials are "trustees" of this information for the people.[63]

The main thrust of the movement for the right to information in India has seen this right as being closely related to survival. Food security, shelter, environment, and employment are all bound up with the RTI. In the absence of information on these issues, people remain marginalized and excluded from their rightful place in society. It is for this reason that in India, the movement for RTI has been as vibrant in the hearts of marginalized people as it is on the pages of academic journals and in media coverage.

It is generally argued that

> Administrative India puts the greatest weight on keeping happening within its corridors secret, thereby denying the citizens access to information about them. Such orientations produce deep contradictions in the larger socio-political system of the land which itself is in a state requiring nourishment and care. As the latter is still relatively new and in its infancy, its growth processes inevitably

get retarded for want of information about the government, which means from the government. Over concealment of governmental, the governors and the governed, and its persistence beyond a point is apt to create an alienated citizenry. This makes democracy itself weak and insecure. Besides secrecy renders administrative accountability unenforceable in an effective way and thus induces administrative behaviour, which is apt to degenerate into arbitrariness and absolutism. This is not all.[64]

The Government, today, is called upon to make policies on an ever-increasing range of subjects and many of these policies must necessarily impinge or the lives of the citizens. It must sometimes happen that the data made available to the policymakers is of a selective nature and even the policymakers and their advisers may deliberately suppress certain viewpoints and favour others. Such bureaucratic habits get encouragement in an environment of secrecy; and openness in governmental work is possibly the only effective corrective to it, also raising, in the process, the quality of decision-making. Besides openness has an educational role in as much as citizens are enabled to acquire a fuller view of the pros and cons of matter of major importance, which naturally helps in building informed public opinion of matter of major importance, which naturally helps in building informed public opinion, no less than good will for the Government.[65]

Aruna Roy points out that the RTI touches all levels of governance.[66] "If even one per cent of the country uses it, it can shape democracy in the country. Central debates like corruption in public office, corruption in political parties and the corrupt deals of national governments will all be set against the context of real facts," she says. For instance, the actual working out of a system or a project can be made transparent and "one can challenge the conditionalities of a license," she goes on, "there need not be any more disasters like Bhopal or Enron even." Also, any institution that raises and uses public money should come under this law, suggests Ms. Roy. Along with a comprehensive RTI there should be a push for a Lok Pal Bill and a Whistleblower's Act that would protect those who used the RTI against intimidation and violence.

Jean Dreze goes further in saying that there should be steps to open up military organization.[67] He says that defense contracts are attractive channels for illegal inducements: the deals are sheltered from the public gaze, the number of "partners" tend to be small, and the amounts are huge. In India, most of the biggest scams that have taken place, from Bofors to Tehelka, have taken place in the defense sector. There is a greater need for transparency and accountability in the nuclear industry. India's reactors are among the most dangerous in the world: according to the Stockholm International Peace Research Institute, all of them are among the world's 50 least reliable reactors and 4 are among the worst 6. The precarious conditions of India's nuclear facilities have been kept under the heavy lid of secrecy, consolidated with the liberal use of OSA. There is a greater need to open up these anti-democratic influences on the military establishment.

RIGHT TO INFORMATION: AN INSTRUMENT TO ACHIEVE PUBLIC ACCOUNTABILITY

Marian Koren talks about the importance of RTI as an important ingredient for the growth of a child. The study of the right of the child to information is necessarily related to a child's development, the processes involved in seeking information, the availability and accessibility of sources of information, and the relevant legal protection. The child's developmental process reveals that information plays an indispensable role. The informational process begins even before birth and accompanies the child throughout childhood and further stages of human development. Information affects the physical, emotional, cognitive, and social development of the child. The way in which a child learns to walk and to talk and how he plays and communicates with others is also due to the information he has received. The idea that information plays an important role, both in the development of his identity and personality, and, in his social participation, has far-reaching implications for the child's providers of information. Parents are the main source of information for the child. As both verbal and non-verbal behavior of parents is imitated, the example set by parents cannot be underestimated and is crucial to the child's development. The human values of which parents are aware and which they have integrated into their way of behaving form the frame of reference for the child in developing his views on the world and himself. Parents should also be attentive to the uniqueness of the child, listening carefully when communicating with the child.

The RTI considered in the light of human development requires a stronger visibility and protection from the perspective of the seeker or receiver of information. Therefore, a general RTI, which provides for the right to inform oneself from generally available sources and to educate oneself as a human being, should be acknowledged for the sake of children as well and should be enshrined explicitly in international treaties and other human rights instruments and be implemented in national constitutions.[68]

Andrew Puddephat[69] calls it a fundamental human right and gives five reasons so as to give its importance. He says:

- In any democracy, if you don't have access to information, it is impossible to have an informed public debate. It is impossible to discuss range of political options that are freely open to you. It is impossible to vote in ways that are in your own best interests, or in accordance with your own beliefs and values.

- Secretive societies bring with them a political culture of rumour and conspiracy that makes healthy public debate very difficult to achieve.
- The twin of secrecy is corruption. Nobody knows what decisions and policies are formed, sheltered behind the veil of secrecy. But if secrecy is the disease then sunshine is the best disinfectant. If economic activity is to take place in public, accounts have to be published and the people who organise these deals know that one day every detail may be exposed in the public arena then one has a fighting chance of dealing with corruption. Without that openness tackling corruption is an impossible uphill struggle.
- Openness is important because it is essential to the development of society. For instance it was earlier believed that AIDS is a contagious disease, which could spread by mere touching. But it is now a well-known fact that it is a disease that is spread through contact of blood or other body fluids. We know all this but in order to achieve these fundamental basic developments one needs to have a completely open and transparent regime of information.

Right to information is crucial because it is only through access to information that we can hold governments to account. If governments are made to publish annual reports and accounts, and if their files are open so that the people are made to see what the government has been doing, we can make accountability a real and effective source.

Information is power, and as the former prime minister Atal Behari Vajpayee stated, "The government wants to share power with the humblest; it wants to empower the weakest. It is precisely because of this reason that the Right to Information has to be ensured for all."[70] Even as steps are taken to ensure openness in matters affecting the public, there has to be a greater sense of responsibility on the part of users of information in the media and elsewhere. Even the journalists must ensure that they seek information in public interest and not as agents of interested political parties or organizations, so as to promote transparency in government institutions.

RESTRICTIONS OF RIGHT TO INFORMATION

The information under the Act can be denied if

- Disclosure prejudicially effects of sovereignty and integrity of India, security strategic scientific or economic interests of the state, relation with the foreign state of lead to incitement of an offence.
- Publication of information is expressly forbidden by court of law or tribunal and disclosure constitute contempt of court.

- Information disclosure of which causes breach of privilege of the parliament or state legislature
- Information includes commercial confidence trade secrets or intellectual property & disclosure would harm competitive position of the third party unless the competent authority is satisfied that the public interest warrants disclosure of such information.
- Information available to the person in his fiduciary relationship unless the competent authority is satisfied that larger public interest requires disclosure of such information.
- Information received in confidence from the foreign government.
- Information which disclosure endanger the life or the physical safety of any person or identities the source or assistance given in confidence for the enforcement of the law or security purposes.
- Information which would impede the process of investigation or apprehension or prosecution of offender.
- Cabinet papers including records of deliberations of the council of musters, secretaries and other officers. However, the decision of the council of minister and the reasons and material on which the decision were taken shall be public after the decision has been taken provided it is not covered under any of the exemption clauses mentioned.
- Personal information which has no correlation to any public activity or interest or which comes unwarranted invasion of the privacy of the individual unless larger public interest justifies the disclosure of such information.
- Providing information involves an infringement of copyright subsisting in a person other than state.[71]

The enactment of RTI is indeed a bold step and will go a long way in creating enabling involvement in favor of maturation of our constitutional democracy. Keeping in view the intent of the framers of the RTI Act, 2005 (22 of 2005) and its spirit, the Odisha Information Commission (commission for short) is a process of making continuous efforts for effective implementation of the provision of the Act despite all the initial hurdles and infrastructural inadequacies be facing a new institution.

PREAMBLE OF THE RIGHT TO INFORMATION ACT, 2005

An Act to provide for the setting out the practical regime of the RTI for the citizens to secure access to information under the control of public authorities, in order to promote transparency and accountability in the working of every public authorities, the Constitution of Central Information Commission and the State Information Commission (SIC) for the matter connected there-with or incidental thereto.

Whereas[72] the constitution of India has establish democratic Republic;

And whereas democracy requires an inform citizenry and transparency of information which are vital to its functioning and also to contain corruption and to hold Governments and their instrumentalities accountable to the governed;

And whereas revelation of information in actual practice is likely to conflict with other public interests including efficient operations of the Governments, optimum use of limited fiscal resources and the preservation of confidentiality of sensitive information;

And whereas it is necessary to harmonise these conflicting interests while preserving the paramountcy of the democratic ideal; Now, therefore, it is expedient to provide for furnishing certain information to the citizens who desire to have it.

PURPOSE OF THE RIGHT TO INFORMATION ACT

As per the preamble of the Act the purposes are

- To provide citizen right to information which will enable them to have access to information under control of the public authorities which will promote transparency and accountability in the working of every public authority and
- To provide for the constitution of a central information commission and state information commissions. The Act will extend to whole of India except the state of Jammu & Kashmir.[73] The Act gives every citizen of India a Right to information.[74]

OBJECTIVES OF RIGHT TO INFORMATION ACT

(a) To provide for setting out practical regime or right to information for citizens to secure access to information under the control of public authorities.

(b) To promote transparency and accountability in the working of every public authority.

(c) To set up central information commission and state information commission and for matter connected there with.

(d) To contain corruption and to hold government and their instrumentalities accountable to the people. And

(e) To harmonies revelation of information with public interest, including efficient operations of the governments' optimum use of limited fiscal resources and preservation of confidentiality of sensitized information.[75]

CONSTITUTIONAL GUARANTEES FOR RIGHT TO INFORMATION

Article 19(1) (a) of the Constitution guarantees the fundamental rights to freedom of speech and expression. The prerequisite for enjoying this right is knowledge and information. The absence of authentic information on matters of public interest will only encourage wild rumors and speculations and avoidable allegations against individuals and institutions. Therefore, the RTI becomes a constitutional right, being an aspect of the right to freedom of speech and expression which includes the right to receive and collect information. This will also help the citizens perform their fundamental duties as set out in Article 51A of the Constitution. A fu1ly informed citizen will certainly be better equipped for the performance of these duties. Thus, access to information would assist citizens in fulfilling these obligations.

The recognition of RTI, as being included in the constitutional guarantees of freedom of speech and expression finds its genesis in Supreme Court decisions challenging governmental control over newsprint and bans on the distribution of newspapers. In a landmark case the petitioners, publishers of one of the leading national dailies challenged restrictions in the Newsprint Control Order on the acquisition, sale, and use of newsprint. The Supreme Court struck down the restrictions on the basis that they interfered with the petitioners' right to publish and circulate their paper freely, which was included in their right to freedom of speech and expression.

The judges remarked: "It is indisputable that by freedom of the press is meant the right of all citizens to speak, publish and express their views Freedom of speech and expression includes within its compass the right of all citizens to read and be informed."

The dissenting judgment of Justice K. K. Mathew emphasized two aspects of freedom of speech: the individual interest in expressing oneself and the social interest in the attainment of truth. Regarding the latter, Mathew noted: "Now in the method of political government the point of ultimate interest is not in the words of the speakers but in the hearts of the hearers."[76]

In a subsequent case, the Supreme Court held that media controlled by public bodies were required to allow both sides of an issue to be aired. Mr Shah, the director of a nongovernmental consumer rights organization, wrote a paper highlighting discriminatory practices by the Life Insurance Corporation, a government-controlled body. The Corporation published a critique of this paper in its institutional publication but refused to publish Mr Shah's rejoinder. The Court held that a state instrumentality having monopolistic control over any publication is under an obligation to publish views contesting those it had presented.[77]

The principle that the public has a right to receive information was even more clearly enunciated a few years later when the Court stated: "The basic purpose of freedom of speech and expression is that all members should be able to form their beliefs and communicate them freely to others, In sum, the fundamental principle involved here is *the people's right to know*."[78]

In the area of civil liberties, the courts have tried to ensure a transparent criminal justice system, free from arbitrariness. The Supreme Court has specifically detailed all the information, which must be recorded and provided to the accused or his or her family in order to achieve this objective. Listing the procedural safeguards for arrest and custody, the Supreme Court said, "Transparency of action and accountability perhaps are the two possible safeguards which this Court must insist upon."[79]

Furthermore, in *Prabha Dutt v. Union of India*,[80] the Court held that there could be no reason for refusing permission to the media to interview prisoners on death row, unless there was clear evidence that the prisoners had refused to be interviewed. Thus, the right to acquire information includes the right to access sources of information. The linkage between the right to life and liberty, guaranteed by Article 21 of the Constitution, and the right to know was clearly affirmed in another case by Justice Mukhatji, who stated: "We must remember that the people at large have a right to know in order to take part in a participatory development in the industrial life and democracy. Right to know is a basic right to which citizens of a country aspire under Article 21 of our Constitution."[81]

The right to access official information was further developed in a case where the respondent sought access to documents pertaining to the security arrangements, and the expenses thereof, of the prime minister. The prime minister claimed the right to decide whether disclosure of certain privileged documents was in the public interest or not. The Supreme Court noted:

> While there are overwhelming arguments for giving to the executive the power to determine what matters may prejudice public security, those arguments give no sanction to giving the executive exclusive power to determine what matters may prejudice the public interest. Once considerations of national security are left out there are few matters of public interest, which cannot be safely discussed in public.[82]

The right to know has been reaffirmed in the context of environmental issues which have an impact on people's very survival. Several High Court decisions have upheld the right of citizens' groups to access information where an environmental issue was concerned. For example, in different cases, the right to inspect copies of applications for building permissions and the accompanying plans, and the right to have full information about the municipality's sanitation program have been affirmed. The overall impact of these decisions has been to establish clearly that the right to freedom of information, or the public's right to know, is embedded in the fundamental rights provisions of the Constitution. This position has been relied upon not only by independent advocates of the right but also by official committees, as well as in the Objects and Reasons of the Bill on Right to Information, 2004.

PROBLEMS IN THE ACCESS OF THE RTI

In many regions, the standard of record-keeping is extremely poor. A typical picture of a government office is stacks of dusty files in cupboards, on shelves, and on the floor providing an easy excuse for refusing access to records on the grounds that they have been "misplaced.". Usually, getting information from the "records section" of an office is accompanied by delays and demands for bribes.

When "computerization" started, most of the computers found their way into the offices of senior staff. In the last few years, some states have started large-scale computerization programs to reach out to village-level communities. The rapid growth of the information technology business has meant that most states are now trying to promote technology, primarily to attract investment, and this is certainly making a significant contribution to increasing the flow of information.

As N. Vittal has noted:

> IT makes the best use of information . . . it lets people access information. Breakthrough in IT will expand our reach. This can empower our rural masses. We ought to put information related to all kinds of government projects on our websites. It will lead to better management of our resources. People in villages can actually get to know of the projects aimed at their development and the kind of funds that are available. They can demand better management from the administration.

Another problem is that local personnel may not be properly trained to use computers to good effect, even when they are available. Investment in technology has had positive results. For example, the "Gyandoot"[83] project in Dhar District, Madhya Pradesh, which started in January, 2000, has established a network of about 600 villages (about half a million people). A computer installed in the *Gram Panchayat* office can give information about market prices or land records to any villager upon payment of a fee.

Complaints can be sent to the authorities through e-mail. States such as Andhra Pradesh and Rajasthan are also using computers to provide villagers with information. However, these "success stories"[84] need to be viewed with some caution. A recent appraisal notes that three factors have limited the impact of these projects: lack of electricity, lack of connectivity, and lack of software in regional languages.

Two factors, low levels of literacy and the absence of effective communication methods, compound the poor flow of information. Methods of communication are unimaginative and there is a surprising overdependence on the written word, which is inappropriate for the largely illiterate population. Traditional means of communication such as *munadi* have not been considered sufficiently.

There is also excessive reliance on English, instead of vernacular languages. For example, for many years the traffic authorities in New Delhi used the slogan "Lane driving is sane driving" to encourage people to adhere to traffic safety, although the majority of bus and truck drivers are, if not illiterate, at least unable to understand this rather cryptic English. Three years ago, a cyclone warning to fishermen in coastal Gujarat was flashed across the screen of the national TV channel while a popular film was being screened. The warning was flashed in English, which few fishermen can read, instead of Gujarati or Hindi. The same problem applies to style. Laws, rules, notifications, orders, and other official documents are drafted in an excessively legal style, which the common person cannot comprehend. Even notices designed to inform the public are often poorly worded, without keeping the user group in mind. The mass media has been used effectively in recent times to inform people and to promote social change. Many radio programs have been fruitful to the society especially the lower strata. However, much more could be done, particularly by the publicly funded broadcast media. For example, a listener complained that on the day of the earthquake in Gujarat, *All India Radio* only provided information on the situation in the late afternoon.

DEVELOPMENTS TOWARD RIGHT TO INFORMATION IN THE COUNTRY

The campaign for a RTI has sought two key legal reforms: the amendment or repeal of the OSA, 1923, and enactment of a specific law giving effect to the RTI. Objections to the OSA have been raised ever since 1948, when the Press Laws Enquiry Committee recommended that "the application of the Act must be confined, as the recent Geneva Conference on Freedom of Information has recommended, only to matters which must remain secret in the interests of national security."[85]

Amending the Official Secrets Act

Objections to the OSA have been raised ever since 1948, when the Press Laws Enquiry Committee recommended that "the application of the Act must be confined, as the recent Geneva Conference on Freedom of Information has recommended, only to matters which must remain secret in the interests of national security."

In 1977, a Working Group was formed by the government to look into the idea of amending the OSA by relaxing its prohibitions on the dissemination of information to the public. Unfortunately, the Working Group did not recommend changes to the Act, as they were of the view that it related to the protection of national safety and did not prevent the release of information in the public interest, despite overwhelming evidence to the contrary. In 1989, a Committee was set up which recommended limiting the areas where governmental information could be hidden and opening up of all other spheres of information. No legislation followed these recommendations. In 1991, there were reports in the press to the effect that a task force had recommended amendment of the OSA and enactment of a Freedom of Information Act, but again, no legislative action followed[86] until now through the implementation of the new RTI Act, 2005.

THE "PRESS COUNCIL" DRAFT

The first major draft of legislation on the RTI was circulated in 1996 by the Press Council of India. This draft was derived from an earlier one which had been prepared in October 1995, at a meeting of social activists, civil servants, and lawyers at the Lal Bahadur Shastri National Academy of Administration, Mussoorie.[87]

The fact that serving officials of this institute took the initiative to convene this meeting made it a watershed in the national movement for the RTI. Importantly, the Press Council draft affirmed in its preamble that the RTI is already protected under the Constitution as an aspect of the fundamental right to free speech and expression, in line with a number of superior court rulings, noted earlier. The draft affirmed the right of every citizen to information from any public body. Significantly, the term "public body" included not only the state, as defined in the Constitution,[88] but also all privatelyowned undertakings, non-statutory authorities, companies, and other non-state bodies whose activities affect the public interest. Thus, both the commercial sector and nongovernmental organizations were included in the ambit of this draft.

The draft did provide for a limited number of restrictions on the RTI in line with those allowed in relation to other fundamental rights. These included where disclosure would prejudicially affect the sovereignty and integrity of India, the security of the state, and friendly relations with foreign states, public order, investigation of an offense, or where disclosure would lead to incitement to an offense. Bona fide grounds of individual privacy and trade and commercial interests were also included as exceptions.

A significant saving provision was that information which cannot be denied to parliament or the state legislature shall not be denied to a citizen. This would have been a powerful defense against want on withholding of information by public bodies because the agency seeking to withhold the information would have had to commit itself to the position that it would also withhold the information from parliament or the state legislature. The draft also provided for personal fines for failing to provide information and for appeals to the local civil judiciary against a failure or refusal to supply the requested information.

THE "CERC" DRAFT

By far the most detailed proposed freedom of information legislation in India was drafted by the Consumer Education Research Council (CERC). This draft, in line with international standards, gives the RTI to anyone, except "alien enemies," whether or not they are a citizen. It requires public agencies at the federal and state levels to maintain their records in good order, to provide a directory of all records under their control, to promote the computerization of records in interconnected networks, and to publish all laws, regulations, guidelines, and circulars related to or issued by government departments and any information concerning welfare schemes. Requesters are liable only for the cost of supplying copies of records, with fees being waived for journalists, newspaper organizations, and public interest groups. The CERC draft contains a class exception for cabinet documents but documents relating to security, defense, international relations, and economic and commercial affairs are subject to a "grave and significant damage" test. There are also exceptions for personal information in the interests of privacy and the research activities of voluntary organizations if disclosure would undermine their functioning or result in "grave and significant damage" to another person. Records relating to the internal deliberative processes of government—the one exception being the cabinet documents—and center-state relations are not excepted under the CERC draft.

The draft also provides for the outright repeal of the OSA but does not provide specific protection for whistleblowers. Finally, the CERC draft provides for an appeal against refusals to disclose information, first to a network of independent information commissioners at the national, state, and district levels and then to an Information Tribunal.[89]

The draft was introduced as a private member's Bill in the Parliament, but was never taken up for discussion. The election manifestos of most of the major political parties in the last decade have promised transparency and administrative reform. These promises were given impetus at the May 24, 1997, Conference of Chief Ministers of Indian States, which discussed an Action Plan for Effective and Responsive Government at the Central and State Levels.

The prime minister presided over the deliberations and the Conference was also attended by the central home minister, the finance minister, the law minister, the minister of state for personnel, public grievances and pensions, the cabinet secretary, the chief secretaries of the states and Union Territories, and other senior Government of India officials.

The 1997 Conference represented the culmination of a national debate on "effective and responsive administration," initiated at the Conference of Chief Secretaries in 1996. It was agreed that immediate steps must be taken to restore the faith of the people in the fairness, integrity, and responsiveness of the administration. The prime minister favored a RTI to combat undue secrecy in the government and the idea of social audit as an instrument of greater accountability was emphasized.

The Conference resolved that the central and state governments would work together on a number of themes, including transparency and the RTI. The Conference recognized that secrecy and lack of openness are largely responsible for corruption in official dealings and is also contrary to accountable and democratic government. To address this, the Government of India agreed to take immediate steps, in consultation with states, to introduce freedom of information legislation, along with amendments to the OSA and the Indian Evidence Act, before the end of 1997. Those states which had not already provided for a RTI would take the necessary steps to do so. Two states passed RTI legislation that year and the Government of India appointed a Working Group to draft the Freedom of Information Bill, 1997.

The central and state governments also agreed to a number of other measures to promote openness. These included establishing accessible computerized information centers to provide information to the public on essential services, and speeding up ongoing efforts to computerize government operations. In this process, particular attention would be given to computerization of records of particular importance to the people, such as land records, passports, investigation of offenses, administration of justice, tax collection, and issuance of permits and licenses.

THE "SHOURIE COMMITTEE" DRAFT

The Working Group appointed by the government in 1997 was known as the "Shourie Committee" since it was headed by former bureaucrat and consumer rights activist H. D. Shourie. It had the mandate to make recommendations regarding secrecy legislation and to prepare draft legislation on freedom of information. Unfortunately, the legitimacy and effectiveness of the work of this Committee were undermined by a lack of public consultation and the fact that the recommendations were never sufficiently publicized.[90]

The Shourie Committee itself consisted of 10 persons; 8 of whom were senior bureaucrats from the Central Government. The salient features of the Bill were

1. When enacted, it will also apply to state governments over riding state legislations to the extent they clash with the Central legislation;
2. A fee would be paid by the citizen while seeking information from Government, and the officer or the department concerned can be held responsible and taken to a Consumer Court for not providing the information within the prescribed time limit of 30 days;
3. Every Government department should appoint a Public Information Officer for this purpose;
4. Section 5 of the Official Secrets Act should be suitably amended to make it easier for a citizen to obtain official information, and information can be withheld only in respect of especially, exempted. items;
5. Clauses 123 and 124 of the Indian Evidence Act which inhibit public officials from submitting information to Courts, should be suitably amended, and the basis and the procedure for classification of official documents (as top Secret?, Secret? and confidential?) should be suitably amended so that availability of information to the public becomes the rule rather than the exception.[91]

The Shourie Committee's draft freedom of information law was significantly diluted by comparison with the civil society drafts. The scope of exceptions was very wide and included a remarkable clause, seriously undermining the whole project, whereby public authorities could withhold "information the disclosure of which would not sub serves any public interest." The draft also failed to provide for penalties for groundless refusals to disclose. Appeals were allowed to consumer courts, providing a simple remedy to consumers. However, these courts are already overburdened and have serious backlogs. The draft excluded the private sector and nongovernmental organizations not "substantially funded or controlled" by the government from its ambit. The draft did, however, include the judiciary and legislatures within its purview.

THE FREEDOM OF INFORMATION BILL, 2000[92]

With the demise of two governments in quick succession, the Shourie draft was never introduced into Parliament. However, it was revived with some changes, in July 2000, when it was introduced as the Freedom of Information Bill, 2000. Prior to the Bill being introduced in Parliament, there was no official effort to publicize the draft or engage in a debate over its provisions. There was a debate on the expected law in certain media, academic, nongovernmental organizations, and other interested circles, but it was based primarily on conjecture as to the Bill's contents. At the time of writing, the Freedom of Information Bill, 2000, was before the Parliamentary Standing Committee on Home Affairs, which was receiving submissions from various groups and individuals.

Overall, the Bill fails in important ways to conform to international standards and best comparative practice on access to information. Nor does it reflect a serious attempt to address information issues in the Indian context, as the laws of South Aflica and Japan do for their countries. Overall, the weakness of the Bill reflects the lack of political will to implement a good information disclosure system. Indeed, the Bill is so weak that civil society has debated whether this Bill should be resisted outright at the risk of losing the opportunity to have legislation on the right to know, until at least the non-negotiable standards are included.

Most freedom of information advocates in the country now concurs in their name criticisms of the Freedom of Information Bill, 2000.[93] Perhaps the most serious problem with the Bill was that it failed to provide for an independent review of refusals to disclose information, either by an independent administrative body or by the courts. This means that decisions on whether or not to release information rest entirely within the government. A blanket exclusion of key intelligence and security organizations and an excessively broad regime of exemptions significantly undermine the potential for the Bill to promote the public's right to know. The lack of a public interest override for these exclusions and exemptions further undermines the Bill.

FREEDOM OF INFORMATION 2002[94]

There are four criteria on which the strength of a RTI Act can be judged:

1. The width of application of the Act, (the nature of organizations or institutions to which it applies or does not apply);
2. The range and kind of information that it can be used to access and the kinds of information that are exempted from disclosure;

3. The independence of the institutions, which would adjudicate disputes between the citizens and the state regarding the disclosure of particular pieces of information;
4. The sanctions in the Law against wilful and *mala fide* refusal to disclose information or against incorrect disclosure of information.[95]

The Bill was quite weak in each of these four indicia. Section 16 of the Act exempts a large number of investigative, intelligence, and security organizations specified in the schedule from the operation of the Act. The government's justification for excluding information regarding such organizations was that its release might compromise national security. But any information regarding any organizations which might compromise national security can always be denied on the basis of the first exclusionary clause in Section 8 which specifies what kind of information should be exempted from disclosure. But all information about such organizations need not compromise national security. For example, the budget and funding of such organizations, and the manner in which such funds have been expended, are matters of public interest since it is public money that is being expended.

Section 8's Clauses C, D, and E, discussed earlier, exempt several categories of information. The exemption from disclosure of information which might prejudice center- state relations is also objectionable. Another serious weakness of the Central Act is that there is no provision for an appeal to an independent authority. Moreover, the Act does not provide any penalty for wilful nondisclosure of information or for wilfully incorrect disclosure of information by a government authority.

THE RIGHT TO INFORMATION BILL, 2004[96]

The Right to Information Bill passed in December 2004 perhaps is one of the best Bills but certain flaws in this Bill too have lent it for the criticism of the Act by the Civil Society groups.[97]

Brief Analysis of Various State Laws and Orders on the Right to Information

Several Indian states have, in the last three years, passed either RTI laws or executive orders to implement this right. A comparative overview of these state laws shows that the various models adopted have different kinds of pros and cons. Some of the state laws have a long list of exceptions and few have adequate provisions for imposing liability for not providing information. Moreover, as pointed out by a legal expert,

> the somewhat sparse public debate of the peoples' right to know began to concentrate on the need for legislation rather than providing and making information available to the public immediately . . . somehow, the basic strategy that seems to have evolved in public discourse became "legislation first, information later."

Today almost nine states of the country including Jammu and Kashmir have the RTI Act but here too there is a debate regarding that in case of a clash which would prevail.

Ever since the RTI Act of 2005 has been passed by the Government of India, the whole question of the durability of the RTI Act of the states arises. Though the citizens are given more choices on the RTI, there can be occasions when there can even be a clash between the center and the states on the Acts.

Prakash Kardaley says, "If states do not repeal their existing and allow national laws to coexist perhaps the Article 254 of the constitution might come into play."[98] Article 254 reads that

> If any Law made by the Legislature of a State is repugnant to any provision of a Law made by the Parliament which the Parliament is competent to enactment the Law made by the Parliament whether passed before or after the Law made by the Legislature of such State, or, as the case may be, the existing Law shall prevail and the Law made by the Legislature of the State shall, to the extent of repugnancy, be void.

THE GOA RIGHT TO INFORMATION ACT, 1997[99]

This is, so far, the best of the laws passed in any Indian state, although it still has shortcomings. It has the fewest categories of exceptions, a provision for urgent processing of requests pertaining to life and liberty, a penalty clause, and it applies to private bodies executing government works. One weakness is that it has no provision for proactive disclosure by the government.

TAMIL NADU RIGHT TO INFORMATION ACT, 1997[100]

Perhaps Tamil Nadu seems to be the only state where there is no evidence of even a single tenacious citizen extracting any tangible information through the Act though the Act was formulated eight years before the present central RTI Act.

This law contains 21 categories of exceptions, including 12 sub-clauses within them. The information must be provided within 30 "working" days from the date of receipt of the application. There is no penalty clause and requesters may appeal only to the state government, or any such authority as may be notified by the government. The law is vague in its description of certain key areas, such as "public interest," "public order," and "public harm." It does not have any provision for proactive disclosure of information.

THE MADHYA PRADESH RIGHT TO INFORMATION ACT AND ORDERS ON THE RTI[101]

Although the State of Madhya Pradesh passed a RTI Act in March 1998, presidential assent was refused and so it has not come into force. The apparent reason is that the legislative competence to pass such a law is with parliament. Executive orders on the Right to Information are, however, operational in close to 50 departments.

The Act puts an unusual and welcome obligation on public bodies to make information available proactively, especially information relating to health and security, through electronic and print media or any other method deemed fit. An application requesting information must be accepted or refused within 30 days of its receipt and reasons for any rejection must be given. The Act has 11 categories of exceptions, with procedures for appeals and revision. An official who breaches the law can be fined up to ₹2,000 (US$42.40). The Act sets up an Advisory Board with the chief minister as its chairperson, and including two members from nongovernmental organizations, the press, and the legal profession.

A series of executive orders was made to about 50 governmental departments to provide information on request as well as a mandatory direction to put up information boards outside various departments that are operational in Madhya Pradesh and now also in the new State of Jharkhand. Monitored by the Department of Administrative Reforms, these orders have not been widely used by the public. However, they do have the potential to create a culture of information sharing if enforced properly. The orders have a provision for charging a nominal fee for the inspection of records as well as for obtaining copies of records. Time limits are specified and internal appeals are provided for. Disciplinary action can be taken under these orders against erring officials.

THE RAJASTHAN RIGHT TO INFORMATION ACT, 2000[102]

The Act came into force after the prolonged struggle of MKSS headed by Aruna Roy, Nikhil Dey, and Shankar Singh when the poor peasants of Rajasthan could not tolerate the government injustices toward them.[103]

The Rajasthan Act has 13 sections in all, 10 of which establish categories of exceptions. It has exceptionally weak clauses for proactive disclosure and penalties. There is provision for one internal appeal and one appeal to an independent body.

THE KARNATAKA RIGHT TO INFORMATION ACT, 2000[104]

The Act contains standard exception clauses covering 12 categories of information. It has limited provisions for proactive disclosure, contains a penalty clause, and provides for an appeal to an independent tribunal. The Act has been used widely for environmental purposes in the state; moreover, some economists have even founded a group called PROOF,[105] in Bangalore, to use the Right to Information law to expose access and analyze information about government budgets.

MAHARASHTRA RIGHT TO INFORMATION ACT, 2003[106]

This state came into effect after a prolonged struggle by Gandhian activist Anna Hazare.[107] Through his Gandhian tactics, he compelled the Maharashtra Government to repeal an earlier weak Act and to pass a much stronger RTI Act. It is perhaps one of the best State acts passed in 2003.

The Maharashtra Act has only nine sections in all but appears to be the most restrictive state law to date, with 21 categories of exceptions. It does not provide for the establishment of an appellate authority which would review refusals to disclose and purports to bar the jurisdiction of the courts. It has neither provision for providing information proactively nor penalties for withholding or destroying information.

DELHI RIGHT TO INFORMATION ACT AND ORDERS ON RIGHT TO INFORMATION[108]

The Delhi Assembly passed the Delhi Right to Information Act in 2001. This regulation is as per the assent of the Lt. Governor of Delhi, containing the standard exceptions providing for an appeal to an independent body, as well as establishing an advisory body, the State Council for Right to Information. 119 Departments of Delhi Government have been brought under the purview of the Act. In each department, one senior officer has been designated as the competent authority under the Act to accept the request forms and to provide the information sought by the people.[109]

Under this Act any person can seek information on government work. He can file an application under the competent authority. An application fee of Rs 25 per application has to be paid at the time of submitting the application. In addition, a sum of Rs 5 per page is charged when information is supplied. For inspection of documents, a fee of Rs 15 is charged for every 15 minutes of inspection. The Government makes sure that the person gets the information in like 30 days failing which he can file an appeal to the public grievance commission. The appeal costs another 25 rupees. In case an appeal is allowed, the information is to be supplied to the applicant by the competent authority within such period as ordered by the appellate authority. This period shall not exceed 30 days from the date of receipt of the order. After 30 days, if the person bound to give information fails to give information then he pays Rs.50 per day for a delayed period beyond the 30 days subject to a maximum of Rs 500 per application and if the information found is false then he is liable to pay a penalty of Rs.1,000 per application.

UTTAR PRADESH CODE OF PRACTICE ON ACCESS TO INFORMATION

The State of Uttar Pradesh has prepared a "Code of Practice on Access to Information," which it has applied to three areas on a priority basis, namely the Agricultural Production Commissioner, the Public Works Department, and the Tax and Consolidations Department. These departments have been asked to supply information forth with in accordance with the Code and to report back to the Department of Administrative Reforms annually.[110]

CONCLUSION

It is in the backdrop of the theoretical analysis, discussed previously, on Right to Information in India. The complex systems that have been formed as a result of the enormous bureaucracy in India, which seek to diminish the effect of the public sphere primarily through barring of dissemination of information or curtailing the amount and quality of knowledge and information available to the general public, are sought to be made transparent to the general public through the RTI Act in India. The extent to which the answerability and accountability of these institutions have been affected by the implementation of the RTI Act on a national level is one of the questions that are sought to be examined in this chapter.

NOTES

1. Vleugels, R. (2011), "Overview of All Freedom of Information Laws", *Fringe Special*, October 9, 2011

2. Kothari, Rajni. (1998), *State Against Democracy: In Search of Humane Governance*. New Delhi: Ajanta Publication.

3. Mill Stuart Mill, De Tocqueville on democracy in America: The collected works of John Stuart Mills, Volume XVIII- *Essays on Politics and Society* part I. 1832.

4. Gujral, I.K. (2007), *Democracy: A View from India. An Essay in the Construction of Democracy: Lessons from Practice and Research*. Ed. Jorge I. Dominguez and Anthony Jones. John Hopkins University Press.

5. Mathur, Kuldeep. (2009), *From Government to Governance*. National Book Trust, India.

6. United Nations Development Programme. (1997), *Governance for Sustainable Human Development*. New York: UNDP.

7. Dreze, Jean and Sen, Amartya. (1997), *India: Economic Development and Social Opportunity*. New Delhi: Oxford University Press.

8. Pierre Elliot Trudeau (1997), quoted by Gerald Baldwin, cited in Murray Rankin. *Speech of right to Freedom of Information in Canada: Will the doors stay shut?* Ottawa: Canadian Bar Association.

9. Brandt, Karl. (1965), *The German Resistance in American Perspective: Eternal Vigilance the Price of Freedom*, delivered at Berlin, July 20.

10. Blau, Peter. (1956), *Bureaucracy in Modern Society*. New York: Crown Publishing Group/Random House.

11. Mc Turner. (1956), "Access to Official Information: A Neglected Constitutional Right", *Indian Law Journal*, 27: 209–214.

12. Ibid. See Blau, Peter. (1956). *Bureaucracy in Modern Government.*

13. Peter, Hernon and R. McClure Charles. (1984), *Public Access to Government Information: Issues Trends and Strategies*.

14. Ghuman, B.S. (2012), *Right to Information in India Rhetoric and Reality*. A Keynote Address at National Seminar on "Six years of RTI in India: Challenges and Opportunities", Khalsa College Gardhiwala, Hoshiarpur, 17 March 2012.

15. Ghuman, B.S. (2012), *Right to Information in India Rhetoric and Reality*. A keynote Address at National Seminar on "Six years of RTI in India: Challenges and Opportunities", Khalsa College Gardhiwala, Hoshiarpur, 17 March 2012.

16. See Fenester, M. (2006), "The Opacity of Transparency", *Lowa Review*, 91: 885949, Retrived from http://scholarship.law.ufl.edu/cgi/viewcontent.cgi?article=1059&context=facultypub/.

17. Ibid.

18. See Fenester, M. (2006), "The Opacity of Transparency", *Lowa Law Review*, 91: 885–949. Retrived from http://scholarship.law.ufl.edu/cgi/viewcontent.cgi?article=1059&context=facultypub/.

19. Ibid.

20. See Fenester, M. (2015). "Transparency in Search of a Theory", *European Journal of Social Theory*, 18(2): 150–167.

21. Hayek, F.A. (1945). "The Use of Knowledge in Society", *The American Economic Review*, 35(4): 519–530.

22. Gillespie, J.S. (2006), *Transplanting Commercial Law Reforms: Developing a 'rule of law' in Vietnam*. Surrey, UK: Ashgate Publishing Limited.

23. Hildreth, W.Bartley. (2005), "Tax Transparency", in Joseph J. Cordes, Robert D. Ebel & Jane G. Gravelle (eds.), *The Encyclopaedia of Taxation and Tax Policy*. Washington, DC: The Urban Institute Press.

24. See Fenester, M. (2006). "The Opacity of Transparency", *Lowa Law Review*, 91: 885–949. Retrived from http://scholarship.law.ufl.edu/cgi/viewcontent.cgi?article =1059&context=facultypub/

25. Kindornay, S., J. Ron, and C. Carpenter. (2012), "The Right based Approaches to development implications for NGOs", *Human Rights Quarterly*, 34(2): 472–506.

26. Kapur, A., and Duvvery, N. (2008). *A Right-based Approach to Realizing the Economic and Social Rights of Poor and Marginalised Women*. Washington, DC: International Centre for Research on Women.

27. Public Affairs Centre. (2009). *National Assessment of Degree of Compliance to Sou Motu Disclosure Provisions of Right to Information Act, 2005*. Bangalore: Public Affair Centre.

28. See Centre for Good Governance, 2009; Government of India, 2006; Shreyaskar, 2013 et al.

29. See Godbole, Madhav. (2003), *Public Accountability and Transparency: The Imperatives of Good Governance*. New Delhi: Orient Longman, p. 32.

30. Ibid., p. 37.

31. See Handbook for the Training on RTI Act, 2005, Administrative Training Institute, Government of West Bengal, Available at http://www.atiwb.gov.in.

32. See Fritz, Machlup. (1962), Introduces the Concept of Information Economy in his book, *The Distribution and Production of Knowledge in the United States*. Princeton University Press.

33. Habermas, Jurgen. (1996), *Between Facts and Norms: Contributions to a Discourse Theory of Law and Democracy*, Cambridge, MA: MIT Press.

34. See Hazel, 1999, Hood and Herald, 2006.

35. Chapman, Richard A. and Michael Hunt. (2010). *Freedom of Information. Local Government and Accountability*. Surrey, UK: Ashgate Publishing Ltd.

36. Harry, M. Kibirige. (1983), *The Information Dilemma: A Critical Analysis of Information Pricing and the Fees Controversy*. Greenwood Press, 1983.

37. Thomas G. (2000), "Governance, Good Governance and Global Governance: Conceptual and Actual challenges", *Third World Quarterly*, 21(5): 795–814.

38. D. F. Thompson. (1980), "Moral Responsibilities of Public Official: The Problem of Many Hands", *The American Political Science Review*, 74(4): 905–916.

39. Keohane, Robert O. (1984), *After Hegemony: Cooperation and Discord in the World Political Economy*. Princeton: Princeton University Press.

Also See Held, David, Anthony McGrew, David Goldblatt, and Jonathan Perraton (1999). *Global Transformations: Politics, Economics and Culture*. Stanford: Stanford University Press.

40. Davis, G. et al. (1999), *Public Policy in Australia* (2nd Edition). North Sydney: Allen & Unwin Australia Pty Ltd.

41. Keohane, Robert (2003), "Global Governance and Democratic Accountability in Taming globalization", in David Held and Mathias Koenig-Archibugi (eds.), *Frontiers of Governance*. Polity.

42. Roy, Aruna and Nikhil Dey. (2002), "Fighting for the Right to Know in India", *Development Dialogue*, 1: 77–90.

43. See Universal Declaration on Human Rights- http://www.un.org/Overview/rights.html accessed on 20.10.2017, 11 a.m.

44. Dicey, A.V. (1959), *An Introduction to the Study of the Law of the Constitution* (10th Edition). London: Macmillan and Company Ltd.

45. Fishkin, J.S. and R.C. Luskin. (2005) "Experimenting with a Democratic Ideal: Deliberative Polling and Public Opinion", *Acta Politica* 40(3): 284–298.

Also see Fishkin, J.S. (2009), *When the People Speak: Deliberative Democracy and Public Consultation*. Oxford: Oxford University Press.

46. Olson, J.P. (2008), "The Ups and Downs of Bureaucratic Organization", *Annual Review of Political Science*, 11: 13–37.

47. Baxi, Upendra. (1985), "Taking Suffering Seriously: Social Action Litigation in the Supreme Court of India", *Third World Legal Studies*, 4: Article 6. Available at: http://scholar.valpo.edu/twls/vol4/iss1/6.

48. See James, Boyle. (2003), *The Second Enclosure Movement and the Construction of the Public Domain*. Available at http://www.law.duke.edu/journals/ 66LCPBoyle.

49. Kyle, Jensen and Murray Fiona. (2005), "Intellectual Property Landscape of Human Genome", American Association for the Advancement of Science. Available at science.sciencemag.org.

50. Boyle, James. (2003), *The Second Enclosure Movement and the Construction of the Public Domain*. http://creativecommons.org/licenses/by-sa/1.0, 2003.

51. Roy, Jaytilak. (2007), "Second Administrative Reforms Commission on Right to Information: Critical review", *Indian Journal of Public Administration*, 53(3): 558–570.

52. Roy, Jaytilak Guha. (2003), "Right to Information: A Key to Accountable and Transparent Administration", in Alka Dhameja (ed.), *Contemporary Debates in Public Administration*. New Delhi, Prentice-Hall of India Pvt. Ltd, pp. 312–314.

53. Roy, Jaytilak. (2006), "Administrative Reform Initiatives for Excellence in Public Services", *Indian Journal of Public Administration*. Special Number on Excellence in Public Service, LII(3).

54. See selected works of Edmund, Burke. (1999), *Thoughts on the Present Discontents* and *Two Speeches in America*, A New Imprint of the Payne Edition, Liberty fund Inc.

55. Wilson Woodrow quoted in William, E. Simon. (1978), *A Time for Truth*. New York: Mc Graw Hill.

56. The Canadian Information Commissioner's report 2000.

57. See "Global Corruption Report. Available at www.transparency.org.

58. Godbole, Madhav. (1999), "Right to Information: A Long Way to Go", *Lokayan Bulletin,* 3.

59. The Right to Information Bill, 2005, Bill No.107-F of 2004.

60. Bulent, Yilmaz. (1998), "The Right to Information: Is It Possible for Developing Countries?", Paper presented at Amsterdam, *64th FLA General Conference,* Netherlands, August 16–21, www.ifla.org.

61. Marian Koren. (1997), "The Right to Information as a Condition for Human Development", At 63rd IFLA General Conference, August 31–September 5, Copenhagen, Denmark, www.itla.org/IV/ifla64.

62. Jagwanth Saras. (2002), "The Right to Information as a Leverage Right", in Calland Richard and Tilly Allison (eds.), *The Right to Know the Right to Live, Access to Information and Socio-Economic Justice*. Cape Town: ODAC.

63. Mander and Joshi. (1998), "The Right to Information Movement in India-People's Power for the Control of Corruption", *CHRJ*. New Delhi.

64. Maheshwari Shriram. (1981), *Open Government in India*, Macmillan, pp. 95–96.

65. Ibid.

66. See www.righttoinformation.com.

67. Jeane, Dreze. (2002), "Information, Democracy and Military Establishment", *Vidura*, 39(4).

68. Koren, Marian, *The Right to information: A Human Right of Children*, www .ifla.org/faife/papers/others/koren.htm.

69. Puddephat, Andrew. (2002), "Flow of Information Empowers Ordinary People", in Calland Richard and Tilly Allison (eds.), *The Right to Know the Right to Live, Access to information and Socio-Economic Justice*. Cape Town: ODAC.

70. This was said by Mr Vajpayee while introducing the FOI Bill in the Parliament in July, 2000. See "National Documentation Centre on Mass Communication, Research, Reference and Training Division", by Ministry of Information and Broadcasting, www.nic.in/rrtd.

71. See Section 15(2) of the Right to Information Act, 2005.

72. See Section 19(6) of the Right to Information Act, 2005.

73. See Section 4 of Right to Information Act, 2005.

74. See Section 2(f) of Right to Information Act, 2005.

75. Pande, Sachi and Sekhar Singh. (2008), *Right to information Act-2005: A Primer*. New Delhi: NBT.

76. *Bennett Coleman & Co. v. Union of India*, AIR 1973 SC 783

77. *Manubhai D. Shah v. Life Insurance Corporation*, AIR 1981.

78. *Indian Express Newspapers (Bombay) Pvt. Ltd.v. India* (1985) I SCC 64 I.

79. *D.K. Basu v. State of West Bengal* (1997) I SCC 216.

80. *Prabha Dutt v. Union of India,* AIR 1982 SC 6.

81. *Reliance Petrochemicals Ltd. v. Proprietors of Indian Express Newspapers Bombay Pvt. Ltd*, AIR 1989 SC 190.

82. *State of UP v. Raj Narain*, AIR 1975 SC 865. See also *S.P. Gupta v. Union of India*, AIR 1982 SC 149, which strengthened this position.

83. "Gyandoot" means "Messenger of Knowledge." The project won the Stockholm Challenge Award for Public Service and Democracy, See Article 19, "Global trends on the Right to Information: A South Asia Survey", *Article 19*, www.articlel9.org.

84. Reference to *Down to Earth*, an Indian magazine on the environment is made, Ibid.

85. Sec Guhan and Paul, *Corruption in India: Agenda for Action*, Vision/Orient: New Delhi, 1997.

86. *The Hindu*, December 13, 1991.

87. The institute where recruits to the elite branches of the civil services are trained.

88. Article 12 of the Constitution defines the State for the purposes of enforcing fundamental rights.

89. Cited by Chand Vikram Khub (1999), "Legislating Freedom of information in India", *CHR!:* New Delhi, www.humanrightsinitiative.org.

90. Ministry of Information and Broadcasting, "National Documentation Centre on Mass Communication, Research, Reference and Training Division", *Ministry of Information and Broadcasting,* http://www.nic.in/rrtd.

91. Ministry of Information and Broadcasting, "National Documentation Centre on Mass Communication, Research, Reference and Training Division", *Ministry of Information and Broadcasting,* http://www.nic.in/rrtd.

92. Appendix A that is Preamble of Right to Information Act, 2005.

93. A detailed critique of the Bill can be seen on CHRI's website, www.humanri ghtsinitiative.org. For an international perspective, see www.articlel9.org.

94. See Appendix A.

95. Prashant, Shushan. (2002), "A Long Struggle Ahead, A critique of the Freedom of Information Bill 2002", *NCPRI:* New Delhi.

96. See Appendix B.

97. Groups like the MKSS, NCPRI, and Parivartan, See www.righttoinformation .info.

98. Prakash, Kardaley. (2005), "A New Era", *Seminar* 551.

99. See Frederick, Noronha. (2001), "Goa: Perils of Knowing, Right to Information Act 1997", *Economic and Political Weekly.* Also see www.goacom.com/rti/ thelaw.html.

100. Government of Tamil Nadu, tamil Nadu, Right to Information Act No. 24 of 1997, http://www.tn.gov .in/acts-rules/right2info.htm.

101. Government of Madhya Pradesh, Madhya Pradesh Right to Information Bill, 2003, Act no. of 2003.

102. Government of Rajasthan, The Rajasthan Right to Information Act, 2000, Act no. 13 of 2000, www.righttoinformation.info/raj_rti_ac.t.htm.

103. Detailed studies on the Right to Information see www.righttoinformation .info.

104. Government of Karnataka, Karnataka Right to Information Act of 2000, no. 28 of 2000, www.righttoinformation.info/karnataka_act.htm.

105. Public Record of Operations and Finances (PROOF), see www.voicesforall .org/proof.

106. Government of Maharashtra, Maharashtra Act 2003, www.righttoinformation.info/maharashtra_act.htm.

107. See www.geocities.com/ mahadhikar and www.prajanet. org/partners/ma hadhikar/resource_persons.htm.

108. See www.ar.delhigovt.nic.in.

109. Ibid.

110. Government of Uttar Pradesh, Prepared by the Department of Administrative Reforms, State Secretariat (Sachivalaya Bhawan), Lucknow-226 001, India. Also see www.righttoinformation.info/uprti_act.htm.

Chapter 3

Global Trajectory and Legal Framework of Right to Information

INTRODUCTION

Interface between the right to know in India and a similar right that exists across the world is best understood through a comparative cross-country analysis. The dissemination, sharing, and release of information by public agencies to the stakeholders are directly related to the state of constitutional democracy, civil society activism, and responsive governance in any country. Laws and statutory initiatives arrive only when the public institutions are able to inculcate confidence in their performance vis-a-vis people, failing which democracy and rights of citizens may be jeopardized.

The present chapter attempts to study many such interactions between the state of country governance and the legal framework of RTI Act. This work attempts to study the information laws of most prominently active countries where freedom of information law is thriving within the democratic constitutional framework. At the same time, this chapter aims to trace the research problem in the existing and available legal framework for the right to the freedom of information especially since placing the problem in its present legal context would help to answer one of the very important questions, that is, What are the key areas of judicial grievance redressal mechanisms available to the citizens at large? An attempt has been made to locate the argument that the RTI Act in its present form cannot be an effective tool for citizens' empowerment. Many issues and lacunas such as absence of an in-built performance appraisal system, monitoring within departments, and scope and haziness of the "exemption" clause weaken and delay access to the right and correct information.

LEGISLATIVE HISTORY OF THE RIGHT TO INFORMATION IN GLOBAL CONTEXT

In India, before 2005, there is a complete absence of information as far as providing access to the government records is concerned. This chapter aims to compare this Act with that of the United States, United Kingdom, Canada, Australia, New Zealand, and Ireland. Freedom of information laws now exist in 40 countries across the world (including Australia, Belgium, Belize, Bosnia and Herzegovina, Bulgaria, Canada, Czech Republic, Denmark, Estonia, Finland, Greece, Hungary, Iceland, Israel, Japan, Latvia, Lithuania, the Netherlands, New Zealand, Norway, Poland, Portugal, Slovakia, South Africa, South Korea, Spain, Sweden, Thailand, Trinidad and Tobago, Ukraine, United Kingdom, and United States) (Macdonald and Jones, 2003).[1]

In all of these countries, information from public authorities is a matter of right and the exemptions from access to the information and the appeals procedure is outlined. The right to access information held by public authorities has existed in Sweden since the eighteenth century, in the United States since 1966, in France and the Netherlands since 1978, in Australia since 1982, in Ireland since 1983, and in the UK since 2000. There is a lot that can be learnt in the context of India, from these mature democracies with a varied range of experience in freedom of information laws.

Present Status of Information Law: Canadian Experience

For example, upon study of the patterns of use of the Access to Information Act of Canada, it is important to note that the largest user group has been business, that is, 43% in 1992–1993 (The Canadian Information Commissioner's Office report, 1994).[2] It is noted that many business houses sought information from the government that would in an indirect manner help the businesses to seek government contracts. Another category of business use is by persons or companies who obtain government information so that they sell it on to other interested parties at a profit. Even though this may seem as a misuse of the Freedom of Information Act (FOIA), however, according to the Information Commissioner in Canada, this does not pose as a problem since he says that such persons and companies pay taxes and the same information could be exploited by the government itself, if it so desired or the need for such information arises. Individuals formed the next largest group (39% in 1992–1993), followed by media (7–10%), academics (around 2%), and lawyers make up the rest. The use by parliamentarians had been very low and minimal. The Canadian Task Force Report 9 for the year 2000–2001 shows that business users still predominate, with 40.9% of requests emanating from them. About 31.5% came from the general public, which includes parliamentarians, who are estimated to have made about 10%, 16% from organizations,

10.8% from the media, and 0.8% from academics. (The Canadian Information Commissioner's report, 2000, 1:17)[3]

United States

However, it is the developments in the United States that are very interesting to note. The highest seekers of information in the United States as in Canada are the business community and an entire industry has grown up of data brokers or surrogate requesters who gather information under the statute and then sell it forward to interested parties. Individuals and media are usually far behind in the case of the United States (*AEI Journal*, March/April 1982:16).[4]

Ireland

In Ireland, 64% of the queries under the freedom of information laws has been from individuals and the requests for purely personal information is around 45%.

Australia

A similar case is that of Australia where there has been a predominance of requests for personal information and over 90% of requests were being made to four agencies wherein the applicant's own information was being requested, that is, the Australian Taxation Office (ATO), the Department of Veteran Affairs, Immigration and Ethnic (now multicultural) Affairs, and Social Security (now known as Centre link) (Australian Law Reform Commission report, 1977).[5]

The degree and extent of the availability of information are different and differs from time to time in different societies around the world. The history of the restrictions on the free flow of information can be traced back to 1476, with the advent of the first British Printing Press by William Caxton in Westminster. There existed no restrictions on the free flow of information in the garb of laws and legislation on the curtailment of information and the printing endeavors of individuals were only restricted by their ability and imagination. However, shortly after the pursuits of William Caxton, the British Crown initiated to control and regulate the printing presses in England (Dubuque, Brown, 1984:39).[6] The importance of daily discussion and the power of debate and dialogue have been advocated by ancient scholars. Plato has said in his Apology for Socrates:

> In me you have a stimulating critic persistently urging you on with persuasion and reproaches, persistently testing your opinions and trying to show you that you are really ignorant of what you suppose you know. Daily discussion of the matters about which you hear me conversing is the highest good for man, Life that is not tested by such discussion is not worth living. (Bury, 1975:23)[7]

FREEDOM OF INFORMATION TREND IN INTERNATIONAL COMMUNICATION

It is widely acknowledged that the role of freedom of expression is a corollary to freedom of information. Various terminologies such as self-government, checking value, democratic process, and so on are frequently invoked in the defense of freedom of expression (Mehra, 1986).[8] There has existed in this world an information order that directs the flow of information in the world through press agencies and government releases. However, this arrangement has been quite often been accused by the world to be a tool that has been used by developed countries to exploit developing countries by monopolization of the resources of communication. In fact, in the 1980s more than 100 nations rallied together to challenge long-standing information principles and pledged to create a new international information order (NIIO) (Richstad and Anderson, 1981:20).[9]

It has often been a criticism of the UN documents, many of which have become templates for other countries to follow, that most of the early documents of the United Nations were drafted when a clear majority of the 51 original members of the United Nations were from Western countries or countries which were closely allied with the West. Thus it is important to understand that Western liberal traditions unquestionably had a strong influence on UN deliberations at the time (Mehra, 1986).[10] The former U.S. ambassador to the United Nations Daniel Patrick Moynihan has said that the UN Charter is a "'constitutional document' drafted in the tradition of Western liberal societies . . . utterly opposed in spirit and hostile in its provisions to totalitarianism." He points to the "obvious" similarities with the US Constitution:

We the people of the United States . . .
We the people of the United Nations . . .

Similar templates have been followed in the Indian context, wherein the model that has been initiated by the United Nations has been used and the freedom of information laws of most countries that have followed this model have a distinguishing similarity. The rhetorical Anglo-American stress on "fundamental human rights," "dignity and worth of the human person," and "the equal rights of men and women" is noticed right at the outset of the documents and recurrently thereafter. The Charter takes as given those propositions about "human rights and . . . fundamental freedoms for all," which are common philosophical foundation on which the democratic societies of the West have been constructed (Moynihan, 1976:473).[11] The UN debates that the reaction of the emerging nations was extremely quiet and unconcerned as far as the early years of the UN discussion on the free flow of information are concerned. Thirteen of the developing countries, that is, Egypt, Guatemala, India, Iran, Pakistan, Saudi Arabia, Siam, Syria, Afghanistan, Argentina, Belgium, Burma, and China abstained on the vote taken on the "Convention on the Gathering of News and the International Right of Correction" (Official record of the U.N. General Assembly, 209th meeting: 357).[12] In such a scenario, it is important to mention for the purpose of this research the position as far as India is concerned, India wanted the press to "recognize the obligation of preserving the integrity of the state and public order and morality." It was stated that "certain restrictions were inevitable (on freedom of information) in the era of political instability in which most underdeveloped countries currently found themselves" (Fascell, 1979:114-128).[13]

FREEDOM OF INFORMATION AND THE UNITED STATES

The United States of America has consistently upheld the freedom of information and was one of the key countries which were instrumental in promoting the freedom of information in the United Nations in the form of the US- backed Philippine draft resolution by the General Assembly of the United Nations on December 14, 1946. The resolution noted as follows:

> Freedom of information is a fundamental human right and is the touchstone of all the freedoms to which the United Nations is consecrated; Freedom of information implies the right to gather, transmit and publish news anywhere and everywhere without fetters. As such it is an essential factor in any serious effort to promote the peace and progress of the world. . . .Understanding and cooperation among nations are impossible without an alert and sound world opinion, which, in turn, is wholly dependent upon freedom of information. (U.N. G.A. resolution 59(I): www.un.org/documents/ga/res/1/ares1.htm)[14]
>
> The U.S. was a reticent part of the wars and conflicts of the world and mostly the experience of the U.S. as a British colony and in the American Revolution defined the conceptions of presidential powers of the U.S. leaders. However, during the twentieth century the U.S. no longer avoided involvement in foreign conflicts and participated in both the World War I and World War II which changed its policy of information. The presidential right of executive privilege was reaffirmed by President Nixon to deny Congress access to official documents and presidents since Truman have issued orders classifying "national security" information. There is documented material available that analyses and discusses the history of FBI, CIA, and NSA official's efforts to avoid releasing their agency's records. There have been very many instances of American administrators, including the Office of the President himself, who have tried to destroy official documents in the fear of having to provide them to the public or

> the press. The most notable example of the same is the Nixongate. Many U.S. Presidents preferred to take official records with them upon the end of their term or upon relinquishing office and then decided the terms of the conditions as to when these records would become available and accessible to the public. However, this era of official secrecy was taken to the next level when under the Nixon-Sampson agreement of 1974 the former President of the USA claimed as his right the destruction of Oval Office Tapes claiming that they were his personal property. This culture of secrecy was further intensified in 1976 when there was a public outrage over Nixon's destruction of records which resulted in a flurry of FOIA requests for FBI records which led to the FBI to record a disposition plan to the National Archives to destroy all closed FBI field office files on the pretext that their contents were duplicated in FBI headquarter files. (Theoharis, 1989: 85)[15]

As in the case of the debate over cabinet papers in the Indian context, there has been an ongoing controversy regarding the release of documents by the Federal Bureau of Investigation (FBI) of the United States under the FOIA of the United States. However, during the 1970s the government was affected by the Watergate affair and the Vietnam war happenings and the Federal intelligence agencies were forced by the Congress to open their records to public scrutiny. The FBI tried to defend its position by giving several lame justifications. Acting FBI director L. Patrick Gray (Theoharis 1989)[16] criticized one proposal to limit exemptions to disclosure to only those FBI records which were kept for a particular official law enforcement purpose. He was also of the view that instead of broadening the 1966 FOIA so that more transparency can be brought into the system, the Justice Department should seek an amendment for the complete exemption of FBI files. In their private deliberations, FBI officials worried that if the official files were open for the scrutiny of the public, they may be misused by twisting and rephrasing factual information which would lead to the loss of reputation of the FBI (Theoharis 1989).[17] Similar excuses can be cited from the Indian experience wherein government officials have refused to part with official information and documents citing similar reasons. Recently, the Government of India has made the CBI exempt from the aegis of the RTI Act. Further, the Indian experience now seems more similar to the reaction of the FBI because when the attempt to protect the FBI records from exemption under the FOIA failed the FBI officials executed the Act by interpreting the Act very broadly and capriciously. As a result, resultant documents have not furthered the goal of development at all because they reveal almost nothing of concrete nature. In many instances, applicants have found that the information that has been revealed after a FOIA request is so innocuous that it is unclear as to why it was not revealed in the first place or in some cases official who blacked out the information was unaware that the portion that he was blacking out was actually information that was under public domain. A similar case is witnessed by this researcher when the responses of the PIOs under the RTI Act and some other organizations were reviewed. Most PIOs are either very reluctant to part with information and when they do part with information, they usually black out the portions in the documents which are actually a part of the information that should be provided under the Act, that is, information in public domain. Further, the first attempt is to try to not provide the information by the public authority and the second attempt is usually to block as much information as possible. Theoharis (1989)[18] has shared how it took him 16 years to ensure the fullest release of Hoover's office files. Various exemptions such as personal privacy were used to disallow access to information which was challenged by Theoharis and a summarized version of the documents that were requested for were provided to him.

Historians in the United States have faced a multitude of problems in accessing records and have resorted to litigation. In some cases, it took 11 to 15 years to challenge the denial of information from public authorities. Apart from the time consumed, the cost of litigation is a major setback for applicants seeking information under the freedom of information laws. The FBI and CBI have claimed the national security clause to withhold documents that are more than 30 years old in issues such as the Kennedy Assassination that led to the creation of the Kennedy Assassination Records Review Board.

The argument for openness has been best offered by a former CIA insider, William Colby, that "intelligence substance can be disseminated to the public while its sources are kept secret." Further, in his book *Honourable Men*, Colby wrote:

> In a political debate where knowledge can be power, intelligence judgements must be supplied impartially to all factions, to help the best solutions to emerge, rather than the favoured one. Photographs must be declassified, backgrounders attributed, publications edited to protect the sources but allow the substance of the reports and assessments to circulate to Congress and the public. The estimates will then be debated and the sage unanimity of the cloistered world of intelligence will be challenged by those close to the struggle and fearful of the irrational and foolhardy, but real, surprises. Out of the process will come a better understanding of the role and value of modern intelligence, as well as better intelligence itself. (Colby and Forbath, 1978:465 66)[19]

Many historians and researchers have tried to access the records of the Central Intelligence Agency (CIA) of the United States since it had information about everything important that was going on in the world. However, as Theoharis (1998)[20] opines, the history of CIA is in part the history of the conflict between secrecy and publicity and that is why a brief analysis of the public disclosure policies, or the lack of the same, is empirically a requirement for the purpose of this research. It is observed by the United States post its cold war experience that secrecy can endanger a democratic system by denying the people information about the functioning of their own government and it has a corrosive effect on the popular trust necessary for any democracy to function. Also, even though it is an accepted fact that it is necessary for intelligence, however, secrecy can harm the effective conduct of intelligence by allowing errors, foolhardiness, and criminal conduct to develop and remain uncorrected (Theoharis 1998).[21] The same situation can be translated into the Indian experience wherein the problem of corruption coupled with secrecy has made the bureaucracy become totally despotic and unaccountable to the people. Unlike the Indian RTI Act 2005, the FOIA 1966 of the United States, which created an enforceable right to access government records, the CIA, and other government agencies were not exempted from disclosure of information from the Act. However, to protect the interests of national security and protection of governmental interests, certain exemptions were provided in the statute on which any agency including the CIA could rely. One of the exemptions related to national security and permitted agencies to withhold information specifically required by executive order to be kept secret in the interest of the national defense or foreign policy. The authority to withhold information that was exempt under the Act was offset by empowering requesters with the right to challenge in federal courts any wrongful withholding of records by agency personnel. The courts were given the authority to conduct de novo review (i.e., to make a fresh determination) of agency claims.

The report of the Senate that accompanied the legislation clearly establishes the Congress's intent, stating that de novo review was "essential in order that the ultimate decision as to the propriety of the agency's action is made by the court and (to) prevent (judicial review) from becoming meaningless judicial sanctioning of agency discretion." The most important aspect of this being that the courts were given the authority to reject the denial of information orders of the executives using methods such as in-camera examination of documents and order the release of documents that were improperly classified. However, it is seen that the courts were from the outset reluctant to enforce the Act against the CIA since it is an established principle that the decision to examine disputed documents in any particular case is the discretion of the courts. In the light of the guidance of sound discretion, most appeals panels have held that a court need not conduct its own in-camera inspection of contested documents if three conditions are satisfied: (1) the FBI has claimed a reasonable basis for finding potential harm in the release of documents, (2) the information logically falls under national security, and (3) no evidence can be found that contradicts the government's claim or that suggests bad faith. Upon only an affidavit claiming that the information was classified, the courts granted permission to the agency for not disclosing the requested information. The process of judicial examination of classified documents exists also in India, however, in the United States, even though the judicial examination of secret documents provides a check on government abuse of power, it has one undemocratic aspect, that is, the judicial examinations themselves are secret. The plaintiff who is seeking the information is not allowed to be present in the in-camera discussion that takes place between the judge and the government. Courts have tried to rectify this anomaly by making the public records as descriptive as possible. A few years later, not succumbing to the pressure from the Reagan administration to exempt the CIA entirely from the mandatory review and disclosure requirements of the FOIA, the Congress instead adopted the CIA Information Act. The CIA Information Act reaffirmed the application of the FOIA to the CIA but exempted from search and review what Congress thought would be only a small category of operational files. As is seen through the course of this research and as is in most cases of public disclosure that reach the courts in India, intelligence agencies such as the CIA are never forced to reveal information by courts but are instead compelled to reexamine the initial, overbroad claims of nondisclosure and more often than not, the CIA voluntarily releases more information.

However, the case of India is peculiar because courts are actually refusing to grant information about them under the RTI Act and therefore there is little faith that is left in judicial redressal of complaints regarding the denial of information. Thus, the FOIA worked to open up substantial quantities of CIA information, and, in 1980, the Centre for National Security Studies made available to interested researchers a list of CIA documents releases through the FOIA based on which numerous books and articles have been written. However, what has become routine in CIA responses are GLOMLAR responses wherein if the FOIA applicant seeks CIA records which relate to a foreign national or a specific event abroad, a frequent and common CIA response states that in all requests such as yours, the CIA can neither confirm nor deny the existence or nonexistence of any CIA records responsive to your request. As is the case in India, journalists, scholars, and activists in the United States have used the FOIA to scrutinize the operations of government agencies and to expose official misconduct and lying, including the FBI's illegal efforts to harass, intimidate, disrupt, and otherwise interfere with lawful political actions (Theoharis 1998).[22] The experience with the FOIA has been a success in the United States, according to statistics, in 1990 federal agencies received 491,000 FOIA requests and spent $83 million responding to them. The defense department received 118,000 requests; the justice department, 62,000: the INS, 45,000; the EPA, 39,000; the FBI 11,000; and the CIA, 4,000. The FOIA further requires that agencies report the extent of their denials of such requests: the agency with the highest denial rate in

1990 was the Office of Ethics, which refused to release 75% of requested documents. In contrast, the Department of Health and Human Services denied only 2% of the requests received (Access Reports 17, Oct 30 1991:5).[23] David M. Walker (Radin Chanin, 2010)[24] has written that what one expects from his or her country's government is commitment to the Constitution of the country; competency to focus on things that will generate value, mitigate risk, and avoid crises; and caring for the less fortunate in our society, integrity, that is, knowledge of the truth and innovation meaning thereby that new ways to address old problems should be found for which dramatic fundamental transformational change is needed and not incrementalism.

There is the latest question of digital information that is held with the government that needs to be tackled. Even though this is not a major part of this research, yet the secrecy that is generated by the e-mails exchanged within government offices that are related to work needs to be examined. Especially, in the light of the fact that these are actually records of the government that are easily destructible. A pertinent comparison in this respect is the experience of Scott Armstrong that he has underlined in the essay titled "The War over Secrecy: Democracy's most Important Low—Intensity Conflict" (Theoharis 1998)[25] in which he had to engage in a battle with the US administration to dissuade them from purging email exchanges in the White House. Armstrong also fought a long and hard legal battle with the courts in the United States and the US Supreme Court refused to grant the writ of certiorari in his case which was against the president.[26] Thereafter, through its decision, the Supreme Court has assured that the activities of the National Security Council (NSC) remain secret for 12 years after Clinton leaves office and more importantly that the president and his national security adviser can decide which records they will and will not retain.[27] In the essay titled "We Can't Yet Read our Own Mail: Access to the Records of the Department of State by Page Putnam Miller" (Theoharis 1998),[28] it has been explained how documents related to the Foreign Relations of the United States (FRUS)[29] which is the State Department's respected documentary record of US diplomacy have become increasingly out of reach of the government. The first FRUS volume which was a 441-page executive document, which included circulars, notes, instructions, and dispatches related to foreign policy, appeared on December 3, 1861, and was a supplement to President Abraham Lincoln's annual message to Congress. Until 1906, the FRUS volumes were released the year following the events recorded in the documents. However, it is important to note in the context of this research, since there is a continuous discussion on the increasing secrecy in the world, that by 1914, personnel shortages and constraints on access to pertinent records stretched the one-year time gap to four years and by 1921 it had grown to eight years. Following World War I, a 15-year time gap between the date of the documents and their publication became the practice, and this continued for a number of years (Leopold, 1963: 595-601).[30] In the 1920s, there was a drive to ensure the historical integrity of such records, and in 1925, Secretary of State Frank Kellogg ordered that the volumes contain the correspondence "relating to all major policies and decisions of the Department . . . together with events which contributed to the formation of each decision or policy." There are four points contained in Kellogg's order which are still printed at the beginning of each volume which make clear that there are to be no deletions without an indication of where the deletions occurred, no omissions to conceal or gloss over what might be regarded as a defect of policy, and no facts omitted that were of major importance in reaching a decision. Kellogg's final point specified the criteria under which omissions are permissible: if the published information would impede current diplomatic negotiations or would contravene the confidences US officials had given to foreign governments (Leopold, 1963: 595-601).[31] President John Kennedy issued a National Security Action Memorandum in 1961 observing that the publication of the Foreign Relations series has fallen in number and the time gap that approaches twenty years is unfortunate and undesirable because a democracy should have an informed citizenry. Kennedy emphasized that "any official should have a clear and precise case involving the national interest before seeking to withhold from publication documents or papers fifteen or more years old" (National Security Action Memorandum no.91, Kennedy, 1961:21).[32] Another intriguing example of the secrecy of the American administration is the tight secrecy under which the FBI and CBI functioned after the murder of President John F. Kennedy which led to the creation of The John F. Kennedy Assassination Records Collection Act of 1992 (Public Law 102-526, 102d Congress), which was an important milestone in the people's right to know and the culture of secrecy that evolved during 50 years of the cold war. The main purpose of the Act was to placate theories that implicated federal agencies in a conspiracy to murder the young president; however, the unintended consequence has been to reveal some deeply buried secrets of the FBI, CIA, and other intelligence agencies. The absence of information breeds totalitarianism and dictatorship in the context of the concept of information as given in, where it is said that "just as secrecy and democracy are incompatible, so totalitarianism and an informed public cannot coexist" (Indiana Law Journal 1952: 209-214).[33]

OFFICIAL SECRECY AND THE ISSUE OF NATIONAL DEFENSE

When an RTI application is received from an applicant, the question that a public authority should ask is (1) whether the public authority has the information and (2) whether the public authority desires to disclose the information. The trial of Peter Treu4 who was an electronics engineer who was accused of violating the Official Secrets Act created a furor in Canada over the high-handedness of the government as far as official secrecy is concerned. This was because it was the first criminal trial in Canada that was held entirely in secret and the image of a Canadian citizen being tried in utter secrecy led to a lot of media attention and wrath of journalists (Rowat1979).[34] In the early twentieth century, Max Weber (Macy 1975)[35] opined that some secrets are to be kept secrets in functional interest and he placed military secrets as one of them. He stated that tendencies toward secrecy follow the material interest of some administrative fields. He also said that secrecy is found where the power of the dominant structure is at stake, whether in the face of an economic competitor or a foreign or hostile state. Military secrets that are vital for the defense of a country are the ones that are regarded by authorities as most important. Even in the United States, even though three major kinds of classifications exist, that is, top secret, secret, and confidential—yet the general attitude is to overclassify material rather than to underclassify it. If one were to delve into the history of FOI laws, then it is found that Sweden has the longest experience with the principle of openness which goes as far back as 1766. This trend in Sweden started with the adoption of the Freedom of the Press Act which is one of the basic constitutional laws of Sweden.

Therefore, now for over two hundred years, the government of Sweden has provided full information to citizens about government matters. The road till here has not been smooth and arose out of a fierce struggle in the last half of the eighteenth century and after the end of a period of absolutism between 1772 and 1809, the freedom of the press and parliamentary form of government were reestablished and this principle was soon established as part of the normal political life of Sweden. Therefore, a reverse provision is applicable in Sweden wherein all administrative documents are open to the public until under some law they are made private. The Swedish tradition of open access for all citizens is so deeply embedded in the psyche of the institutions and for the people who run the institutions that both courts and ombudsmen place a great weight on an open government initiative. Moreover, there is no permanent time period under Swedish law under which documents can be kept secret from the public which means that the Secrecy Act keeps the documents of the foreign office or of the armed services secret only temporarily. However, one important point of difference is that the Swedish Act creates a distinction between official documents and internal working papers, which is a distinction that does not exist in the Indian context. Under the Swedish Act, the right to access documents exists only in the case of documents that are sent from one organization to another and not otherwise. However, this is not the case with India.

Moreover, the most important feature in the Swedish context is the entire spirit in which the issue of transparency is created, which means that due to the open attitudes of the public officials, the entire nature and manner in which the business is conducted changes and there is a much lesser feeling of public suspicion and distrust of officials, which gives a greater confidence to individuals. However, despite this, there is tremendous amount of administrative secrecy in Sweden. As in the case of India, the law provides that to protect public interest and personal privacy, certain information may be exempt from disclosure. Premature access and publicity are avoided by making a distinction between working papers and official documents.

Lastly, there is constant pressure by government and officials to keep matters confidential for their own convenience. A critique of such openness in administrative societies is that government officials communicate important information to each other orally instead of putting it down on paper (Donald C. Rowat 1979).[36] B. Wennergren, a former ombudsman, concluded in his book that the right of access is very seldom abused in Sweden and that it does not impede the daily work of administration "to any degree worth mentioning" (Wennergren, 1970:249).[37]

It is interesting to note that countries which top the human development index such as Finland, Denmark, and Norway have only recently adopted laws related to public access to information. This throws light on the disjunctions prevailing between development and RTI as the RTI cannot be taken at its face value but has to be looked into as one of the many other constitutional tools required for the development. Finland, Denmark, and Norway have only recently adopted laws related to public access to information. In Denmark and Norway, citizens, including reporters, are required to ask for specific documents, that is, they must know that a document exists and then only they can ask for the document. Moreover, another important point of distinction in Scandinavian countries is that appeals against the denial of information can be made to more than one independent authority. For example, in Finland and Sweden, an appeal can be made to the ombudsmen, the Chancellor of Justice, or the Supreme Administrative Court, while in Denmark and Norway, it can be made to the ombudsman or the ordinary courts. However, even though openness exists in Sweden to a much greater extent than in other countries, however, its exemptions are very specific and certain. However, in the case of countries such as the United States and India, the categories of exemption are much broader and therefore leave more room for official discretion and judicial interpretation. Through the applications filed for FOI in the United States, various new pictures have come to light such as disclosure of the CIA files in MK-ULTRA5 case and planned assassinations of foreign leaders. In 1976, of the estimated 150,000 requests under both the Information and Privacy Acts, about 25,000 or 17% were denied in whole or in part. About 4,200 of these denials or again about 17% produced appeals to the head of the organization. In over half of these cases, the head changed the original decision and released part of the information requested (46%) or all of it (12%). The result is that only about 15% of the documents requested were wholly denied by the departments and agencies on the ground that they fell under one of the secrecy provisions of the Act. Mainly responsible for these denials were the security and law enforcement agencies which still deny large numbers of requests for personal documents. Due to the large number of requests under both acts, compliance problems do exist for the administration, especially the welfare, defense, treasury, security, and law enforcement agencies, which receive the bulk of the requests. Thus, the department of justice claims that, including the FBI, the amount of time it devoted to freedom of information and related privacy requests rose from 120,000 man-hours in 1975 to more than 600,000 in 1976 and has protested that the increased workload and the potential revelation of secret information weakens its law enforcement capacity. Most business houses in the United States has used the Act to collect information about their competitors. New business and law firms have sprung up which specialize in freedom of information laws and carry appeals to courts. There is a movement of reverse freedom of information cases in which a court injunction is sought to release the requested documents and the government is having greater difficulty in collecting sensitive information from business corporations (Donald C. Rowat 1981).[38]

The reasons for nondisclosure need to be given while refusing to give information. In the UK, the FOI Act came quite late in 2000 and was made enforceable only in 2005. The White Paper that was presented to the British Parliament in December 1997 which was titled "Your Right to Know—The Government's Proposals for a Freedom of Information Act" starts with the following sentence, unnecessary secrecy in government leads to arrogance and defective decision-making. The report on the government of India website, that is, www.rti.gov.in gives the report on Mexico and one more country that is conducted by Price Waterhouse Coopers which serves as an insight into the workings of the comparative RTI in these two countries.

In the Netherlands, there exists a combination of discretionary secrecy which is combined with specific provisions for openness and access. A very unique feature of the FOI Act in the Netherlands is that it provides a RTI in administrative documents rather than to the documents themselves. This leaves a lot of discretionary power in the hands of the government officials and gives a lot of opportunity to the officials to interpret the contents of the documents to suit their own interests, rather than giving the document straight away to the applicant. It is seen that keeping in view the Swedish example, there is a need to reverse the principle that everything is public unless it is made secret by law. The Swedish experience depicts that there is a possibility to have a system where the abovementioned principle is reversed by law and a strong tradition of openness can be developed, without the workings of the government coming to a halt. On the other hand, according to Donald C. Rowat (1979),[39] where there is no such tradition of openness that exists, the full establishment of the principle of public access will require a radical change in law, practices, and attitudes.

Moreover, the adoption of a law which clearly declares a reversal of the principle of secrecy has great symbolic and dramatic value in altering both public and official attitudes. However, a lesson can be learnt from the failure of the first American law of 1946 and the limited success of the law of 1966 until its amendment in 1974, such a law will not succeed unless it contains strong provisions for its enforcement. Public officials are too used to the old system of discretionary secrecy under which they arbitrarily withhold information for their own convenience or for fear of disapproval by their superiors and will not change their ways unless they are required by law to do so.

Moreover, in a parliamentary system of democracy, such as that exists in India, where the executive government controls the introduction of legislation, there usually exists resistance from the government to initiate such a strong law, since the promulgation of such a law would result in the government losing its power and strength and because the system of discretionary secrecy suits the government in power. In the United States, the House of Representatives, sub-committee on Government Operations, after speaking with 142 witnesses in the summer of 1972 noted that the bureaucracy "already set in its ways never got the message about freedom of information." As a result of this, federal agencies took an average of 33 days to respond to initial inquiries for information. And moreover, people requesting government documents were often faced with excessive charges from the agencies for finding and reproducing records. However, it is important to note that The Federal Drug Administration received around 13,000 requests in 1975 and within a year this figure stood at 21,800. Mark Feldman, the deputy legal advisor of the Department of State, testified before a senate subcommittee that an estimated 3,500 requests were expected for the calendar year of 1977 as compared with 1,812 two years earlier (U.S. Senate hearings, 1977:342).[40]

Moreover, a 1977 overview of ninety agency reports concerning the FOIA revealed that the Departments of Justice, State, and the Treasury denied, respectively, 30%, 40%, and 31% of their initial requests. Only 12.5% of the administrative appeals conducted in 1977 were granted, while 53.5 were denied in full and 34% were denied in part (Relyea, 1978:217).[41] If negotiations that the government enters into with various parties are kept a secret from the public then the government negates the claims of a democracy. This is the basic tenet of a vibrant and participatory democracy, in the light of the current debate with regard to transparency and accountability for which the RTI is seen as a vital instrument.

CONCLUSION

The chapter on global trajectories and legal framework of RTI, as the name suggests, the chapter divided into two parts, global trajectories and legal framework. This chapter deals with the Indian experience with regard to the RTI Act vis-à-vis other countries. The Indian experience has been fairly recent since the Act was promulgated only in the year 2005. The final draft of the present Act also underwent quite a few changes till the current version saw the light of the day. In comparison with countries such as the United States, the Indian experience is fairly new and is evolving at its own pace. The chapter makes a comparative analysis of the implementation of the RTI Act of India with that of the United States, Ireland, Australia, a few Scandinavia countries, and so on. The ethos and democratic makeup of each country with whom the comparisons are drawn is a very different, therefore the experience with regard to the freedom of information laws also varies. In the course of the comparative analysis, it is seen that as a democracy matures, there is demand and pressure for more and more transparency and accountability in government functioning. The content of the chapter toward the end throws light on the major issues of participatory democracy vis-à-vis information dissemination. The continuous effort to throttle the free flow of information in democracies wherein the freedom of information act has existed for a much longer time than in India serves as an example for our country because in many ways as elucidated earlier, history is being repeated as far as curbing the total implementation and effect of the RTI Act is concerned.

The second part of the chapter outlines the legal framework within which the RTI Act has been promulgated and subsequently being implemented. The chapter analyzes the RTI Act in the backdrop of the various legal provision and national and international case laws. The chapter locates the RTI Act within the Constitution of India. It also explains in detail the importance of the RTI Act and briefly mentions provisions of other statutes that are in consonance with the spirit of the RTI Act. The chapter also outlines the various important judgments of the Supreme Court and the High Court pertaining to the RTI Act; it outlines the process of promulgation of the RTI Act in India. The chapter outlines through its various components, how the RTI Act is not a clear and precise piece of legislation in as much as it leaves a lot of scope for interpretation. It has also created a quasi-judicial body of institution which has not lessened the burden of judicial courts as RTI-related matters are still reaching courts of law for adjudication under the writ jurisdiction of courts.

Moreover, the Information Commissioners who are appointed under the Act give many contradictory orders which dilute the efficacy of the legislation. The exemption clause of the Act leaves much to be desired. Undoubtedly, the new information law is a substantial achievement, however, it needs to be implemented in the right spirit and there is need to strengthen it.

NOTES

1. John, Macdonald, Q. C. Clive, and H. Jones. (2003), *The Law of Freedom of Information*, Editors.
2. Canadian Information Commissioner's Report 1994-1.
3. See the Canadian Information Commissioner's Report 2000-1.
4. Vaughn, R. G. (ed.). (2000), *Freedom of Information*, Also See *The Freedom of Information Act Has No Clothes: Regulation:* AEI Journal on Government and Society (March/April, 1982) 16, reprinted in R. G. Vaughn (ed.) freedom of Information (2000).
5. See Australian Law Reform Commission. (1995), *Open Government: A Review of the Federal freedom of Information 1982*. Also See Report 77.
6. See Pember, Donald R. (1984), *Mass Media Law* (Dubuque, Ia).
7. Bury, John B. (1975), *A History of Freedom of Thought.* Greenwood Press.
8. Mehra, Achal. (1986), *Free Flow of Information - A New Paradigm.* Greenwood Press.
9. Jim, Richstad and Michael Anderson (eds.). (1981), *Crisis in International News: Policies and Prospects.* New York: Columbia University Press.
10. Mehra, Achal. (1986), *Free flow of Information - A New Paradigm.* Greenwood Press.
11. Daniel, Moynihan. (1976), "Abiotrophy at Turtle Bay: The United Nations in 1975", *Harvard Journal of International Law,* 17(3): 473.
12. See U.S. Department of Health, Education and Welfare, *Report of the Secretary's Advisory Committee on Automated Personal Data Systems: Records*, Computers, and the Rights of Citizens 1973 (Official Records of the General Assembly, 209th meeting, p. 357).
13. Fascell, Dante (ed.). (1979), *International News: Freedom Under Attack.* Beverly Hills: Sage.
14. See *U.N. G.A. Resolution 59(I)*: www.un.org/documents/ga/res/1/ares1.html.
15. Theoharis, Athan G. (1989), *A Culture of Secrecy: The Government Versus the People's Right to Know.* University Press of Kansan.
16. Theoharis, Athan G. (1989), *A Culture of Secrecy: The Government Versus the People's Right to Know.* University Press of Kansan.
17. Ibid.
18. Ibid.
19. Colby, William and Peter Forbath. (1978), *Honourable Men: My life in the CIA*. New York: Simon and Schuster.

20. Theoharis, Athan G. (1998), *A Culture of Secrecy: The Government Versus the People's Right to Know*. University Press of Kansan.

21. See Theoharis, Athan G. (1998), *A Culture of Secrecy: The Government Versus the People's Right to Know*. University Press of Kansan.

22. Theoharis, Athan G. (1998), *A Culture of Secrecy: The Government Versus the People's Right to Know*. University Press of Kansan.

23. See Access Reports *Department of Health and Human Services* (1991:5), 17, Oct 30.

24. Beryl A., Radin and Joshua M. Chanin (ed.). (2010), *What Do We Expect from Our Government*?

25. Theoharis, Athan G. (1998), *A Culture of Secrecy: The Government Versus the People's Right to Know*. University Press of Kansan.

26. See The Court Case that Armstrong fought against the president's office is titled *Scott Armstrong v. Reagan* which later became *Scott Armstrong et al. v. Executive Office of the President et al.*

27. See *Armstrong v. Executive Office of the President,* 90 F. 3d 553 (D.C. Cir. 1996).

28. Theoharis, Athan G. (1998), *A Culture of Secrecy: The Government Versus the People's Right to Know*. University Press of Kansan.

29. The foreign relations of the *United States series is the official documentary historical record of major U.S. policy decisions* which first began in 1861. Its volumes contain documents from presidential libraries, Departments of State and Defence, National Security Council, Central Intelligence Agency, Agency for International Development, and so on. www.state.gov/www/about_state/history/fruswhat.html

30. Richard, Leopold W. (1963), *The Foreign Relations Series: A Centennial Estimate*. Mississippi Valley *Historical Review* 49.

31. Ibid.

32. See *National Security Action Memorandum (1961) No.91*, President John Kennedy, September 6.

33. Access to official information: A Neglected Constitutional Right, *27 Indiana Law Journal* 209, 214. 1952.

34. Rowat, D.C. and Niels E. Holm (eds.). (1979), *Denmark Administrative Secrecy in Developed Countries,* New York: Columbia University Press.

35. Macy, Arthur. (1975), *The Myths of National Security, The Peril of Secret Government.* Boston: Beacon Press.

36. Rowat, D.C. and Niels E. Holm (eds.). (1979), *Denmark Administrative Secrecy in Developed Countries.* New York: Columbia University Press.

37. Wennergren, B. (1970), *Civic Information- Administrative Publicity, International Review of Administrative Science,* XXXVI(24).

38. See Rowat, Donald C. (ed.). (1981), *The Right to Know : Essays on Governmental Publicity and Public Access to Information.* Columbia University Press.

39. Rowat, D.C. and Niels E. Holm (eds). (1979), *Denmark Administrative Secrecy in Developed Countries.* New York: Columbia University Press.

40. See *U.S. Privacy Protection Study Commission: Personal Privacy in an Information Society*. Washington, DC: Government Printing Office, 1977—Also known as the Study Commission Report.

41. See Relyea, H. (1978), *The Administration of the FOI Act: A Brief Overview of Executive Branch*, Annual Reports for 1977. Washington, DC: Congressional Research Service.

Chapter 4

Functioning of Right to Information Act in Odisha Secretariat

INTRODUCTION

This chapter provides an overview of the implementation of RTI Act in Odisha since its inception. More particularly, it explains the compliance with RTI Act by different PAs, receipt and disposal of RTI applications and first appeals (FAs) in different years, and disposal of second appeals (SAs), complainant cases (CCs), and charges collected from RTI applicants. The review is based on the data collected from the annual reports of OIC published in different years and primary data from all the departments of the Odisha Secretariat. Applications received by public authorities in the different departments of the Odisha Secretariat since the inception of the Act were reviewed. The RTI authorities include Public Information Officer/Assistant Public Information Officer, Secretariat Information Cell.

ODISHA RIGHT TO INFORMATION RULES, 2005

In exercise of the power conferred by the Government of Odisha, Information and Public Relation Department (I & PR) notification on October 1, 2005, while exercising power conferred by Section 27 of the RTI Act (No.22 of 2005)[1] has made a Rule to make RTI Act 2005 more operational in the State. This Rule is called the Odisha Right to Information Rules 2005. The Rule clearly defines the functional categories such BPL households, fee, form, identity, nodal officer, PIO, schedule, and State government. The Rule also clearly delineates the process and procedures of appointment and obligations of PIO, procedure to obtain information, information regarding rejection, meeting the recommending committee, memorandum of appeal, penalties, and maintenance of registers and deposit of expenditure. In addition the Rule also provides different forms, A, B, C, D, E, F, and G, to make the process of implementation smooth.

The amendments incorporated in the Odisha Right to Information (Amendment) Rules, 2006, are as follows:

(i) PIO is to maintain a register in Form-F for recording the details of the applications received and application supplied by him/her and keep the Heads of the Departments informed after furnishing any information and it shall be the duty of the Head to ensure required assistance if any. The PIO is to facilitate in providing information and the registers shall remain open to the inception by the members of public as required in respect of the proactive disclosures under the Section 4 (1) (b) of the Act.
(ii) Each PA is to maintain a Register for day-to-day record of the members of the public who visit the office in connection with accessing or inspecting sua motto information proactively disclosed by the authority under the Section 4 of the Act.
(iii) The PIO shall maintain a cash register in Form-G for recording the details of money received by him/her relating to providing information and deposit the money in any scheduled bank in the name of such officials as decided by the concerned office head.
(iv) The postal charge will be charged if any information is supplied through post.

STUDY PROFILE

The study profile covers all the respondents of the employees of different departments of Odisha Secretariat. The study profile covers the CCs and SA cases of RTI applicants (Employees of Odisha Secretariat). The primary data collected from PIOs and APIOs of the 40 departments of Odisha Secretariat. The secondary data are collected from the Information and Public Relation Department (Nodal Department) of RTI. The 400 respondents' CCs and SA cases are thoroughly studied (2006–2016)[2] to know the grievance redressal of the employees of Odisha Secretariat through the RTI.

SAMPLE SIZE

This section covers distribution of different categories of RTI personnels and employees of Odisha Secretariat. The study has covered 400 RTI CCs of the employees (RTI applicants)[3] in form of FA and SA and 40 PIOs of Odisha

Table 4.1 PAs and RTI-Designated Personnel Covered under the Study

Sl. No.	*PA Categories*	*Total PIOs*	*FAA*	*HOD*	*Premises*
1.	Secretariat Departments	40	30	10	40
2.	Heads of the Departments	10	07	03	10
3.	RTI Applicants Cases	400 (Random Sample)	300 (Complaint Cases)	100 (Second Appeals)	400 (Information and Public Relation Department)
4.	Total	450	337	113	450

Source: Primary and Secondary Survey, 2019.

Secretariat (Secretariat Information Cell). The details of Random Sample size covered from different PAs are given in table 4.1.

Gender Distribution

A look into the gender distribution of the respondents shows that among the PIOs female accounts for only 5 (9.38%). Among the First Appellate Authorities (FAAs), female accounts for only 10 (7.69%), while among the Heads of Departments female accounts for 3 (20.00%). A look into the variations according to the PAs shows that in Secretariat Departments the share of female PIOs tunes to only 5 (9.38%), female FAA tunes to 10 (7.69%), and the female Heads of Departments account for only 3 (15.38%). In the Heads of the Departments the female PIOs share is 0 (00.00%), while 2 (30.00) female is represented in FAA and Heads of Departments category there is not a single female. Similarly, among the other RTI applicants, the female PIOs share is only 50 (17.74%), the female FAA is only 50 (2.63%), and female Heads of Departments is also 10 (5.88%). The study finally indicates that female representation in the sample is less than their share as per the representation for women.[4] The details of the distribution of females in different RTI positions in PAs are given in table 4.2.

As regards the previous experiences of the PIOs working as PIO, the data indicate that in the Secretariat Departments, 15 (31.25%) had one year experience, 18 (46.88%) had 1 to 2 years experience, 4 (12, 50%) had 2 to 3 years experience, and the rest 3 (9.38%) had more than 3 years of experiences as PIO. In other departments, this indicates that none of the PIOs during the time of Study were new to the responsibility. The PIOs of the Heads of the Departments also have early experiences of working as PIO, which covers 12 (46.15%) PIOs who had 1 year experience, 8(30.77%) had 1 to 2 years

Table 4.2 Distribution of RTI-Designated Personnel According to Their Gender

			Gender Distribution								
			PIO			*FAA*			*HOD*		
Sl. No.	*Categories of PAs*	*Total PAs covered*	*Male*	*Female*	*Total*	*Male*	*Female*	*Total*	*Male*	*Female*	*Total*
1.	Secretariat Department	40	35 (90.63)	5 (9.38)	40 (100)	20 (92.31)	10 (7.69)	30 (100)	7 (80.00)	3 (20.00)	10 (100)
2.	Heads of the Departments	10	7 (84.62)	3 (15.38)	10 (100)	5 (100)	2 (30.00)	7 (100)	3 (100)	0 (0.00)	3 (100)
3.	RTI Applicants Cases	400	350 (82.26)	50 (17.74)	400 (100)	250 (97.37)	50 (2.63)	300 (100)	90 (94.12)	10 (5.88)	100 (100)
4.	Total	450	392 (85.00)	58 (15.00)	450 (100)	275 (96.47)	62 (3.53)	337 (100)	50 (90.91)	5 (9.09)	113 (100)

Source: Primary and Secondary Survey, 2019 (figures in the bracket are per cent of total).

of experience, 4 (15.38%) had 2 to 3 years of experience, and 2 (7.69%) had more than 3 years of experiences of working as PIO. In other PAs around 30 (48.39%) PIOs had 1 year experience, 18 (29.03%) PIOs had 1 to 2 years experiences, 7 (11.29%) had 2 to 3 years of experiences and equal number of 7 (11.29%) also had 3 years of experiences of working as PIO during the study.[5] Thus, the majority of PIOs for all categories of PAs had only one year experience.

In total, 22.50% PIOs had early experience of more than 2 years, 34.17%had the work experience of more than 2 years, and 34.17% had the work experience of 2 years as PIO previous to the present assignment. The details of their previous experiences of the PIOs are given in table 4.3.

RESPONSES OF RTI USERS AND NONUSERS

This part of the study focuses on operational constraints and critical gaps faced by the Civil Society which includes RTI users and nonusers at various levels to access the benefits of RTI Act in Odisha. In addition to the RTI-designated personnel in different PAs, the study also covered RTI users and nonusers so as to find out the operational constraints from secretariat employees perspective. Thus, the study has covered 400 RTI Users (applicants RTI cases) and 40 PIOs and APIOs responses of the different department of Odisha Secretariat. A list of RTI users was collected from the Information and Public Relation Department and depending on their availability 400 RTI users were randomly interviewed in different department of Odisha Secretariat with the help of a specific interview schedule for my study. Similarly 10 RTI cases from each department were covered in the study. Based on the age and education criteria, around 400 respondents of almost equal numbers were covered in the study from both male and female category. The study of RTI users covered various aspects of the RTI Act. They are knowledge of the users on RTI Act; use of the RTI Act by the user with respect to the period of use, purpose of use, number of questions asked, frequency of visit by the user to the PAs for information, knowledge of the user on the timeline for the disposal of information; perception of the people and the government functionaries on the RTI users; and knowledge of the users on various aspects of OIC and punishment and penalty provisions in the RTI Act. Similarly, the RTI like the Non- User Schedule covered their knowledge and understanding on various aspects of the RTI Act like the processes of submitting RTI application; timeline for information delivery by the RTI authorities; duties of the RTI authorities; and on various aspects of OIC and punishment/penalty provision in the RTI Act. The socioeconomic profile of both the user and nonuser

Table 4.3 Distribution of Previous Experiences Worked as PIOs since 2005

Sl.			*Previous experience as PIO*			
No.	*PA Categories*	*Total PIOs*	*<1 year*	*1–2 yrs*	*2– 3 yrs*	*3 yrs and Above*
1.	Secretariat Departments	40(100)	15(31.25)	18(46.48)	4(12.50)	3(9.38)
2.	Heads of the Departments	26(100)	12(46.15)	8(30.77)	4(15.38)	2(7.69)
3.	Other PAs	62(100)	30(48.39)	18(29.03)	7(11.29)	7(11.29)
	Total	120(100)	52(43.33)	41(34.17)	15(12.50)	12(10.00)

Source: Primary Survey, 2019
(figures in the bracket are percent of the total).

groups was collected with respect to gender distribution, their occupations, and educational distribution.

Socioeconomic Profile of RTI Users and Nonusers

Gender Distribution

The gender distribution of RTI users show that out of 400 RTI users, 200 (50.00%) were males and 100 (25%) were females. The female RTI users were covered in the different department of Odisha Secretariat employee's perspective and gender distribution of the RTI nonusers shows that out of 400 RTI applicant cases respondents, female respondents account 40 (10.00%), and male respondents account 100 (25.00%). The proportion of male and female nonuser respondents select in each department of Odisha Secretariat 50 (15.00%) and male nonuser 114 (28.00%) level of comparison (table 4.4).[6]

Age Distribution

Both the RTI users and nonusers are divided into three age classifications. They were 20 to 35, 36 to 45, and 46 and above. Around 7 (23.33%) RTI users were within the age group of 20 to 35, while 10 (33.33%) were within the age group of 36 to 45, and 13 (43.33%) were above 45 years. Similarly, among the nonusers group 70 (64.22%) were within the age group of 20 to 35 years, while 27 (24.77%) were within the age group of 36 to 45, and 12 (11.01%) were within the age group of 46 and above.[7] The district-wise distribution of both RTI users and nonusers as per their age distribution in different districts is given in table 4.5.

Occupational Distribution

As a part of the socioeconomic profile and considering its importance, the study finds out the occupational categories of both RTI users and nonusers. The data reflect that among the RTI nonusers 19 (17.43%) had ASO, followed by 28 (25.69%) who had adopted LO/ALO, 3 (2.75%) were engaged in DO/SO, and 49 (44.96%) had various services. Similarly, among the RTI users, out of total 30, 21 (70.00%) had LO/ALO, 6 (20%) had US, and 2 (6.67) had other employees of different departments.[8] The details of occupational distribution of both RTI users and nonusers in the different department are given in table 4.6.

Educational Background

A look into the educational background of the RTI users and nonusers was explored. The educational status of the respondents is divided into four

Table 4.4 Gender Distribution of RTI Users and Nonusers

Sl.		*Male*		*Female*		*Total*	
No.	*Category*	*User*	*Nonuser*	*User*	*Nonuser*	*User*	*Nonuser*
1	400 (AP)	200(50.00)	100(25.00)	60(15.00)	40(10.00)	260(100)	140(100)
2	40 (PIO)	16(40.00)	8(20.00)	10(25.00)	6(15.00)	26(100)	14(100)
3	30 (HOD)	12(40.00)	6(20.00)	8(27.00)	4(12.44)	20(100)	10(100)
	Total	**228(58.00)**	**114(28.00)**	**78(29.00)**	**50(15.00)**	**306(100)**	**164(100)**

Source: Primary and Secondary Survey, 2019.

Table 4.5 Age Classification of RTI User and Nonuser Respondents

		Age Distribution							
Sl.		*20-30*		*36-45*		*46 and Above*		*Total*	
No.	*Departments*	*User*	*Nonuser*	*User*	*Nonuser*	*User*	*Nonuser*	*User*	*Non- user*
1.	Women and Child Development	1(25.00)	9(50.00)	1(25.00)	4(22.22)	2(50.00)	5(27.78)	4(100)	18(100)
2.	Rural Development	2(28.57)	13(72.22)	2(28.57)	3(16.67)	3(72.86)	2(11.11)	7(100)	18(100)
3.	Energy	0(00)	8(44.44)	2(66.67)	7(38.89)	1(33.33)	3(16.67)	3(100)	18(100)
4.	Panchayati Raj	3(60.00)	12(63.16)	0(00)	7(36.84)	2(40.00)	0(00)	5(100)	19(100)
5.	Agriculture	1(20.00)	16(88.88)	3(60.00)	1(5.56)	1(20.00)	1(5.56)	5(100)	18(100)
6.	Finance	0(00)	12(66.67)	2(33.33)	5(27.78)	4(66.67)	1(5.55)	6(100)	18(100)
	Total	**7(23.33)**	**70(64.22)**	**10(33.33)**	**27(24.77)**	**13(43.33)**	**12(11.01)**	**30(100)**	**109(100)**

Source: Primary Survey and Secondary Survey, 2019.

Table 4.6 Occupational Distribution of RTI Users and Nonusers

	Occupational Categories									
Sl.	*ASO*		*DO/SO*		*LO/ALO*		*US*		*Others Employees*	
No.	*User*	*Nonuser*	*User*	*Nonuser*	*User*	*Nonuser*	*User*	*Nonuser*	*User*	*Nonuser*
1.	4(100)	1(5.56)	0(00)	1(5.56)	2(50.00)	8(44.44)	2(50.00)	1(5.56)	0(00)	7(38.88)
2.	7(100)	3(16.67)	0(00)	0(00)	5(71.43)	1(5.55)	2(28.57)	5(27.78)	0(00)	9(50.00)
3.	3(100)	5(27.78)	0(00)	0(00)	2(66.67)	4(22.22)	1(33.33)	1(5.56)	0(00)	8(44.44)
4.	5(100)	4(21.05)	1(20.00)	1(5.26)	2(40.00)	8(42.11)	0(00)	0(00)	2(4.00)	6(31.58)
5.	5(100)	4(22.22)	0(00)	1(5.56)	5(100)	3(16.66)	0(00)	1(5.56)	0(00)	9(50.00)
6.	6(100)	2(11.11)	0(00)	0(00)	5(83.33)	4(22.22)	1(16.67)	2(11.11)	0(00)	10(55.56)
	30(100)	**19(17.43)**	**1(3.33)**	**3(2.75)**	**21(70.00)**	**28(25.69)**	**6(20.00)**	**10(9.17)**	**2(6.67)**	**49(44.96)**

Source: Primary Survey, 2019.

categories which includes undergraduate, graduate, and graduate and above. The educational status of the RTI users shows that around 5 (16.67%) were graduate and 25 (83.33%) have education including graduate and above. Among the nonusers, 16 (14.68%) reported having undergraduate, 57 (52.29%) had graduate, and 36 (33.03%) had graduate and above education.[9] The details of the educational status of the RTI users and nonusers according to different Secretariat Departments are given in table 4.7.

Responses from RTI Nonusers

Knowledge of Nonusers on RTI Act 2005

The study first attempted to find out the knowledge level of the nonusers on RTI Act. Around 57.62% male replied with a positive knowledge on the Act, while among the women 62% replied knowing the Act. In Women and Child Development Department, Rural Development, and Energy Department 16.88%, 13%, and 9% know the RTI Act, respectively. Among female, not a single replied of knowing the Act in Panchayati Raj Department. In Panchayati Raj Department out of 19 respondents, only 2 could tell about the Act. In Agriculture and Finance Department among both males and females around 80% and 87.5%, respectively, could replay the schedule data sheet[10] given in the table 4.8.

Knowledge of the Nonusers about the Location of OIC

The nonusers were asked about their knowledge in OIC. In total among the males only 38.98% could tell that they know the location of Odisha Information Commission, while among the females only 18% could tell about it. Thus, in total, study found that 29.36% nonuser respondents could tell about the OIC and its location. Women and Child Development Department (55.56%) and Rural Development Department (50%) in none of the respondent knowledge level on OIC was satisfactory. Among the female respondents, not a single respondent knew about OIC in the case of Panchayati Raj and Finance. The responses of the females in Women and Child Development (33.33%), Rural Development (37.5%), Energy (25.00%), and Agriculture (10.00%) with regards to their knowledge were very minimal and not encouraging[11] (table 4.9).

DISTRIBUTION OF RTI-DESIGNATED PERSONS IN DIFFERENT DEPARTMENTAL POSITION

Heads of the Departments (HODs)

The study focuses on various positions that are designated as RTI officials. In the Secretariat Departments Heads of the Departments are consisting of

Table 4.7 Educational Status of the RTI Users and Nonusers

		Educational Distribution					
		Under graduate		*Graduate*		*Graduate/Above*	
Sl. No.	*Total Respondents*	*User*	*Nonuser*	*User*	*Nonuser*	*User*	*Nonuser*
1.	22	0	3(16.67)	1(25.00)	13(72.22)	3(100)	2(11.11)
2.	27	0	4(22.22)	0	8(44.45)	7(100)	6(33.33)
3.	21	0	2(11.11)	0	11(61.11)	3(100)	5(27.78)
4.	24	0	1(5.26)	3(60.00)	10(52.63)	2(40.00)	8(42.11)
5.	23	0	4(22.22)	0	9(50.00)	5(100.00)	5(27.78)
6.	24	0	2(11.11)	1(16.67)	6(33.33)	5(83.33)	10(55.56)
	Total-	**0**	**16(14.68)**	**5(16.67)**	**57(52.29)**	**25(83.33)**	**36(33.03)**

Source: Primary Survey, 2019.

Table 4.8 Distribution of Knowledge of the Nonusers on the RTI Act 2005

			Gender Distribution					
			Yes			*No*		
Sl. No.	*Departments*	*Total*	*Male*	*Female*	*Total*	*Male*	*Female*	*Total*
1.	Women and Child Development	18 (100)	8(88.88)	8(88.88)	16(88.89)	1(11.12)	1(11.12)	2(11.11)
2.	Rural Development	18 (100)	8(80.00)	5(62.5)	13(72.22)	2(20.00)	3(37.5)	5(27.78)
3.	Energy	18(100)	4(40.00)	5(62.5)	9(50.00)	6(60.00)	3(37.5)	9(50.00)
4.	Panchayati Raj	19(100)	2(16.66)	0	2(10.53)	10(83.34)	7(100)	17(89.47)
5.	Agriculture	18 (100)	4(50.00)	6(60.00)	10(55.56)	4(50.00)	4(40.00)	8(44.44)
6.	Finance	18(100)	8(80.00)	7(87.5)	15(83.33)	2(20.00)	1(12.5)	3(16.67)
	Total	**109(100)**	**34(57.62)**	**31(62.00)**	**65(59.63)**	**25(42.37)**	**19(38.00)**	**44(40.37)**

Source: Primary Survey, 2019.

Table 4.9 Knowledge of the Nonusers about the Location of OIC

Sl. No.	Departments	Total	*Gender Distribution*					
			Yes			*No*		
			Male	*Female*	*Total*	*Male*	*Female*	*Total*
1.	Women and Child Development	18 (100)	7(77.77)	3(33.33)	10(55.56)	2(22.23)	6(66.66)	8(44.44)
2.	Rural Development	18 (100)	6(60.00)	3(37.5)	9(50.00)	4(40.00)	5(62.5)	9(50.00)
3.	Energy	18(100)	3(30.00)	2(25.00)	5(27.78)	7(70.00)	6(75.00)	13(72.22)
4.	Panchayati Raj	19(100)	2(16.66)	0	2(10.53)	10(83.34)	7(100)	17(89.47)
5.	Agriculture	18 (100)	1(14.28)	1(10.00)	2(11.11)	7(85.72)	9(90.00)	16(88.89)
6.	Finance	18(100)	4(40.00)	0	4(22.22)	6(60.00)	8(100)	14(77.78)
	Total	**109(100)**	**23(38.98)**	**9(18.00)**	**32(29.36)**	**36(61.02)**	**41(82.00)**	**77(70.64)**

Source: Primary Survey, 2019.

Table 4.10 Distribution of HODs Interviewed in Different PAs (N = 55)

Sl. No.	*Different Positions*	*Responses*	*%*
A. Secretariat Departments (N = 20)			
1.	Principal Secretary/Commissioner-cum- Secretary	18	90.00
2.	Director-cum-Additional Secretary	1	5.00
3.	Engineering-in Chief	1	5.00
B. Heads of the Department (N = 18)			
1.	Directors	13	72.22
2.	Chief Engineers	4	22.22
3.	Deputy Commissioner	1	5.55
C. Other PAs (N = 17)			
1.	Director	5	29.41
2.	Secretary/Addl. Secretary	3	17.61
3.	CMD/MD/CE	7	41.17
4.	Superintendent	1	5.88
5.	Vice-Chairman	1	5.88

Source: Primary Survey, 2019 and figures in the bracket are percentage of total.

principal secretaries and commissioner-cum-secretary (18), director-cum-additional secretary (1), and engineer in chief-cum-secretary (1). The HODs in the Heads of the Departments interviewed consist of directors (13), chief engineers (4), and deputy commissioner (1). In other PAs the Heads of the Departments include directors (5), secretary/additional secretary (3), CC/CMD/MD (7) superintendent (1), and vice-chairman (1).[12] The details of positions which were interviewed in the study as Heads of the Department of different PAs are given in table 4.10.

First Appellate Authority (FAA)

Out of a total of 85 FAAs, the study covered 26 FAAs in Secretariat Departments, which includes different positions like commissioner-cum-secretary (3), joint secretary (5), additional secretary (26), and director (1), in the Heads of the Departments the study covered 21 Heads of Departments representing directors (3), joint directors (9), deputy directors (5), chief engineers (2), SO/ESO(1), and CCF (1). The study covered 38 FAAs in other PAs which included different positions like Joint Directors, Additional Secretary, Additional Directors, Program Coordinators, Superintendent Engineers, GM, CEO, PD, DGM, FA, CGM, MD, and so on.[13] The details of FAA positions and their numbers are given in table 4.11.

Table 4.11 Distribution of FAAs According to their Positions in Different PAs (N = 85)

Sl. No.	*Positions*	*Response*	*%*
A. Secretariat Department (N = 26)			
1.	Commissioner-cum-Secretary	3	11.53
2.	Additional Secretary	15	57.69
3.	Joint Secretary	5	19.23
4.	Deputy Secretary	2	7.69
5.	Director	0	0.00
B. Heads of the Department (N = 21))			
1.	Director	3	14.28
2.	Chief Conservation of Forest	1	4.76
3.	Joint Director	9	42.85
4.	Chief Engineer	2	9.52
5.	Deputy Director	5	23.80
6.	SO/ESO	1	4.76
Sl. No.	*Positions*	*Response*	*%*
C. Other PAs (N = 38)			
1.	Joint Director	2	5.26
2.	Additional Director	2	5.26
3.	Superintendent Engineer	1	2.63
4.	Executive Engineer	3	7.89
5.	General Manager	3	7.89
6.	Chief Executive Officer	2	5.26
7.	Program Coordinator/PD	4	10.52
8.	DGM	2	5.26
9.	Chief Executive Officer	1	2.63
10.	Managing Director	1	2.63
11.	Chief Executive Officer	2	5.26
12.	Assistant Conservator of Forest	1	2.63
13.	APO	1	2.63
14.	Director	3	7.89
15.	Member Secretary	1	2.63
16.	Financial Advisor	1	2.63
17.	Secretary	8	21.05

Source: Primary survey, 2019.

Public Information Officers (PIO)

The study covered a total of 120 PIOs in different PAs, representing 40 PIOs in Secretariat Departments which included different positions like Joint Secretary (1), Deputy Secretary (9), Under Secretary (16), and Desk Officers (6); 26 PIOs from the Heads of the Departments representing positions like Assistant Directors (5), Deputy Director (6), Establishment Officer (4), Executive Engineer (1), DIG Police (1), Conservator of Forest, and Additional Commissioner (16); and 62 PIOs from other PAs which covered

Table 4.12 Distribution of PIOs According to Their Positions in Different PAs

Sl. No.	Positions	Response	%
A. Secretariat Departments (N = 40)			
1.	Joint Secretary	1	3.12
2.	Deputy Secretary	9	28.12
3.	Under Secretary	20	50.00
4.	AFA/Desk Officer	10	18.75
B. Heads of the Departments (N = 26)			
1.	Assistant Director	5	19.23
2.	Dy. Director	6	23.07
3.	EE/conservator of Forest DIG/Sr. Research Officer Additional Commissioner	11	42.30
4.	Establishment Officer	4	15.38
C. Other Public Authorities (62)			
1.	Executive Engineer/Asst. Engineer	5	8.06
2.	Section Officer /AO/Sr. Asst.	16	25.80
3.	Research Officer	3	4.83
4.	Program Coordinator	2	3.22
5.	Joint/Dy./Asst. Director	20	32.25
6.	GM/AGM/Dy. Manager/Manager	14	22.58
7.	Statistical Officer	1	1.61

Source: Primary Survey, 2019.

a range of officials/positions like Statistical Office (1), EE/AE (5), Section Officer/Administrative Officer, Senior Assistant (16), Program Coordinator (2), Joint/Deputy Assistant Director (20), and GM/AGM/Dy. Manager and Manager (14). Table 4.12 gives the details of the positions of PIOs in different PAs.[14] The details of respondents in different departments and their position are given next.

ROLE PLAYED BY INFORMATION AND PUBLIC RELATION DEPARTMENT THE NODAL DEPARTMENT TO IMPLEMENT RTI ACT IN ODISHA

As per the institutional arrangement made by the Government of Odisha, Information and Public Relation Department is the Nodal Department to implement RTI Act in the State. The Nodal Department has carried out various programs for providing support to different stakeholders involved in the implementation of the Act. It is suggested that the Nodal Department is yet to establish reporting and monitoring channel for operation on regular basis starting from GPs at the ground level to the Secretariat Department at the State level. Major roles played by Information and Public Relation

Department the Nodal Department, Government of Odisha, in relation to the implementation of RTI Act in Odisha includes the translation of RTI Act, 2005, into Oriya and preparation of the Odisha Right to Information Rules, 2006. The department has effected the amendment as "Odisha Right to Information (Amendment, Rules, 2006)."[15]

Issue of Operational Guidelines

Information and Public Relation Department the Nodal Department has taken various steps to designate PIOs, and first appellate authorities in all public authorities. For better understanding of the people of the state on the RTI Act and the RTI Rule the Nodal Department has published the salient features of the RTI Act in electronic and print media through vernacular language. The department has formed State Right to Information Implementation Cell in Information and Public Relation Department. It has devised various formats for collecting data for fortnightly, monthly, and annual reports.

As per the Clause 4(1) (b) of the RTI Act Information and Public Relation Department within 120 days ensured the preparation of the revised 17 points manual by each public authority designation the PIOs and APIOs (Clause 5 (1), designating the authorities to whom the FA lies (Clause 19 (1), Constitution of SIC (Clause 15) carried out the amendments to the existing Acts and Rules (Clause 22), framed rules (Clause 27) with respect to cost of the information, the fee, procedure to be adopted by the Commission in deciding appeals under sub-section (10) of section 16, preparing detail guideline regarding the preparation of annual report by SIC, and the submission of data to PA[16] (Clause 25).

The operational guidelines were also issued by the Chief Secretary & Chief Development Commissioner, Government of Odisha, Bhubaneswar to all Secretaries to the Government on October 28, 2005. The specific guideline issued by Information and Public Relation Department with respect to the implementation of RTI Rule (Clause 8 of the Rule) includes payment of various forms, maintenance of cash registers, bank account by the PIO, procedure required to maintain the cash book, information register, the file movement to provide information, display board, and so on etc. In order to maintain the uniformity in the maintenance of receipt of book, Information and Public Relation Department circulated specimen copies for receipt book, cash book, expenditure, and so on. The third set of operational guidelines was issued to all principal secretaries and commissioner-cum-secretaries/and secretaries of all Government Departments with respect to the proactive disclosure of information under RTI Act, 2005, by the public authorities.[17]

After a request from Nodal Department Hon'ble High Court of Odisha has also formulated their own Rules and facilitated the implementation of RT1

Act, 2005, in all courts. Collecting feedback from public authorities and getting indication from SIC, a committee in being constituted to effect suitable changes to Rules and forwarding the recommendation of the Hon'ble Commission in Annual Report.[18]

TRAINING

In addition to the training programs organized by different training institutes of the Government, Information and Public Relation Department the Nodal Department in collaboration with the SIC has also organized training programs for the participants representing Secretariat Departments and Directorates of the State Government to create Master Trainers and Resource Persons,[19] who will again provide training to other stakeholders like PIO, APIO, and FAAs. The training was imparted to Master Trainers at Gopabandhu Academy of Administration and to Resource Persons at State Institute of Rural Development for Panchayati Raj functionaries. In addition, programs were organized to orient the MLAs at State Legislative Assembly. The first batch of training was organized from January 15 to 17, 2009. A total of 40 participants have been trained in both the training programs.

PROACTIVE DISCLOSURE

In order to make the proactive disclosure as prescribed under Section 4(1)(b) by all the public authorities, and in response to the instruction of SIC and Informatin and Public Relation, the Nodal Department, has entered into a MOU with Ms. Luminous Infoways Pvt. Ltd, who has developed a software to ensure an online management of the proactive disclosure in respect of all PAs of the state. Hosting of proactive disclosure of Government Departments in the website of Government of Orissa on November 10, 2005 at 11 a.m. was carried out. Steps have been taken to initiate suitable disciplinary action against the heads of the defaulting PAs. The Collector and District Magistrates have been requested through communications to ensure voluntary disclosure as stipulated in the Act and also to update regularly.

RECORD MANAGEMENT

In response to the order of chief secretary and chief development commissioner, Odisha, regarding placing the foolproof arrangement to ensure handing over and taking over of files and documents, at different levels by the officers, officials to their successors in order to prevent loss/dislocation of files/documents resulting in denial of information to the applicants and avoid imposition of penalty on the PIO and referred PIO, commissioner-cum-secretary, 1&PR, has issued instructions to different districts, divisions, and block level public authorities reminding the above fact. Officers of Nodal Departments have also undertaken visits to different districts to assess the progress in implementation of the RTI Act including the designation of PIO/APIO/FAA in different public authorities.[20]

MONITORING AND REVIEW

A review process of the RTI Act 2005 was carried out by I &PR under the Chairmanship of the chief secretary and chief development commissioner, Odisha, in the second quarter of 2009. It was recommended that the Head of the Public Authorities is expected to provide templates and revised norms setting and appropriate guidelines for subordinate's offices under their control for compliance of Section 4 of the RTI Act. Public authorities of all departments of the State Government shall also ensure computerization and maintenance of all records remaining under their administrative control to be connected with Central Monitoring Mechanism of the Nodal Departments per provision of Section 4 (a)[21] of the RTI Act 2005. Information and Public Relation Department has taken initiative to implement a successful program in the light of Jankar,i an ICT initiative the Government of Bihar effecting state specific features. Periodic monitoring and periodic review of implementation of RTI Act 2005 in all PAs is undertaken by the Nodal Department. In order to facilitate the process a Central RTI Application Receiving Cell the Reception Centre of State Secretariat has been started.

AWARENESS ABOUT OBLIGATIONS UNDER THE RTI ACT

The study attempted to find out the awareness levels of the PIOs regarding their position. It was presumed that the PIOs are well aware of the relevance of their position. Their awareness level has relevance to their role performance with respect to RTI issues. The responses were collected on three-point scales. They are agree to the proposed relevance of the PIO position and do not agree to the proposition and cannot say. The responses of the PIO in the Secretariat Departments indicate that only 59.38% of them agreed that PIO position has relevance, while 37.50% did not express any view in this respect. In case of the Heads of the Departments, 76.92% agreed to the

Table 4.13 Distribution of Responses of the PIOs on the Relevance of PIO Position

		Public Authorities			
Sl. No.	*Relevance of PIO*	*Secretariat Departments*	*Heads of Departments*	*Other PAs*	*Total*
1.	Yes	19(59.38)	20(76.92)	40(64.52)	79(65.83)
2.	No	1(3.13)	0(0.00)	1(1.61)	2(1.67)
3.	Can't Say	12(37.50)	6(23.08)	21(33.87)	39(32.50)
	Total PIOs	3(100)	26(100)	62(100)	120(100)

Source: Primary Survey, 2019 (figures in the bracket are per cent to total).

proposal that PIO position has relevance and 23.08% did not express their views on it. In other public authorities 64.58% PIOs feel that the position of PIO has relevance. In total the study found out that of the 120 PIOs only 65.83% PIOs feel that the position of PIOs has relevance in the functioning of RTI Act, while 32.50% PIOs did not give any view in this regard. It is important to find that only 2(1.67%) felt that there is no relevance of the post of PIOs. However, When they were asked the reasons they could not substantiate anything. By and large, a few reasons common to all the PIO respondents as regards full appreciation of their important role are

- Quite a good number of PIOs are not well-trained. Lack of knowledge of the PIOs makes them feel the position and the responsibilities as a routine work of the department. They do not feel the importance of the RTI Act.
- Second, around 52.50 per cent PIOs ranging from 59.38 per cent in case of Secretariat Departments, 65.38 per cent in case of Heads of the Departments, and 43.55 per cent in case of other public authorities were not consulted when they were entrusted with the new responsibility of PIO. This has some possible bearing on few PIOs not to feel the importance of their post.
- The Heads of Departments when asked in this regard opined that as a part of the RTI Act around 160 (54.98%) PIOs were declared as PIO within 100 days of the promulgation of the RTI Act on a requirement basis. The proposal of consultation with the concerned persons did not arise. The details of the responses in different categories of public authorities are given in table 4.13.[22]

IMPORTANCE OF PIO ROLE

Role of PIO is very important in the smooth and successful implementation of the RTI Act. The study gave adequate importance to understanding various aspects of the role and responsibilities of the PIOs. Reactions were sought from the PIOs whether they consider their new role as a burden. In total, around 30 (25.00%) PIOs viewed that they feel this new assignment a burden, which is to the tune of 28.13% in case of Secretariat Departments, 26.92% in case of Heads of the Departments, and 22.56% in other PAs. Around 4.17% PIOs did not give any view regarding the consideration of the new responsibility as a burden. The details of the responses of the PIOs in this regard are given in the Table 4.14.[23] The reasons for treating PIO responsibility as a burden were put forth by a few PIOs. They are as follows:

- The PIOs by and large feel that it is a thankless job, but has time-bound implications for cash punishment, in case any deviation takes place in fulfilling the duties as per the RTI Act.
- In the departments, if we do not get cooperation to comply information sought by the applicants, it became difficult for the PIOs to carry out the total responsibility.
- There is no financial reward for the extra responsibility shouldered by the PIOs under the RTI Act.
- Record keeping and its management in Government Departments are very poor, but the responsibility of tracking the records lies with the PIOs under the RTI Act. Still POs consider that RTI Act is the best tool to bring good governance in government functioning.

Knowledge of PIO about the Provision of Referred PIO

Attempt was made to find out the knowledge level of the PIOs about the referred PIO within the department. Few questions were asked relating to APIO and the role of APIO. The study found out that around 69.17% could tell about the APIO, while 20.83% could not tell about the APIO, and 10.00% did not have given any answer. The knowledge of PIO about APIO tunes to 71.88% in Secretariat Departments, 84.62% in Heads of the Departments, and

Table 4.14 Responses of PIO Whether They Feel the New Role as Burden

			Responses		
Sl. No.	*PA Categories*	*Total PIO*	*Feel Burden*	*Don't Feel Burden*	*Can't Say*
1.	Secretariat Departments	32(100)	9(28.13)	22(68.75)	1(3.13)
2.	Heads of the Departments	26(100)	7(26.92)	19(73.08)	0(0.00)
3.	Other PAs	62(100)	14(22.58)	44(70.97)	4(6.45)
	Total	120(100)	3(25.00)	85(70.83)	5(4.17)

Source: Primary Survey, 2019 (Figures in the bracket are per cent to total).

Table 4.15 Distribution of Responses on the Knowledge of PIO about the Referred PIO

Sl. No.	PA Categories	Total PIO	Responses		
			Yes	No	No answer
1.	Secretariat Department	32(100)	23(71.88)	4(12.50)	5(15.63)
2.	Heads of the Department	26(100)	22(84.62)	3(11.54)	1(3.85)
3.	Other Pas	62(100)	38(61.29)	18(29.03)	6(9.68)
	Total	120(100)	83(69.17)	25(20.83)	12(10.00)

Source: Primary Survey, 2019 (Figures in the bracket are per cent to total).

61.29% among the PIOs of other public authorities. Those who knew about APIO, they were asked about the functions of APIO. Most of them told that APIO is to assist in the information compilation process and to perform the role of PIO in the absence of PIO.

This sufficiently indicates the inadequate knowledge of the PIO about the RTI functionaries in a public authority. The details of the responses are given in Table 4.15.[24]

PIO KNOWLEDGE ON TIMELINE OF RTI APPLICATION

Timeline for the disposal of the RTI applications is the heart of the RTI Act. This ensures the disposal of RTI applications and responds to the applicant's needs in time. The study attempted to find out the knowledge of the PIO about different timelines spelt out in the RTI Act.

The study sought to find out the knowledge level of the PIOs in this respect. It is observed that only 16 (13.33%) PIOs could tell partially about the timeline, while around 86.67% PIOs could tell about total timeline links to comply information with the RTI applications. The details of the responses and their variations regarding the timeline given in tables 4.16 and 4.17.[25] Those who could not respond to the questions (13.33%) were mostly confused while replying.

KNOWLEDGE OF PIO REGARDING RESPONSES TO RTI APPLICANTS

Knowledge of PIO regarding responses to RTI applicants was also assessed in the study. Two specific questions were asked to PIO through close-ended questions regarding the mandatory nature of giving name and address while forwarding information to the applicants and secondly mandatory nature of intimating the receipt and transfer of applications. As regards the forwarding of the applications, PIOs were asked whether it is necessary to give name

Table 4.16 Timeline for the Disposal of RTI Applications as per the RTI Act

Sl. No.	Period	Specific Assignment
1.	5 days	As per the 6 (3) regarding the request for obtaining information, where an applicant is made to a public authority requesting for an information which is held by another public authority or the subject matter which is more closely connected with the functions of another public authority to which such application is made shall transfer the application or such part of it as may be appropriate to that public authority and inform the applicant immediately about such transfer. The transfer of such application will be made as soon as practicable but in no case later than five days from the date of receipt of the application.
2.	30 days	As per 7 (1) regarding the disposal of request where information sought subject to the provision in the sub-Section 2 of Section 5 of the proviso to sub-section 3 of Section 6 the case may be, on receipt of a request under Section 6 shall, as expeditiously as possible and in any Case within 30 days of the receipt of the request, either provide the information on payment of such fees as may be prescribed or reject the request for any of the reasons specified in Section 8 and 9.
3.	35 days	If the request is made to an APIO for information, compliance is expected within 35 days
4.	45 days	Information about Human Rights violation by Security agencies have to be provided within 45 day
5.	48 hours	As per 7 (1) regarding the disposal of request where information sought for concerns the life or liberty of a person, the same shall be provided within 48 hours of the receipt of the request.

and address to the applicants. The study found out that as high as 88.33% PIOs have the knowledge regarding this provision while only 11.67% did not agree to the proposal. However, PIOs who did not agree to the proposal when asked further did not give enough reason to substantiate their arguments. It is understood that the PIOs are yet to be informed about various provisions of the department.

As regards the intimation to the applicants about the transfer of application under Section 6(3) RTI 87.50% PIOs are aware that it is necessary to inform the party, while 12.50% did not agree to the proposal. The details of responses and their variations are given in table 4.18.[26]

Proactive Disclosure by PAs under Section 4(1) B of the RTI Act 2005

The data with respect to proactive disclosure under Section 4 of the RTI Act 2005 by PAs was collected from PIOs and the Heads of Departments. The

Table 4.17 Distribution of Responses on the Knowledge about Timeline of RTI Application of PIO

Sl. No.	*PA Category*	*Total no of PIOs*	*Knowledge on Timelines*				
			5 days	*30 days*	*40 days*	*45 days*	*48 days*
1.	Secretariat Departments	32	5(84.63)	27(84.38)	27(84.38)	27(84.38)	27(84.38)
2.	Heads of the Departments	26	2(7.69)	24(92.31)	24(92.31)	24(92.31)	24(92.31)
3.	Other PAs	62	9(14.52)	53(85.48)	53(85.48)	53(85.48)	53(85.48)
	Total	120	16(13.33)	104(86.67)	104(86.67)	104(86.67)	104(86.67)

Source: Primary Survey, 2019 (figures in the bracket are percent of the total).

Table 4.18 Knowledge of PIOs Regarding Responses of RTI Applicants

Sl. No.	*PA category*	*No. of PIO*	*Mandatory to*			
			Yes	*No*	*Yes*	*No*
1.	Secretariat Departments	32(100)	29(90.625)	3(9.375)	28(87.5)	4(12.5)
2.	Heads of the Departments	26(100)	25(96.15)	1(3.85)	25(96.15)	1(3.85)
3.	Other PAs	62(100)	52(83.87)	10(16.13)	52(83.87)	10(16.13)
	Total	120(100)	106(88.33)	14(11.67)	105(87.5)	15(12.5)

Source: Primary Survey, 2019 (Figures in the bracket are percent of the total)

data with respect to the proactive disclosure under Section 4 of the RTI Act by different PAs table 4.19 and figure 4.1[27] brought out that all the Secretariat Departments have their own website; however, quite a few have not maintained the format as given in the Act. For State Directorates maintenance of information is found in website only in case of 15 (57.70%) PAs and in case of other 22 PAs both the website and the hard copy are maintained. Around 7 (26.92%) State Directorates have only hard copy, while 4 (15.38%) did not have any information under proactive disclosure. Similarly, in case of other PAs 9 (18%) have only hard copy to preserve the information, while 38% PAs did not have any information base as demanded by the RTI Act.

Table 4.19 Knowledge of PIOs Regarding Responses of RTI Applicants includes Directorates

		Sources of Data Declaration		
Sl. No.	*From the Disclosure*	*Secretariat, N-33*	*Directorates, N-26*	*Other PAs, N-50*
1.	Secretariat Departments	33(100.00%)	15(57.70%)	22(44.00%)
2.	Heads of the Departments	0	7(26.92%)	9(18%)
3	Other PAs	0	4(15.38)	19(38%)

Source: Primary Survey, 2019 (figures in the bracket are percent of the total).

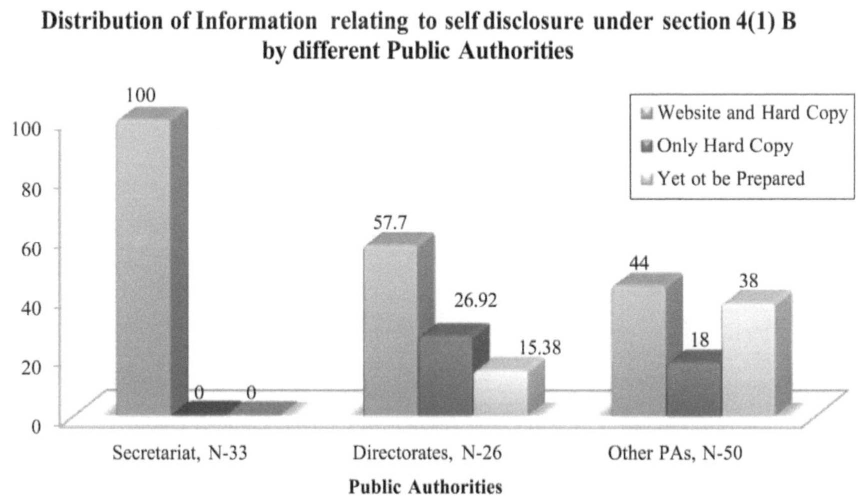

Figure 4.1 Distribution of Information Relating to Self-disclosure under Section 4(1) B by Different Public Authorities. *Source*: Information and Public Relation Department, Government of Odisha, Primary Survey, 2019.

Table 4.20 Distribution of Availability of Information Relating to Self-disclosure under Section 4(1) B

Sl. No.	Public Authorities	Sources of Data Declaration	
		Available with PIO	Not Available with PIO
1.	Secretariat (N-33)	2(6.06)	31(93.94)
2.	Heads of the Dept (N-26)	3(11.53)	23(88.47)
3.	Other Public Authorities (N-50)	4(8.00)	46(92.00)
	Total 109	9(8.25)	100(91.75)

Source: Primary Survey, 2019 (figures in the bracket are percent of the total).

As regards the availability of information relating to the proactive disclosure under Section 4(1) B of the RTI Act with different PIOs of PAs, table 4.20 and Figure 4.2[28] brought out that in the case of Secretariat Departments only 2 (6.06%) PIOs possess the information and the rest PIOs did not have. In case of Heads of the Departments similarly 3 (11.53%) PIOs had the information and in case of other PAs only 4 (8%) PIOs had the information.

The Heads of Departments of various PAs were asked about the language used and the format use for the self-disclosure. A total of 55 Heads of Departments of different PAs were interviewed representing 20 from Secretariat Departments, 18 from Heads of the Departments, and 17 from other public authorities. As regards the language used for disclosure, it is observed that 43 (78.18%) Heads of Departments opined that they maintain the information in English language, 3 (5. 45%) Heads of Departments pointed out that they

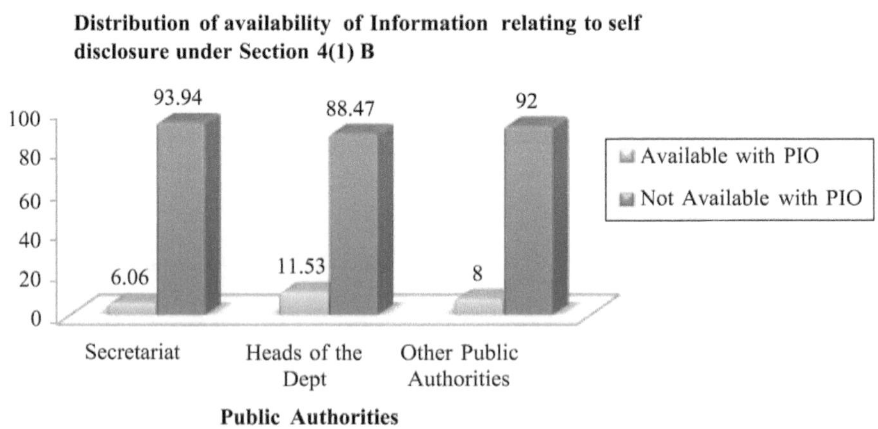

Figure 4.2 Distribution of Availability of Information Relating to Self-disclosure under Section 4(1)B. *Source*: Data Submitted by Information and Public Relation Department (Nodal Department) Government of Odisha, supplied by Odisha Secretariat Information Cell.

maintain in local vernacular language, and only 9 (16.36%) Heads of Departments opined that they maintain information in both English and vernacular language English is the dominant language adopted by a majority of the PAs observed in all the PAs categories.

The format used for the disclosure of the information was also inquired during the study. The data indicate that manual formats are used by 55.00%, while in case of 16.36% electronic mode of disclosure is adopted, while 34.54% pointed out that they have web-based disclosure. By and large manual form of disclosure is still maintained by the PAs as per the RTI Act. These PAs are yet to develop their disclosure as per the RTI Act. The details of each PA are given in table 4.21.[29]

ISSUE OF GUIDELINES FOR IMPLEMENTATION OF SECTION 4(1) B ON SELF-DISCLOSURE

The Heads of Departments are responsible for ensuring the implementation of self-disclosure requirement in time in their PA. The study wanted to find out the steps taken by them to make it successful. It was observed that the Heads of Departments have issued guidelines to their subordinate offices and staffs. In Secretariat Departments around 85.00% Heads of Departments have issued guidelines to their PAs. In total, around 81.82% Heads of Departments have issued guidelines to their subordinates for the purpose. Heads of Departments when asked about the follow up if any they have made to ensure that the disclosure is done in time, the responses were not satisfactory. The following table 4.22[30] provides an overview of the responses of the PAs as regards the issue of guidelines is concerned.

FREQUENCY OF UPDATION OF INFORMATION UNDER PROACTIVE DISCLOSURE

The data with respect to the frequency of updation of information for proactive disclosure were collected. The frequency is divided into three different time periods like annual, half yearly, and quarterly updation. The study findings indicate that around 74.54% Heads of Departments update the information annually which is 80.00% in case of state Secretariat Departments, 94.45% in case of Heads of the Departments, and 47.06% in case of other PAs. Around 14.55% Heads of Departments viewed that they update the required information half yearly and 10.92% update quarterly. It is understood that standardization is yet to be adopted in updating the information by

Table 4.21 Responses of HODs on the Language and Format Used for Voluntary Discloser

		PA Categories			
Sl. No.	*Indicators*	*Secretariat Department. (20)*	*Heads of the Department (18)*	*Other PAs (17)*	*Total*
Language Used for of disclosure					
1.	English only	18(90.00)	12(66.66)	13(76.46)	43(78.18)
2.	Vernacular	1(5.00)	2(11.11)	0(0.00)	3(5.45)
3.	Both English and local	1(5.00)	4(22.22)	4(23.54)	9(16.36)
Format Used for Disclosure					
1.	Manual	11(55.00)	11(61.11)	5(29.16)	27(49.06)
2.	Electronic	0(00)	2(11.11)	7(41.17)	9(16.36)
3.	Web based	9(45.00)	5(27.77)	5(29.41)	19(34.54)

Source: Primary Survey, 2019 (figures in the bracket are percent of the total).

Table 4.22 Issue of Guidelines by the I & PR Department on the Implementation of Section 4(1) B on Self-disclosure

Sl. No.	Categories of PAs	No of PAs	Issue of Guidelines	
			Yes	No
1.	Secretariat Department	21(100)	17(85.00)	3(81.82)
2.	Heads of the Department	18(100)	17(94.44)	1(5.56)
3.	Other PAs	17(100)	11(64.71)	6(35.29)
	Total	55(100)	45(81.82)	10(18.18)

Source: Primary Survey,2019 (figures in the bracket are percent of the total).

Table 4.23 Frequency of Updation of Information Contained in Handbook/Web Page for Proactive Disclosure

Sl. No.	Categories of PAs	No of PAs	Frequency		
			Annually	Half Yearly	Quarterly
1.	Secretariat Department	20(100)	16(80.00)	0(0.0)	4(20.00)
2.	Heads of the Department	18(100)	17(94.45)	1(5.54)	0(0.0)
3.	Other PAs	17(100)	8(47.06)	7(41.18)	2(11.76)
	Total	55(100)	41(74.54)	8(14.55)	6(10.92)

Source: Primary Survey, 2019 (figures in the bracket are percent of the total).

the PAs for self-disclosure. The details of responses of the Heads of Departments in this regard are given in table 4.23.[31]

Medium of Proactive Disclosure

As per the RTI Act the PAs are to disseminate information through different mediums. The mediums to be adopted must be contextually suitable and appropriate. Very popular mediums adopted by the PAs are notice boards (56.36%), followed by internet (41.82%). In case of Secretariat Department, internet (75.00%) is frequently adopted and it is the common mode of disclosure followed by notice board (35.00%), while in case of Heads of the Departments notice board (66.67%) is adopted. Among other PAs use of notice board (70.59%) has been popularly adopted and it is followed by the internet (41.18%). The data indicate that the use of notice board is the major and popular mode of dissemination for all categories of PAs. The details of the responses of different PAs in this regard are presented in the table 4.24.[32]

Table 4.24 Medium of Dissemination of Information of RTI Act under Section 4(3)

Sl.		*Categories of PAs*			
No.	*Medium of Dissemination*	*Secretariat Departments (20)*	*Heads of the Departments (18)*	*Other PAs (17)*	*Total (55)*
1.	Notice Board	7(35.00)	12(66.67)	12(70.59)	31(56.36)
2.	News Paper	0(0.0)	2(11.11)	3(17.65)	5(9.09)
3.	Public announcement	3(15.00)	1(5.56)	1(5.88)	5(9.09)
4.	Media Broadcasts	0(0.0)	2(11.11)	0(0.0)	2(3.64)
5.	Internet	15(75.00)	1(5.56)	7(41.18)	23(41.82)
6.	Any Other	1(6.67)	3(16.67)	1(5.88)	5(9.09)

Source: Primary Survey, 2019 (figures in the bracket are percent of the total).

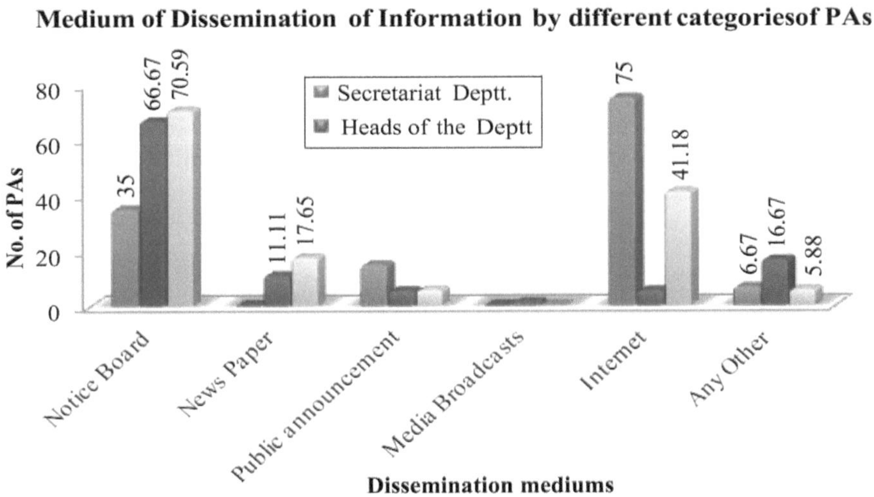

Figure 4.3 Medium of Dissemination of Information by Different Categories of PAs. *Source*: The analysis is based on data compiled by Secretariat Departments, Heads of Departments, and other PAs Primary Survey, 2019.

ATTITUDE TOWARD FULFILLMENT OF OBJECTIVES

The attitude of the designated RTI personnel are very important. RTI Act is one of the very powerful means of information sharing on demand. A positive attitude is necessary to respond to the basic objectives of the RTI Act. Therefore, the study attempted to find out the attitude of PIOs, FAAs, and Heads of Departments in different public authorities relating to the fulfillment of objectives of the RTI Act. Couple of questions were put and the responses are analyzed according to the categories of PAs.

Distribution of Responses of the PIOs on Whether They Like to Act as PIO

The study tried to find out the responses of PIOs on whether they like to act as PIO or not. In all the concerned PAs, PIOs were asked this question. On the whole the data indicate that around 60.83% like the PIO position and are prepared to take on the responsibility, which varies from 65.38 among the Heads of the Departments to 59.68% among PIOs of other PAs and 59.38% among the Secretariat Departments. Around 9.17% in total did not give any view with respect to the holding of to the position of PIO. The details of responses are distributed in table 4.25.[33] Those who expressed their readiness have the following justifications.

Table 4.25 Distribution of Responses of the PIOs on Whether They Like to Act as PIO or Not

Sl. No.	PA Categories	Total PIOs	Responses on Likeness		
			Like well	Don't like	Can't say
1.	Secretariat Departments	32(100.00)	19(59.38)	9(28.13)	4(12.50)
2.	Heads of the Departments	26(100.00)	17(65.38)	8(30.77)	1(3.85)
3.	Other PAs	62(100.00)	37(59.68)	19(30.65)	6(9.68)
	Total	120(100.00)	73(60.83)	36(30.00)	11(9.17)

Source: Primary Survey, 2019 (figures in the bracket are percent of the total).

- It is a new constitutional responsibility, which enjoys some prestige. The people designated as PIO enjoy certain prestige in the bureaucratic functioning.
- This position gives opportunity to widen one's scope of knowledge, since it has to deal with varieties of RTI questions and answers to the RTI applications.
- The designated PIOs have time obligation and responsibility to the public under the RTI Act.
- The PIOs have the power as per the law to cancel the applications if the applicants do not follow the guideline of the Act.
- The PIOs enjoy the work since the RTI Act and RTI Rules are clear cut scope of operation. One cannot exercise one's emotions and authority.

RELEVANCE OF PIOS IN PUBLIC AUTHORITY

The importance of RTI-designated PIOs was asked to each PIO with an aim to understand how the PIOs perceive their roles. Methodologically the responses of all the 120 PIOs of three different public authorities are taken together and analyzed in three categories. The objective is to find distinct trends in their understanding. The common area of importance raised by the PIOs in percent distribution is given in table 4.26.[34] It is found that more responses are observed expressing the fact that PIO can give proper justice to a person by providing correct information (69.17%) followed by the view that PIOs are to coordinate the supply of information to the public (59.17%), PIOs are to provide information in a timely manner to give justice to people (42.50%), and so on. However, less responses of the PIO are found when they said that PIOs are the source for regular supply of information. It is because they are to be supported by the officials to get

Table 4.26 Distribution of Responses of the PIOs on the Relevance of PIO Position

		Public Authorities			
Sl. No.	*Relevance of PIO*	*Secretariat Department*	*Heads of Department*	*Other PAs*	*Total*
1.	Yes	19(59.38)	20(76.92)	40(64.52)	79(65.83)
2.	No	1(3.13)	0(0.00)	1(1.61)	2(1.67)
3.	Can't Say	12(37.50)	6(23.08)	21(33.87)	39(32.50)
	Total PIOs	32(100)	26(100)	62(100)	120(100)

Source: Primary Survey, 2019 (figures in the bracket are percent of the total).

Table 4.27 Distribution of Responses Regarding Relevance of the Responsibility of PIO in a PA

Sl. No.	*Types of Importance*	*Responses (N = 120)*	*In %*
1.	PIO is to interface the public	44	36.67
2.	PIO is to coordinate the supply of information to the public	71	59.17
3.	PIO is to provide information timely to give justice to people	51	42.50
4.	PIO can help in maintaining transparency in a public authority	46	38.33
5.	PIO can give proper justice to a person by providing correct information	83	69.17
6.	PIO can help in checking the corruption level	35	29.17
7.	PIO is a source for regular supply and creating demand for information	12	10.00

Source: Primary Survey, 2019 (figures in the bracket are percent of the total).

information. Information flow from them depends on other's cooperation. Quite a sizeable number of PIOs (21.67%) did not give their responses in this regard.

The responses indicate that around 51.67% considered PIOs responsibility as "relevant" followed by 24.17% who considered it as "very relevant" and "relevant to some extent" (22.50%). While 17.50% did not give their view at all, only 0.83% considered the post of PIO as not relevant. The details of the responses are explained in table 4.27.[35]

In a five-point scale, the responses of the PIOs were also gathered on the relevance of the post of PIO. The responses are categorized as relevant, very relevant, and relevant to some extent, not relevant and no response. Table 4.28[36] explains the responses of the PIOs.

Table 4.28 Distribution of Responses of the PIOs on the Relevance of the PIO Role

Sl. No.	*Responses*	*Public Authorities (N = 120)*	*In %*
1.	Relevant	62	51.67
2.	Very Relevant	29	24.17
3.	To some Extent	27	22.50
4.	Don't know	21	17.50
5.	Not Relevant	1	0.83

Source: Primary Survey, 2019 (figures in the bracket are percent of the total).

ATTITUDE TO IMPROVE THE IMPLEMENTATION OF RTI ACT

The Heads of Departments were asked two questions regarding the possibility of proper implementation of RTI Act in the present structure and whether RTI makes administration responsive and accountable. The responses of the Heads of Departments are analyzed according to the public authorities. Both close- and open-ended responses were collected. As regards the possibility of proper implementation of the RTI Act in the present structure, one find that out of total 55 Heads of Departments, only 58.18% agreed while 41.82% did not agree that improvement is possible. Those who agreed in favor of implementation of RTI Act in the present system tunes to 75.00% in Secretariat Departments, 44.44% in case of Heads of the Departments, and 59.24% in case of other PAs.

Various mechanisms are suggested by the Heads of Departments to improve the implementation RTI Act in the State. The common mechanisms provided by the Heads of Departments of 55 PAs include provision of recommendation to the RTI-designated personnels (89.09%), strengthening RTI cells in each PA (87.27%), review of RTI matter on a regular interval (78.16%), and provision of e-facilities in each PA (72.72%). The details of the responses of the Heads of Departments in this respect are given in table 4.29.[37]

Responses were collected regarding whether RTI Act can make the administration responsive and accountable. The purpose is to understand the conviction of the Heads of Departments in this regard. The data from all the 55 Heads of Departments and 42 Secretariat Departments of different categories of public authorities indicate that all are confident that RTI Act can make the system responsive and functionaries more accountable. Not a single Heads of Departments expressed any doubt in this respect. The Heads of Departments were also asked how RTI Act is helping administration to become more responsive and accountable. The qualitative responses suggested by the Heads of Departments in favor of their stand include the views that under the RTI Act the staffs and officials are accountable (70.91%), followed by the

Table 4.29 Distribution of Responses on Various Mechanisms Required for Proper Implementation of RTI Act

Sl. No.	*Mechanisms*	*Responses (N = 120)*	*In %*
1.	Review of RTI matter on regular interval	43	78.18
2.	Record classification, updation, and compliance	30	54.55
3.	Provision for special pay for RTI-designated officials	49	89.09
4.	Awareness creation by I & PR	38	69.09
5.	Filling the vacant post in the departments	29	52.72
6.	Strengthening the RTI Cells	48	87.27
7.	Provision of E-services in the implementation of RTI Act	40	72.72

Source: Primary Survey, 2019 (figures in the bracket are percent of the total).

Table 4.30 Distribution of Responses of the HODs on Their Attitude to Improve the Implementation of RTI Act

Sl. No.	*Views*	*Responses (N = 55)*	*In %*
1.	Govt. Officials held responsible	30	70.91
2.	Officers are vigilant and sensitized	33	60.00
3.	Improvement ion record management	27	49.09
4.	Job responsibility and responsiveness correlated	21	38.18
5.	Transparency is established	36	65.45
6.	Corruption is made free	33	60.00
7.	Redressal of public grievances	12	21.82

Source: Primary Survey, 2019 (figures in the bracket are percent of the total).

sensitization of the officials (60.00) improvement in the record management (49.09%), transparency is maintained and must be corruption free (65.45%), and so on. The details of these responses are given in table 4.30.[38]

PREMISES

The study covered the inspection of premises of public authorities at Bhubaneswar. As regards the status of basic information available on the sign board (Table 4.31),[39] it is observed that all the Secretariat Departments have their sign boards fixed on the wall, but few of these sign boards were incomplete in many respects. While the name of the PIO was mentioned in case of only 9.09% and the name of the FAA was also mentioned in case of 9.09% no other information like address, telephone number, room number

Table 4.31 Status of Basic Information Displayed by PA in Sign Board under *suo motu* Disclosure (In Nos)

Sl. No.	*Other Particulars on the Sign Board*	*Display by Premises*			
		Secretariat	*Directorates*	*Other PAs*	*Total*
		33(100)	*26(100)*	*50(100)*	*109(100)*
1.	Availability of Sign Board	33(100)	16(61.53)	38(76.00)	87(79.81)
2.	Name of the PIO mentioned	3(9.09)	15(57.69)	27(54.00)	45(41.28)
3.	Address of PIO mentioned	0	5(19.23)	12(24.00)	17(15.59)
4.	Tel. No. of PIO mentioned	0	5(19.23)	4(8.00)	9(8.25)
5.	Room Number of PIO mentioned	1(3.03)	5(19.23)	9(18.00)	15(13.76)
6.	Name of FAA mentioned	3(9.09)	12(46.15)	22(44.00)	37(33.94)
7.	FAA Address mentioned	0	4(15.38)	12(24.00)	16(14.67)
8.	FAA Telephone Number mentioned	0	4(15.38)	2(4.00)	6(5.50)

Source: Primary Survey, 2019 (figures in the bracket are percent of the total).

of both PIO and FAA, were mentioned at all. In case of Directorate Departments, 16 (61.53%) departments had their signboards, while the name of the PIO and FAA were mentioned in case of 57.69% and 46.15% respectively. Other informations were maintained in a few cases. In case of other PAs, 87 (79.81%) had displayed signboards, but for other information, similar trend was observed. Thus, it is observed that the provision of signboards as per the RTI Act in all the public authorities is not available, and even if it is available in a few cases the information furnished on the signboard is incomplete.

Few other indicators relating to the self-disclosure were also assessed. The data found that out of 109 PAs, 64 (58.71%) have used Oriya language as the medium of writing on the signboard, which varies from 72.72% in case of Secretariat Departments to 53.84% in case of Heads of the Departments Directorates and 52.00% in other PAs. As regards the location of the signboards, in case of 58.71% PAs, it is located at visible places, and in case of around 53.21% PAs, the signboards carries accurate information. The details of the responses are given in table 4.32.[40]

Table 4.32 Status of Basic Information Displayed by PAs in Sign Board under *suo motu* Disclosure (In Nos)

Sl. No.	Type of Information	Display by Premises			
		Secretariat	Directorates	Other PAs	Total
		33 (100)	26(100)	50(100)	109(100)
1.	In local language	24(72.72)	14(53.84)	26(52.00)	64(58.71)
2.	Easily Readable	33(100)	16(61.53)	33(66.00)	82(75.22)
3.	Carries Accurate Information	33(100)	8(30.76)	17(34.00)	58(53.21)

Source: Primary Survey, 2019 (figures in the bracket are percent of the total).

APPOINTMENT OF RTI OFFICIALS

As per the RTI Act Section 5(a) (b) of RTI Act the officials like PIO, FAA, and Nodal Officers in each public authority are to be designated within 100 days of the promulgation of the Act. The data collected from 20 Secretariat Departments indicates that out of 80 PIOs only 21 (26.52%) PIOs were appointed within 100 days, and out of 36 FAAs, (41.67%) were designated within 100 days. In 18 Heads of the Departments out of 156 PIOs, 124 (79.24%) PIOs, and out of 36 FAAs 15 FAAs were designated within 100 days that is (41.67%) of the promulgation of the RTI Act. Among the 17 other public authorities out of 55 PIOs, 15 (27.27%) were declared as PIO, and out of 39 FAAs, 13 (33.33%) were designated within 100 days of the promulgation of the RTI Act.

In total, out of 291 PIOs in all PAs, 160 (54.98%) were designated within the time period of 100 days, while among the FAAs out of 184 (64.13%) were declared as FAA within the stipulated time period. As regards the APIOs, out of 334,164 APIOs, 164 APIOs were designated within the time period of 100 days that is (50.60%). The data indicates that most of the Secretariat Departments have not responded to declare RTI personnel in time. The responses of the Heads of the Departments are comparatively much better in the appointment of the PIO and FAA. Most of other PAs have also not responded to the appointment of the RTI-responsible personnel as per the RTI provisions. Table 4.33[41] and gives detail variations of the achievements in this regard.

PRIOR CONSULTATION FOR APPOINTMENT AS PIO

The PIOs were asked whether they were consulted prior to their present assignment to work as PIO. In total out of 120 PIOs in different PAs, 54

Table 4.33 Appointment of Officials as per Section 5 (a)(b) of RTI Act

			PIO			*FAA*		
Sl. No.	*Public Authorities*	*Total Department*	*Within 100 days*	*After 100 days*	*Total*	*Within 100 days*	*After 100 days*	*Total*
1.	Secretariat	20	21(26.25)	59(73.75)	80(100)	15(41.67)	21(58.33)	36(100)
2.	Heads of the Dept.	18	124(79.49)	32(20.51)	156(100)	90(82.57)	19(17.43)	109(100)
3.	Other PAs	17	15(27.27)	40(72.73)	55(100)	13(33.33)	26(66.67)	39(100)
4.	Total	55	160(54.98)	131(45.02)	291(100)	118(64.13)	66(35.87)	184(100)

Source: Primary Survey, 2019 (figures in the bracket are percent of the total).

Table 4.34 Distribution of Responses of PIOs on Prior Consultation by Authorities to Declare them as PIO

			Responses		
Sl. No.	*PA Categories*	*Total PIOs*	*Consulted*	*Not Consulted*	*No responses*
1.	Secretariat Departments	32(100)	11(34.38)	19(59.38)	2(6.25)
2.	Heads of the Departments	26(100)	9(34.62)	17(65.38)	0(0.00)
3.	Other PAs	62(100)	34(54.84)	27(43.55)	1(1.61)
	Total	120(100)	54(45.00)	63(52.50)	3(2.50)

Source: Primary Survey, 2019 (figures in the bracket are percent of the total).

(45.00) viewed that they were consulted and 63 (52.50%) viewed that they were not consulted.

Consultations with the PIOs were more in other PAs (54.84%) followed by Secretariat Departments (34.38%) and Heads of the Departments (34.62%). The details of the distribution in different PAs in this regard are given in table 4.34.[42]

MAINTENANCE OF RECORDS BY PIO

The PIOs were asked about the various types of records in their office relating to the implementation of the RTI Act. In total, the PAs has maintained five different register/records. On the whole, the study found out that 91.67% PIOs have an information register, 86.67% have cash register, 39.17% have register of registers, 69.17% have register of files, and 46.67% have visitor's register. Many of PIOs did not have all the three registers particularly register of registers and the files and visitor's register. More specifically the data when analyzed as per the PAs indicate that in the case of Secretariat Department the register of registers (40.63%) and visitor's register (62.50%) were not maintain fully, while cash register (84.38%) and register of files (81.25%) were maintained. The information register was maintained by (90.63%). Among the Heads of the Department, information register is maintained by all while case register was maintained by (96.15 %), register of files was maintained by (73.08%), visitor's register by (50%), and the register of registers by (42.51%). In other PAs, register of registers (37.10%) and visitor's register (37.10%) were very poorly maintained while the cash register (83.87%) and information register (88.71) were yet to be maintained by all PAs. The details of responses of the PIO on record management in different public authorities are given in table 4.35.[43]

Table 4.35 Distribution of Responses of PIOs on the Maintenance of Records in PAs

Sl.			*Public Authorities*		
No.	*Types of Records*	*Secretariat Departments (32)*	*Heads of Departments (26)*	*Others (62)*	*Total (120)*
1.	Information Register	29(90.63)	26(100.00)	55(88.71)	110(91.67)
2.	Cash Register	27(84.38)	25(96.15)	52(83.87)	104(86.67)
3.	Register of Registers	13(40.63)	11(42.31)	23(37.10)	47(39.17)
4.	Register of Files	26(81.25)	19(73.08)	38(61.29)	83(69.17)
5.	Visitor's Registers	20(62.50)	13(50.00)	23(37.10)	56(46.67)

Source: Primary Survey, 2019 (figures in the bracket are percent of the total).

During the discussion with the PIOs the study wanted to know the reason for not maintaining the registers till date as required under the RTI Act. The following are some of the reasons put forth by the PIOs.

PIOS OF SECRETARIAT DEPARTMENTS ON RECORD MANAGEMENT

Problems

- The heads have never reviewed the progress of the record management as per the requirement under the RTI Act.
- It became very difficult to list out all the records of the departments since many old files (within 20 years) are also not available and many files are always in a move from table to table for operation.
- The Heads of the Departments have to assign this listing of register to somebody else other than the PIO, since PIO is preoccupied with information disposal under the Act and routine work of the department entrusted to him

Suggestions

- Information and Public Relation Department the Nodal Department is to monitor the progress of record management in each department.
- RTI cell to be structured and activated to streamline the functioning of RTI Act in each department.
- The Nodal Officer is to be in charge of tracking various types of registers.

PIOS OF HEADS OF THE DEPARTMENTS ON RECORD MANAGEMENT

Problems

- Many times PIOs are designated from junior rank officers. In such cases, it is difficult for him/her to trace files for making the list.
- All the files of the PA up to 20 years are not available. Many times this became difficult for which registers are not updated.
- Heads of the Departments are yet to give importance to trace out the old records and thus the whole record management as per the demand of the RTI Act becomes difficult.

Suggestions

- RTI cell is to be established in each directorate. It should be the duty of RTI cell to streamline the records and registers in each department.

- Nodal Officers should be appointed in all Heads of the Departments who will look after the management of records and overall functioning of RTI in the departments

PIOS OF OTHER PUBLIC AUTHORITIES ON RECORD MANAGEMENT

Problems

- Many times it is difficult for the PIOs to prepare and maintain the registers. In case a senior officer is in charge of PIO, it became easy for him to yet the work done by others. The Heads of the Departments of the PA should be directly responsible for ensuring the maintenance of records of the office and he/she should be answerable.
- The public authorities may be provided with electronic equipments like computer with printer to store the data of office required under RTI Act and the required software to access them as and when required.
- The PIOs must be trained in computer applications. This will help him/her to maintain related records and information.
- The computerization process and recording of information in all public authorities are to be made on priority basis.

CHANGES IN THE RTI-ACT-RELATED OFFICE MANAGEMENT SYSTEM

Study attempted to find out the perception of PIOs on the changes that have so far taken place in the RTI-Act-related record management system in their office. The responses were documented in three-point-closed tables. The data in total indicated that out of 120 PIO, only 55 (45.83%) feel that the changes have taken place which varies from 59.38% in Secretariat Departments to 41.40% in other public authorities and 38.46% in Heads of the Departments who agreed that some changes have taken place in the overall record management system of the PAs. Around 37.50% PIOs are total viewed that there is no change in the record management system of the office. Another group of 16.67% PIOs did not give any view on the status of record management. The details of responses of the PIOs in different PAs are given in table 4.36.[44]

Those who agreed in favor of changes in the overall record management of the PAs presented the following arguments.

Table 4.36 Distribution of Responses of the PIOs on the Occurrence of Possible Changes in the RTI-Related Office Management System

Sl. No.	PA Category	Total	Responses on possible changes		
			Yes	No	Can't say
1.	Secretariat Department	32(100)	19(59.38)	9(28.13)	4(12.50)
2.	Heads of the Department	26(100)	10(38.46)	12(46.15)	4(15.38)
3.	Other PAs	62(100)	26(41.94)	24(38.71)	12(19.35)
	Grand Total	120(100)	55(45.83)	45(37.50)	20(16.67)

Source: Primary Survey, 2019 (figures in the bracket are percent of the total).

Secretariat Departments

In the Secretariat Departments, the computerization processes have helped to expedite the record management system. The circulars, reviews of RTI-related works by chief minister, chief secretary, and SIC also helped in maintaining the records as per the requirement of the Act. The demand for information in the Secretariat Departments by RTI applicants has created a pressure in the department and the need to streamline the record management system. The other reasons for streamlining the record management system is also partly due to the demand for establishing transparency (28.12%), better record movement (59.37%), formulation and functioning of RTI cell (81.25%), launching of web site (87.50%), and so on.

Suggestions by the PIOs of the Secretariat Departments

- During the training on RTI more importance should be given on teaching various modern office record management systems.
- Full computerization of records and registers and their movement should be made in a very simple manner.
- e-File processing should be introduced in all Secretariat Departments.
- Interdepartmental coordination through e-communication should be started at specific levels.
- Old records beyond 20 years should be kept separately from the regular functioning of the departments.

Heads of the Departments

The reasons for changes in the RTI-related record management are observed due to preparation of job chart, establishment of RTI cell, supply of information in time, discipline maintained in the record management, demand to establish transparency, and introduction of computer in the work. The details of responses are given in table 4.37.[45] The PIOs have also proposed certain suggestions to improve the record management system. They are as follows:

- Introduction of e-communications like computer for all posts where major works are carried out.
- Need of e-processing of files and day-to-day operations.
- Quality of files and folders to be improved.
- File cabinets should be "introduced to store the files instead of dumping on tables."
- Old files and records beyond 20 years should be kept away from normal functioning.
- All officials should be trained in modern record management.

Other Public Authorities

The reasons for changes as expressed by the P1Os of other PAs are as follows the demand has been raised for seeking information. The introduction of Information Technology in record management has helped the overall functioning of offices. Information is supplied in time. A demand is created

Table 4.37 Distribution of Reasons for Changes in the RTI-Related Office Management System

Sl. No.	*Changes Observed*	*Frequency*	*In %*
1.	**Secretariat Departments**	**32(100)**	**100**
	a. Transparency demand increased	9	28.12
	b. Better record movement developed	19	59.37
	c. Launching of Website	28	87.50
	d. Formulation of RTI Cell	26	81.25
	e. Introduction of computer and IT to RTI	30	93.75
2.	**Heads of the Departments**	26(100)	100
	a. Preparation of Job Chart	3	11.54
	b. Establishment of RTI cell	3	11.54
	c. Supply of Information in Time	7	26.92
	d. Discipline in record management	7	26.92
	e. Transparency established	3	11.54
	f. Introduction of Computer and IT	3	11.54
3.	**Other PAs**	62(100)	100
	a. More demand for information	21	33.87
	b. Introduction of Computer and IT to RTI	11	17.74
	c. Supply of Information in Time	7	11.29
	d. Transparency is demanded	21	33.87
	e. Beneficial to streamline information	19	30.65

Source: Primary Survey, 2019 (figures in the bracket are percent of the total).

to establish transparency and everybody realized that proper record management is a pre-condition that simplifies the functioning.

Few PIOs have by and large provided the following suggestions:

- The overall governance in a PA should improve to deliver the Services.
- At every point, responsibility should be fixed and strong action should be takenagainst the deviants.
- Computerization should be introduced fully in public authorities for day-to-day functioning.
- Modern office record management practices should also be taught during RTI training.

Compilation of Annual Data on RTI

Under Section 25(2) on monitoring and reporting, it is clearly mentioned that each department within the jurisdiction collects and providse such information to the SIC, as it is required to prepare the report under this section and comply with the requirements concerning the furnishing of that information and keeping of records.

Section 25(3)[46] mentions that each report shall state in respect of the years to which the report relates the number of requests, number of decisions, number of appeals, particulars of any disciplinary action taken, amount of charges, recommendation for reform, and so on.

The study attempted to collect responses from the Heads of Departments of different PAs. The data indicate that in Secretariat Departments all Heads of Departments agreed that they are compiling the data while in Heads of the Departments only 72.22% agreed to the compilation, which 27.78% viewed that they are not compiling data. The Heads of Departments who responded negatively regarding the compilation of data, viewed that there is no systematic review and monitoring of RTI-related activities. No formats are given to report on quarterly monthly basis. A systematic review process is to be in place so as to regularize the reporting system. Though it is part of the RTI Act, due to the lack of knowledge and lack of seriousness of the system this is not done. Similarly for other public authorities 70.59% Heads of Departments agreed compiling the data, while quite a sizeable of (29.41%) Heads of Departments viewed that they do not compile data. The study (29.41%) also viewed that no systematic guideline has reached them from the Nodal Department. No format in this regard is ever given to them according to which the report is to be submitted. A systematic reporting process needs to be built with proper standard guidelines. Thus, in total 18.18% of Heads of Departments expressed their view that they do not compile the data for the annual report. The details of responses with respect to the compilation of RTI data for annual reporting are given in table 4.38.[47]

Table 4.38 Distribution of Responses of the HODs with Regard to the Compilation of Annual data on RTI as per Section 25(2)

Sl. No.	*Categories of PAs*	*Total No*	*Compilation of Data*	
			Yes	*No*
1.	Secretariat Department	20(100)	20(100)	0(0.00)
2.	Heads of the Department	18(100)	13(72.22)	5(27.78)
3.	Other PAs	17(100)	12(70.59)	5(29.41)
	Total	55(100)	45(81.82)	10(18.18)

Source: Primary Survey, 2019 (figures in the bracket are percent of the total).

BPL Shares in RTI Applicants

The study wanted to know the share of BPI households as RTI applicants in the total RTI applicants in different PAs during 2014–2015 and till the end of 2015–2016. The data indicate that during the year 2014–2015 BPL RTI applications have shares of only 0.44 in Secretariat Departments, 0.72% in Heads of the Departments and 0.35% in other PAs. In total till the end of 2015–2016 the share of BPL applications tunes to only 0.33%, 0.76% and 0.59% in case of Secretariat Departments, Heads of the Department, and other PAs, respectively. As regards the status on the compliance of information to the BPL RTI applications the data indicate that in 2014–2015, 63.15% BPL RTI applications were complied in Secretariat Departments, while all 100% BPL applications complied in Heads of the Departments and 55.55% complied in other PAs. The data on BPL RTI applicants complied when analyzed at the end of 2015–2016, it is observed that 81.57% complied in Secretariat Departments, all 100% in Heads of the Departments, and 76.19% in other PAs. In total around 84.95% BPL RTI applications have been complied. The details are found in table 4.39.[48]

The details of BPL RTI applications received and complied in different years are given in table 4.40.[49] The trend of compliance of RTI applications in general in different years of public authorities is given in table 4.41.[50] The data indicate that during the year 2008–2009 a total of 79.34% RTI applications are complied which range from 98.14% in Secretariat Departments to 89.85% in Heads of the Departments, and 79.05% in other PAs. Until the end of 2008–2009 similarly compilation of information to the applications tunes to 70.35% in Secretariat Departments, 90.79% in Heads of the Departments, and 82.19% in other PAs. The major reasons for noncompliance in different public authorities include non- availability of information within time and difficult to track the RTI applications in case it is transferred to pther PAs.

Table 4.39 Distribution of BPL RTI Applicants in Different PAs

		2014–2015				*Till the End of 2015–2016*			
Sl. No.	*PAs*	*Total Received*	*Total Complied*	*BPL Received*	*BPL Complied*	*Total Received*	*Total Complied*	*BPL Received*	*BPL Complied*
1.	Secretari at Department	4,285	3,220 (0.44)	19 (0.44)	12 (63.15)	11,319 (100)	7,963	38 (0.33)	31 (81.57)
2.	Heads of the Department	1,784	1,603 (0.72)	13 (0.72)	13 (100)	4,336 (100)	3,937	33 (0.76)	33 (100)
3.	Other PAs	2,554	2,019 (0.35)	9 (0.35)	5 (55.55)	7,070 (100)	5,811	42 (0.59)	32 (76.19)
4.	Total	8,623	6,842 (0.47)	41 (0.47)	30 (73.17)	22,725 (100)	17,711	113 (0.49)	96 (84.95)

Source: Primary Survey, 2019 (figures in the bracket are percent of the total); (percentage of BPL applications complied is based on receipt of BPL RTI applications).

Table 4.40 Distribution of BPL RTI Applications during Different Years

Sl. No.	PA Category	*No of BPL Applications*									
		2012–2013		*2013–2014*		*2014–2015*		*2015–2016*		*G. Total*	
		R	*C*	*R*	*C*	*R*	*C*	*R*	*C*	*R*	*C*
1.	Secretariat Department	0	0	6	6	13	13	19	12	38	31
2.	Heads of the Department	0	0	6	6	14	14	13	13	33	33
3.	Others	6	6	14	9	13	12	9	5	42	32
	Total	6	6	26	21	40	39	41	30	113	96

Source: Primary Survey, 2019 R-Received, C-Complied.

Table 4.41 Distribution of RTI Applications Received and Complied

Sl.	PA	*Applications Received & Complied*									
		2012–2013		*2013–2014*		*2014–2015*		*2015–2016*		*G. Total*	
No.	*Category*	*R*	*C*	*R*	*C*	*R*	*C*	*R*	*C*	*R*	*C*
1.	Secretariat Department	328 (100)	229 (68.90)	2,742 (100)	1,685 (61.45)	3,964 (100)	2,829 (71.36)	4,285 (100)	3,220 (75.14)	1,1319 (100)	7,963 (70.35)
2.	Heads of the Department	180 (100)	172 (95.55)	986 (100)	965 (97.87)	1,386 (100)	1,197 (86.36)	1,784 (100)	1,603 (89.85)	4,336 (100)	3,937 (90.97)
3.	Other PAs	295 (100)	292 (98.98)	1,393 (100)	1,255 (90.09)	2,828 (100)	2,245 (79.38)	2,554 (100)	2,019 (79.05)	7,070 (100)	5,811 (82.19)
	Total	803 (100)	693 (86.30)	5,121 (100)	3,905 (76.25)	8,178 (100)	6,271 (76.68)	8,623 (100)	6,842 (79.34)	2,2725 (100)	17,711 (77.93)

R=RTI application Received; C=RTI application Complied (figures in the bracket are percent of the total).

Time Spent by PIO for RTI Activities

The study while exploring data also elicited information relating to the time spent by PIOs for doing RTI-related activities in different PAs with special reference to last three months of 2015–2016. A look into different PAs shows that in Secretariat Departments out of 32 PIOs, 7(21.88%) could not assess the time requirement, while 6 (18.75%) expressed that they have not spent a single day for RTI works and 40.63% viewed that they have spent 1 to 5 days per month for RTI activities. In total the study shows that out of 120 PIOs, 21 (17.50%) have not spent a single day, while 12 (10.00%) did not give any answer, 23 (19.17%) spared 1 to 3 days, 37 (30.83%) spent 4 to 5 days, 17 (14.17%) spared 6 to 10 days, and 10 (8.33%) spent 11 to 15 days per month for accomplishing RTI activities including attending court cases on RTI issues. The details of responses of the PIOs in different PAs in different PAs with regard to the spending of days for doing RTI activities are explained in table 4.42.[51]

Similarly, average days spent to attend the court cases relating to RTI activities were also assessed from each PIO of different PAs. The study found out that 97 (80.83%) PIOs have not spent a single day to attend the court case at SIC, while 18 (15.00%) have spent 1 to 3 days, 4 (3.33%) have spent 4 to 5 days, and 1 (0.83%) has spent 6 to 10 days to attend court cases at SIC. In Secretariat Departments, 21 (65.63%) PIOs have not spent single day, while in Heads of the Departments 92.31% PIOs have not attended court at SIC. The details of the responses in this regard are explained in table 4.43.[52]

Knowledge of FAAs on the Consequences of Deviations of RTI Timeline

Coupl of open questions were asked to all FAAs to find out their level of understanding and perception of the RTI Act. In addition their suggestions were also sought on how to strengthen the functioning of RTI Act in the state. The consequences of not adhering to the timeline while providing information under the RTI Act were collected. The consequences and responses reported by FAAs indicate that they ensure the information within timeline (30–58%) and left out cases are normally cleared within 15 days of the expiry date (23.52%). They intimate the applicants about the noncompliance of the information within time (15.29%) and also refuse to accept RTI application with any valid reasons if it violates the Act (61.17%) and thus liable to get punishment, disciplinary action may also be taken up (45.88%), and penalty/fine may be imposed by SIC @ 250/- per day of denial. The details of responses are given in table 4.44.[53]

Table 4.42 Average Number of Days Spent Per Week by PIO for RTI-Related Works

			Average days per PIO					
Sl. No.	*PA Category*	*Total PIOs*	*Nil*	*1 to 3 days*	*4 to 5days*	*6 to 10 days*	*11 to 15 days*	*No answer*
1.	Secretariat Departments	32(100)	6(18.75)	6(18.75)	7(21.88)	4(12.50)	2(6.25)	7(21.88)
2.	Heads of the Departments	26(100)	4(15.38)	3(11.54)	10(38.46)	4(15.38)	4(15.38)	1(3.85)
3.	Other PAs	62(100)	11(17.74)	14(22.58)	20(32.26)	9(14.52)	4(6.45)	4(6.45)
4.	Total	120(100)	21(17.50)	23(19.17)	37(30.83)	17(14.17)	10(8.33)	12(10.00)

Source: Primary Survey, 2019 (figures in the bracket are percent of the total).

Table 4.43 Average Number of Days Spent by PIO to Attend Court Cases Relating to RTI during May 2016

Sl.			*Average Days Spend*			
No.	*PA Category*	*Total PIOs*	*Nil*	*1 to 3 days*	*4 to 5days*	*6 to 10 days*
1.	Secretariat Department	32(100)	21(65.63)	8(6.66)	2(1.66)	1(0.83)
2.	Heads of the Department	26(100)	24(92.31)	1(3.85)	1(3.85)	0(0.00)
3.	Other PAs	62(100)	52(83.87)	9(14.51)	1(1.61)	0(0.00)
4.	Total	120(100)	97(80.83)	18(15.00)	4(3.33)	1(0.83)

Source: Primary Survey, 2019 (figures in the bracket are percent of the total).

Table 4.44 Responses of FAAs on the Their Knowledge on the Consequences if Timeline not Followed

Sl. No.	*Consequences*	*Number*	*%*
1.	Try to provide Information within the stipulated time	26	30.58
2.	Few left-out cases are disposed within the extended time of 15 days	20	23.52
3.	Intimate to the Applicant about the anticipated time to supply information	13	15.29
4.	Beyond time limit information supply free of cost U/S-7(6)	32	37.64
5.	Reject/Refusal to provide RTI information without authentic reason violates RTI Act.	39	45.88
6.	Complaint case can be lodged at SIC/Second Appeal U/S-18	52	61.17
7.	Disciplinary Action/Departmental proceedings may be initiated against the official for violating the provision of RTI	39	45.88
8.	Penalty/Fine may be imposed by the SIC @250/- for each day of delay upto ₹25,000/-	87	78.82

Source: Primary survey, 2019 (figures in the bracket are percent to total).

Table 4.45 Distribution of Responses of FAAs on Various Reasons for Not Adhering to the Timelines under the RTI Act

Sl. No.	*Reasons of Aadherence*	*Nos*	*%*
1.	Non-adherence to timeline does not arise	16	18.82
2.	Multiple number of information sought in a single application	40	47.06
3.	No such systematic information available with the public authority	25	29.41
4.	Postal delay results tile delay	5	5.88
5.	Absent of applicant in schedule date of hearing	12	14.12
6.	Not processing files with immediate effect by the RTI section	5	5.88

Source: Primary survey, 2019 (figures in the bracket are percent to total).

During the disposal of SAs, it is expected that both the party will be present during the disposal. However, FAAs viewed that in case anybody does not attend the dates the appeal is decided on the basis of merit, while in complicated cases second chance is given to the party to attend the dates, while few viewed that both the parties attend the dates without fail.

Reasons were asked why it is difficult for the FAA to adhere to the timeline while disposing the RTI cases (table 4.45).[54] First, around 47.06% viewed that multiple questions are asked in one application which leads to delay in compliance to all questions since compilation became a delayed one. Around 29.41% opined that the record management and data storage are yet to be systematically maintained. Similarly, the applicants often don't turn to deposit the cost (39.46%) while many viewed that the concerned sections do not make it clear regarding the timely importance of compilation of information (52.18%) which leads to delay in compliance.

The study wanted to know the role of PIO in the compliance process of the RTI applications (table 4.46).[55] It is understood that the PIO place the file and document the data in time while PIO is the person who communicate the date and decisions, PIO explains the decision of denial and clarify the FAA on various reasons of denial. Around 81.67% viewed that PIO is to maintain records and applications.

Role of Training and Workshops

Training is considered as one of the important inputs to improve the delivery of services by the functionaries. The conceptual need for the training for the effective implementation of the RTI Act and various progressive legislations has provided good results in the working environment. Training and workshops are important inputs for the promotion and efficient functioning of progressive Act like RTI Act. It is strongly believed that training of RTI-designated personnel will make the Act more operational. It will develop a positive attitude in the minds of the RTI personnel. Understanding this, Information and Public Relation Department, the Nodal Department for monitoring the implementation of RTI in the State and SICsupport different training programs through different training institutions of the state. Keeping this in mind the Odisha Information Commission supported to organize various training and workshops on RTI. In addition, the training programs were organized at different training institutions located at Bhubaneswar also attended by the RTI-designated personnel.

Table 4.46 Responses of FAAs on the Role of PIOs in the Disposal of RTI Cases

Sl. No	*Role of PIO*	*No.*	*%*
1.	Place the file and documents before the FAA	80	96.47
2.	PIO communicates the data and decision to the party	70	82.35
3.	PIO explains the decision of denial and clarifies in detail to FAA	42	49.41
4.	In timely complying orders passed by FAA	66	77.65
5.	Maintain records and applications	75	88.24

Source: Primary survey, 2019 (figures in the bracket are percent to total).

Training of RTI Personnel

An attempt was made to find out the coverage of training of RTI personnel in different public authorities. The study found out that out of 120 PIOs, only 39.12% have been trained on RTI Act in different training institutions. Similarly, out of 85 FAAs 42 (49.41%) have undergone RTI training. An in depth look into the status of training in different public authorities indicates that in Secretariat Departments the trained PIOs account for 59.38%, while trained FAA covers 69.23%. In Heads of the Departments around 65.38% of PIOs are trained while 52.38% of FAAs have been trained under RTI training. The details of trained RTI-designated personnel in different public authorities can be observed from table 4.47.[56]

The above table indicates that the state has not yet provided training to all the existing PIOs and FAAs even though 12 years have passed since the implementation of the RTI Act. It seems that the special emphasis given by I &PR department to train all the personnel on RTI Act is still inadequate in number and coverage. Many PIOs and FAAs have expressed their willingness to go for special training on RTI Act but no such opportunities have ever come to them.

Usefulness of the Training of PIOs/FAAs on RTI Act

The usefulness of the training provided to PIOs and FAAs was assessed through close-ended responses. The response on the usefulness of the training was collected from all PIOs and FAAs irrespective of their training received. The purpose is to know how they receive training as a method of skill transfer to bring change in the day-to-day operation of the governance of the Act. Out of 120 PIOs, 69.17% agreed that transfer of inputs in the form of training has usefulness in the day-to-day functioning, while 29.17% did not have any response and 1.67% did not agree to this proposition. Similar responses were also sought

Table 4.47 Distribution of PIOs/FAAs Provided with Training on RTI Act

Sl. No.	*Public Authorities*	*Total*		*Trained*		*Untrained*	
		PIO	*FAA*	*PIO*	*FAA*	*PIO*	*FAA*
1.	Secretariat Department	32 (100)	26 (100)	19 (59.38)	18 (69.23)	13 (40.63)	8 (30.77)
2.	Heads of the Department	26 (100)	21 (100)	17 (65.38)	11 (52.38)	9 (34.62)	10 (47.62)
3.	Other PAs	62 (100)	38 (100)	37 (59.68)	13 (34.21)	25 (40.32)	25 (65.79)
	Total	120 (100)	85 (100)	73 (39.17)	42 (49.41)	47 (39.17)	43 (50.59)

Source: Primary Survey, 2019 (figures in the bracket are percent of the total).

from FAAs on the usefulness of the training. The study findings indicate that of the total 85 FAAs, 37 (43.53%) agreed that the training inputs are useful in the day-to-day functioning of the system. Similarly, around 41.18% did not give any view on the use of training inputs. The details of responses of the PIOs and FAAs in different categories of PAs are given in table 4.48.[57]

The usefulness of the training on RTI Act was specifically asked to each trained PIO and FAA. Broadly four specific uses of such trainings on RTI Act were found out. They are viz: training refreshed the knowledge on RTI Act; it helped to establish smooth implementation processes, built transparency in the governance, and helped to find solution to practical problems. A look into the responses in each category of public authorities indicates that in Secretariat Departments, highest of the PIO responses (81.21%) are in favor that training on RTI-related issues refresh knowledge on the RTI Act and the RTI Rules, followed by the fact that it helped in establishing smooth implementation processes in public administration (94.73%) and it helped to find solution to practical problems (73.68%). Among the FAAs of Secretariat Departments they consider that training on RTI Act helped to find solutions to practical problems (66.66%) followed by the fact that it helped to establish smooth implementation processes (61.11%) and refreshed the knowledge of the FAAs on the RTI Act (50.00%). The responses on the usefulness of the training for the PIOs of the Heads of the Departments were also observed who agreed that the training has refreshed their knowledge on RTI Act (82.35%), and solved the problems in day-to-day processing of RTI applications (70.58%). The FAAs of the Heads of the Departments also agreed that the training has helped them to understand the Act (90.90%) and to find practical solutions to the RTI-Act-related problems (100%). Among the other PAs 25.67% PIOs agreed that they have been benefited out of these training which helped to establish smooth implementation processes and in finding practical solution to the RTI-related problems (75.67%). Table 4.49[58] on the usefulness of the training established the fact that both the PIOs and FAAs have been benefited out of these training programs on RTI Act. Very few have pointed out that such training has helped in establishing the transparency in the governance process.

The PIOs and FAAs who agreed that training on RTI is useful put forth the following justifications.

- It acquaints the trainees on various aspects of the RTI Act and empowers them in the operation.
- It brings change in the day-to-day operation of the governance.
- The skill received in RTI training helps in record management, increases the seriousness in the responses to the RTI applications, and in responding to the timeline of the RTI Act.

Table 4.48 Distribution of Responses of PIOs/FAAs on the Usefulness of Training

Sl.		*Total*		*Useful*		*Not Useful*		*Can't Say*	
No.	*Public Authorities*	*PIO*	*FAA*	*PIO*	*FAA*	*PIO*	*FAA*	*PIO*	*FAA*
1.	Secretariat Department	32	26	22	13	2	6	8	7
		(100)	(100)	(68.75)	(50.00)	(6.25)	(23.08)	(25.00)	(26.92)
2.	Heads of the Department	26	21	20	11	0	4	6	6
		(100)	(100)	(76.92)	(52.38)	(0.00)	(19.05)	(23.08)	(28.57)
3.	Other PAs	62	38	41	13	0	3	21	22
		(100)	(100)	(66.13)	(34.21)	(0.00)	(7.89)	(33.87)	(57.89)
	Total	120	85	83	37	2	13	35	35
		(100)	(100)	(69.17)	(43.53)	(1.67)	(15.29)	(29.17)	(41.18)

Source: Primary Survey, 2019 (figures in the bracket are percent of the total).

Table 4.49 Responses of the PIOs and FAAs on the of Usefulness of the Training Inputs

Sl. No.	*Usefulness of the Training Inputs*	*Public Authorities*					
		Secretariat Department		*Heads of the Department*		*Other PAs*	
		PIO (19)	*FAA (18)*	*PIO(17)*	*FAA(11)*	*PIO(37)*	*FAA(13)*
1.	Refreshed Knowledge on RTI Act, Rules and procedures	16 (81.21)	9 (50.00)	14(82.35)	10(90.90)	19(51.35)	8(61.53)
2.	To establish smooth Implementation processes	18 (94.73)	11 (61.11)	11(64.70)	7(63.63)	28(75.67)	6(46.15)
3.	Helped in making transparency in public administration	9 (47.36)	7 (38.88)	9(52.91)	4(36.36)	12(32.43)	5(38.46)
	Finding solution to practical problems	14(73.68)	12(66.66)	12(70.58)	11(100)	28(75.67)	9(69.23)

Source: Primary Survey, 2019 (figures in the bracket are percent of the total)

- Both PIOs and FAAs opined that still many RTI personnel are not given training on the RTI Act. As a result, many of the employees who have been entrusted the RTI assignments are yet to reflect their seriousness. All the employees should be given orientation on RTI Act in different training institutions.
- All the departments of State Secretariat and Directorates should have trained trainers who will carry out the training program on RTI-related issues within the department for all the employees.
- The district-level training programs to be organized to train the employees on RTI Act.

The PIOs in all PAs were asked about the need of training on RTI-related issues. Responses were collected from all PIOs through three point's close-ended scale. In total, the study found out that around 79.17% agreed that training inputs are to be given to the employees on RTI issues. Training is required for the RTI personnel on regular intervals, while 18.33% did not give any response to the question. The details of responses of the PIOs in each PA categories are given in table 4.50.[59]

The PIOs who agreed to the training need justified by providing the following arguments:

- Training on RTI Act at regular interval to the RTI-designated personnel will build their confidence and understanding on various aspects of the Act.
- Such training opportunities will update the knowledge base of the RTI-designated personnel on changing issues relating to the RTI Act.
- Provision of training input at regular interval should be given continuously at least for a period of 5 years, so as to bring a change in the governance processes of the state.

Table 4.50 Responses of PIOs on the Need of Training on Regular Interval to the Government Employees

Sl.		*Total*	*Responses*		
No.	*PA Categories*	*PIO*	*Yes*	*No*	*Can't say*
1.	Secretariat Department	32(100)	28(87.50)	0(0.00)	4(12.50)
2.	Heads of the Department	26(100)	20(76.92)	2(7.69)	4(15.38)
3.	Other PAs	62(100)	47(75.81)	1(1.61)	14(22.58)
	Total	120(100)	95(79.17)	3(2.50)	22(18.33)

Source: Primary Survey, 2019 (figures in the bracket are percent of the total).

Supports to Training Institutions

Training and workshops are one of the activities SIC has also promoted during the year 2008–2009. During the year SIC has provided financial support to seven training institutes functioning under different Government Departments to organize special training on RTI Act. During the study, it was observed that except Gopabandhu Academy of Administration (GAA) and State Institute of Rural Development (SIRD) most of these training institutes are yet to start their training programs on RTI Act. The details of fund support provided by SIC are given in table 4.51.[60]. It is observed that GAA has organized 28 training programs since the inception of the RTI Act. It has provided training to 969 trainees representing different departments of the Government. During the year 2008–2009 GAA has organized seven training programs and trained 223 trainees. Similarly, SIRD has carried out 16 training programs for the promotion of RTI Act and trained 1155 trainees representing different public authority (table 4.52).[61]

Qualitative Responses

In order to substantiate the quantitative responses of the respondents on the usefulness of the training on RTI Act, the study also collected qualitative responses from all 120 PIOs and 85 FAAs. Data (table 4.53)[62] indicate that the PIOs who feel the usefulness of the training input in enhancing the effectiveness in discharging the services under RTI Act tune to 59.17%, followed by 54.17% who are acquainted with RTI Act to a greater extent, 43.33% were helped in strengthening the office records and the lowest benefit (26.67%) were found in the areas of establishing transparency in public administration. Similarly, FAAs (85) were also speaking out the benefits of training to them. Maximum benefits received by them out of these training in the areas of developing effectiveness in discharging services under RTI Act (77.64%), followed by increasing the acquaintance with RTI Act (62.35%), clarification of doubts on RTI Act (71.76%), whereas the lowest benefits are accorded to FAAs also in establishing transparency in governance in public administration.

Suggestions to Improve Training Programs on RTI Act

Suggestions were sought from all PIOs and FAAs to improve the contents of the training programs. All the suggestions are categorized into eight responses including the non-responded category. These responses can broadly be classified as improving training methods, training venues, coverage of training, and budget provision. More number of PIOs have emphasized on the district/

Table 4.51 Distribution of Training Institutions Supported by SIC for Organizing Training/Workshops on RTI during 2008–2009

Sl. No.	*Training Institutions*	*Department*	*Amount Supported*
1.	State Institute of Rural Development, Bhubaneswar	Panchayat Department Raj	₹4.65,200/-
2.	State Institute of Health and Family Welfare, Bhubaneswar	Health and Family Welfare Department	₹1,09,920/-
3.	Biju Patnaik State Police Academy, Bhubaneswar	Home Department	₹2,50.000/-
4.	Scheduled Caste and Scheduled Tribe Research and Training Institute, Bhubaneswar	ST and Development Department SC	₹1,72,240/-
5.	Council for Higher Secondary Education Orissa, Bhubaneswar	School and Mass Education Department	₹5,73,100/-
6.	Madhusudan Institute of Co-operative Management, Bhubaneswar	Cooperation Department	₹87,770/-
7.	Home Economics and Training Centre, Bhubaneswar		₹97,000/-
	Total		₹17,55,230/-

Source: State Information Commission, 2019.

Table 4.52 Distribution of Programmes Organized by Different Institutes Providing Knowledge on RTI Act

	No of Training Programmes			*Total Trainees*		
Years	*GAA*	*SIRD*	*Total*	*GAA*	*SIRD*	*Total*
2005–2006	10	–	10	407	–	407
2006–2007	4	–	4	126	–	126
2007–2008	7	5	12	213	27	240
2008–2009	7	11	18	223	1,128	1,391
Total	28	16	44	969	1,155	2,164

Source: Concerned Training Institutes.

Table 4.53 Responses of the RTI Personnel on the Usefulness of the Training on RTI Act

Sl. No.	*Usefulness*	*PIO (N = 120)*	*In%*	*FAA (N = 85)*	*In%*
1.	Acquainted with RTI Act very much	65	(54.17)	53	(62.35)
2.	Doubts on RTI Act Clarified	51	(42.50)	61	(71.76)
3.	Implementation of RTI Act made smooth	44	(36.33)	38	(44.70)
4.	Helps in establishing the process of transparency in public administration	32	(26.67)	29	(34.11)
5.	Inter- and intra-departmental coordination is expanded	39	(32.5)	34	(40.00)
6.	Mentally prepared to disclose documents of public authorities	46	(38.33)	30	(35.29)
7.	Helped in strengthening the record management	52	(43.33)	49	(57.64)
8.	Effectiveness in discharging services under RTI is ensured	71	(59.17)	66	(77.64)

Source: Primary Survey, 2019 (figures in the bracket are percent of the total).

subdivision and block level training programs (70%), followed by provision of special budget (60.83%), requirement of RTI -experienced/trained trainers (57.50%), and so on. The FAAs also provided their suggestions with respect to the improvement of the training provision of programs. The FAAs emphasized more on the training provision for the government employees in general and designated RTI personnel on regular basis and should be a part of the department (92.94%), which should be organized at district, subdivision and block levels (81.17%) and budget provision (74.11%). The details of the

Table 4.54 Distribution of Responses to Improve the RTI-Related Training Programs

Sl. No.	*Areas of Information*	*PIOs (N = 120)*	*In %*	*FAA (N = 85)*	*In %*
1.	Field exposure to RTI implementing model PAs	56	(46.67)	42	(49.41)
2.	More classroom/mock test, FGD, individual interviews reflecting office situations interactions	61	(50.83)	51	(60.00)
3.	More training program on RTI Act in district subdivision and block levels	84	(70.00)	69	(81.17)
4.	RTI should be a component in all training programs conducted by different training institutions	69	(57.50)	73	(85.88)
5.	Training of RTI Act should be a part of departmental training curriculum	77	(64.17)	79	(92.94)
6.	Group of trainers for each PAs to be created through training	51	(42.50)	54	(63.52)
7.	Provision of special budget on RTI training	73	(60.83)	63	(74.11)
8.	Training should be imparted by field experts and legal luminaries	69	(57.50)	57	(67.05)
9.	No view	26	(21.67)	4	(4.70)

Source: Primary Survey, 2019 (figures in the bracket are percent of the total).

responses on various suggestions of the FAAs are to improve the training programs is given in table 4.54.[63]

CONCLUSION

This chapter on functioning of RTI Act in Odisha Secretariat provides an overview of the profile of employees of Odisha Secretariat (respondent) and Right to Information applicant in the different department of Odisha Secretariat. More particularly, it explains the CCs and SAs with RTI Act by different PAs, Heads of the Department, and other public authorities in the Odisha Secretariat. The review is based on the data collected from the annual reports of OIC published in different years and primary data from all the department of the Odisha Secretariat. Applications received by public authorities in the different departments of the Odisha Secretariat since the inception of the Act were reviewed. The RTI authorities include Public Information Officer/ Assistant Public Information Officer, Secretariat Information Cell. This chapter is based on the primary data from the employees of Odisha Secretariat and secondary data from the Information and Public Relation Department (Nodal Department of RTI). This chapter also focuses on the functional limitation of the Right to Information in the Odisha Secretariat. It highlights the gender distribution, educational distribution, age distribution, sample size, and responses of the respondents of the different departments RTI applicant and status of the BPL applicant of Odisha Secretariat. All the data collected from the Information and Public Relation Department and Secretariat Information Cell of the all the 42 departments of Odisha Secretariat.

NOTES

1. See the Section 27 of the RTI Act (No.22 of 2005) also see Right to Information Rules 2005 published by Odisha Information Commission.
2. Data collected from the Information and Public Relation Department, Government of Odisha and Annual Reports of Odisha Information Commission.
3. Random Sample collected from the Secretariat Information Cell and yearly registered RTI cases of Odisha Secretariat (Information and Public Relation Department, Government of Odisha).
4. Gender distribution of the RTI applicants (Secretariat Employees Perspectives), Primary and Secondary Survey, 2019, and figures in the bracket are percentage of total.
5. Primary Survey, 2019 Response of the previous experiences worked as PIOs (Secretariat Departments) and figures in the bracket are percentage of total.
6. Socioeconomic Profile of the RTI User and Non User Gender Distribution Primary Survey, 2019 (Secretariat Employees Perspectives) and figures in the bracket are percentage of total.
7. Age Distribution of RTI User and Non User, Primary Survey, 2019 (Employees of Odisha Secretariat Perspectives) and figures in the bracket are percentage of total.
8. Occupational Distribution of RTI User and Nonuser Primary Survey, 2019 (Employees of Odisha Secretariat Perspectives) and figures in the bracket are percentage of total.
9. Educational status of RTI User and Nonuser Respondents Primary Survey, 2019 (Employees of Odisha Secretariat Perspectives) and figures in the bracket are percentage of total.
10. Distribution of Gender of the RTI Nonuser Respondents Primary Survey, 2019 of Six Major Departments of Odisha Secretariat and figures in the bracket are percentage of total.
11. Knowledge of the Location of Odisha Information Commission among the RTI Non user in Six Major Departments of Odisha Secretariat and figures in the bracket are percentage of total.

12. Distribution of RTI designated person in the different departmental position and number of responses, Primary Survey, 2019, with percentage.

13. Distribution of FAAs covered under the study according to their positions in different public authorities and number of responses, Primary Survey, 2019 with percentage.

14. Distribution of Public Information Officer covered under the study according to their positions in different public authorities and number of responses , Primary Survey, 2019 with percentage.

15. See Hand book on Right to Information Act, 2005, Yashada, Pune also see Right to Information Rules 2005 published by Odisha Information Commission.

16. See Various Clauses ofRight to Information Rules 2005 published by Odisha Information Commission, Government Press, Cuttack.

17. Ibid.

18. Jain, N.K. (2007), *Right to Information Concept Law Practice*. New Delhi: Regal Publication.

19. See the training program details organized by different training institute of the government, Information and Public Relation Nodal Department in Collaboration with State Information Commission.

20. The computerization and maintenance of all records remaining under administration control connected with Central Monitoring Mechanism of the Nodal Departments also see Handbook on Right to Information Act, 2005, Yashada, Pune.

21. See Section 4 (a) of Right to Information Rules 2005 published by Odisha Information Commission, Government Press, Cuttack.

22. Responses collected from the PIOs Secretariat Departments, Heads of Departments and Other PAs Primary Survey, 2019 (figures in the bracket are percentage to total).

23. Responses collected from the PIOs whether they feel new role as burden, Primary Survey, 2019 (figures in the bracket are percentage to total).

24. Responses collected from the knowledge of PIOs about the referred PIOs , Primary Survey, 2019 (figures in the bracket are percentage to total).

25. Responses on the knowledge about time line of RTI application of PIO, Primary Survey, 2019 (figures in the bracket are percentage to total).

26. Analysis is based on the Knowledge of PIOs Regarding the Responses of RTI Applicants, Secretariat Departments, Heads of Departments and Other PAs Primary Survey, 2019 (figures in the bracket are percentage to total).

27. Ibid.

28. The analysis is based on the data submitted by Information and Public Relation Department (Nodal Department), Primary Survey, 2019 supplied by Public Authorities and Odisha Secretariat Information Cell.

29. Analysis is based on the responses of HODs language format used for voluntary discloser Also see www.orissasoochanacommission.nic.in.

30. The analysis is based on Issue of guidelines by the Information and Public Relation Department on the implementation of Section 4(1) B on Self-Disclosure, Primary Survey, 2019 (figures in the bracket are percentage of total).

31. The analysis is based on Frequency of updation of Information in hand book and web page Secretariat Departments, Heads of Departments and Other PAs Primary Survey, 2019 (figures in the bracket are percentage to total).

32. The analysis is based on the Medium of Dissemination of Information of RTI Act under Section 4(3) Primary Survey, 2019 (figures in the bracket are percentage to total).

33. Analysis is based on the Responses of the PIOs on whether they like to act as PIO Secretariat Departments, Heads of Departments and Other PAs, Primary Survey, 2019 (figures in the bracket are percentage to total).

34. The analysis is based on the responses of the PIOs on the relevance of PIO position Primary Survey, 2019 (figures in the bracket are percentage to total).

35. The analysis is based on the responses regarding relevance of the responsibility of PIO in a PA Primary Survey, 2019 (figures in the bracket are percentage to total).

36. The analysis is based on the responses of PIOs on the relevance of PIO role, Primary Survey, 2019 (figures in the bracket are percentage to total).

37. Responses were collected regarding whether RTI Act can make administration responsive and accountable Primary Survey, 2019 with percentage.

38. Responses were collected from the HODs on their attitude to improve the implementation of RTI Act, Primary Survey, 2019 with percentage.

39. See Status of basic Information displayed by PA in Sign Board, Secretariat Departments, Heads of Departments and Other PAs, Primary Survey, 2019 (figures in the bracket are percentage to total) by Odisha Information Commission.

40. Ibid.

41. Data analysis is based on the Secretariat Departments, Heads of Departments and Other PAs, Primary Survey, 2019 (figures in the bracket are percentage to total) Regarding Appointment of officials as per Section 5(a)(b) of RTI Act, 2005.

42. The analysis is based on the Responses of PIOs on Prior Consultation by authorities to declare them as PIO, Primary Survey, 2019 (figures in the bracket are percentage to total).

43. The analysis is based on the Responses of PIOs on the Maintenance of records in PAs, Primary Survey, 2019 (figures in the bracket are percentage to total).

44. The analysis is based on the responses of the PIOs on the occurrence of possible changes in the RTI-related office management system, Primary Survey, 2019 (Figures in the bracket are percentage to total).

45. The analysis is based on the reasons changes in the RTI-related office management system of Secretariat Departments, Heads of Departments and other PAs, Primary Survey, 2019 (figures in the bracket are percentage to total).

46. See the Section 25(2), (3) of the Right to Information Act – 2005 also see Orissa Right to Information Rules, 2005 published by Orissa Information Commission, Government Press, Cuttack.

47. The compilation of data on RTI as per the Section 25 (2), Secretariat Departments, Heads of Departments and Other PAs, Primary Survey, 2019 (figures in the bracket are percentage to total).

48. Data analysis is based on the Annual Reports of Odisha Information Commission, 2014–2015, 2015–2016 regarding the distribution of BPL RTI applicants in the different public Authorities, Primary Survey, 2019 (Figures in the bracket are percentage to total).

49. Data analysis is based on the Annual Reports of Odisha Information Commission, 2012–2013, 2013–2014, 2014–2015, and 2015–2016 regarding the distribution of BPL RTI applications in the different years, Primary Survey, 2019.

50. Data complied is based on the Annual Reports of Odisha Information Commission, 2012–2013, 2013–2014, 2014–2015, and 2015–2016 RTI applications received and complied in the different years, Primary Survey, 2019.

51. The Responses of PIOs regarding Average number of days spent per week for RTI-related work in Secretariat Departments, Heads of Departments and Other PAs, Primary Survey, 2019 (figures in the bracket are percentage to total).

52. The Responses of PIOs regarding Average number of days spent to attend court cases for RTI-related work in Secretariat Departments, Heads of Departments and Other PAs, Primary Survey, 2019 (figures in the bracket are percentage to total).

53. The data analysis is based on the Responses of FAAs on the their knowledge on the consequences if RTI timeline not followed with percentage.

54. The analysis is based on the responses of FAAs on various reasons for not adhering to the timelines of RTI Act, Primary Survey, 2019 with percentage.

55. The analysis is based on Responses of FAAs on the role of PIOs in the disposal of RTI cases, Primary Survey, 2019 with percentage.

56. The data analysis is based on the Responses of PIOs/FAAs provided with training on RTI Act in Secretariat Departments, Heads of Departments and Other PAs, Primary Survey, 2019 (figures in the bracket are percentage to total).

57. The data analysis is based on the Responses of PIOs/FAAs on the usefulness of training on RTI Act in Secretariat Departments, Heads of Departments and Other PAs, Primary Survey, 2019 (figures in the bracket are percentage to total).

58. The data analysis is based on the Responses of PIOs/FAAs on the usefulness of training inputs on RTI Act in Secretariat Departments, Heads of Departments and Other PAs, Primary Survey, 2019 (figures in the bracket are percentage to total).

59. The analysis is based on the Responses of PIOs on the need of training on regular interval to the government employees in Secretariat Departments, Heads of Departments and Other PAs, Primary Survey, 2019 (figures in the bracket are percentage to total).

60. See the Annual Report of Odisha Information Commission during 2008–2009 regarding the workshop and training on RTI with amount supported by SIC also see www.orissasoochanacommission.nic.in.

61. See the Annual Report of Odisha Information Commission during 2005–2006, 2006-07, 2007–2008, and 2008–2009 regarding the distribution of Programmes organized by different Institutes providing knowledge on RTI Act supported by SIC.

62. The data analysis is based on the Responses of the PIOs and FFAs on the usefulness of the training on RTI Act, Primary Survey, 2019 (figures in the bracket are percent of the total).

63. The data analysis is based on the Responses of the PIOs and FFAs to improve the RTI-related training, Primary Survey, 2019 (figures in the bracket are percent of the total).

Chapter 5

Grievance Redressal and RTI

Secretariat Employee's Perspective

INTRODUCTION

This chapter gives an overview of grievance redressal of employees and RTI in the Odisha Secretariat that deals with the data analysis. This chapter focuses on the statistical figure of the RTI cases in the different department from 2008 to 2018. At the same time, this chapter examines transparency and accountability in the service delivery system in Odisha Secretariat. Recognition of people's rights is one of the important processes of good governance. The RTI provides citizens the right to access information from all the public authorities by way of inspecting works documents and records, taking notes, extract of certified copies of documents or records, certified copies of materials, and obtaining information in electronic form.[1] The chapter deals with the profile of Odisha Secretariat. The analysis based on the data submitted by all 40 Department of Odisha Secretariat and other public authorities.

IMPLEMENTATION OF THE RTI ACT IN THE STATE

The implementation of RTI Act plays a very important role in the grievance redressal of the employees of the Odisha Secretariat. The grievance redressal of employees is based on the data submitted by the various public authorities in the different years on the basis of online and offline RTI applications. The data is collected from various public authorities under control through Information and Public Relation Department (Nodal Department) to prepare the annual reports. As per provision of Section 29(1)[2] of the RTI Act, 2005, the Odisha Information Commission collects the information/materials from various Departments of Government and public authorities under their control through

Information and Public Relations Department of Government (Nodal Department) and prepares an annual report on implementation of the provisions of the Act department-wise on financial year, that is, from April 1 to March 31.

An overview of the receipt and disposal of RTI applications, FAs, CCs, and SAs in the state since the inception of the Commission up to March, 2016, are discussed further in this chapter.

RECEIPT AND DISPOSAL OF RTI APPLICATIONS

Receipt of the RTI Applications

During the period 2015–2016, totally 26,127 RTI applications were stated to have been received in the various departments and the public authorities under their control in the state. The receipt of RTI applications as reported by the different departments of the state is given in table 5.1.

Table 5.1 Number of RTI Applications Received during 2005–2006 to 2015–2016

Sl. No	*Years*	*Total*
1.	2005–2006	447
2.	2006–2007	4,618
3.	2007–2008	9,772
4.	2008–2009	37,997
5.	2009–2010	42,036
6.	2010–2011	35,649
7.	2011–2012	52,305
8.	2012–2013	43,011
9.	2013–2014	60,126
10.	2014–2015	25,172
11.	2015–2016	26,127

Source: Annual Reports, Orissa Information Commission, 2005–2006 to 2015–2016.

The receipt of RTI applications since the inception of Odisha Information Commission are indicated in the table 5.1.[3]

Table 5.1 explains the increasing trend of the RTI application from 2005–2006 to 2013–2014. In the year 2014–2015 and 2015–2016, there was a gradual decrease in RTI application. The table below clearly indicates that people are not satisfied by the replay from PIOs and APIOs of the different departments. The total number of RTI application includes both online and offline applications in the form of FAs, CCs, and SAs.

In figure 5.1 the graphical representation of the RTI application from 2005–2006 to 2015–2016 clearly indicates that there was a continuous increase in the RTI application till the end of 2014.[4] After 2014, the RTI application rate was gradually decreasing. The figure shows receipt of total RTI applications in the different years from 2005–2006 to 2015–2016 (includes both offline and online FAs, CCs, and SAs).

Compliance with RTI Act by Various Public Authorities during 2015–2016

The analysis is based on the data submitted by all 40 government departments of Odisha Secretariat and other public authorities. A total of 26,127 applications were filed during the year 2015–2016. The data indicate that 14 Secretariat Departments have received more than 100 and less than 1,000 RTI applications during the year 2015–2016. School and Mass Education Department has received the highest RTI applications following the steel and mines. The departments that received less than 100 RTI applications during the year include revenue and disaster management, information technology, commerce and transport, public enterprise, and sports and youth services. The

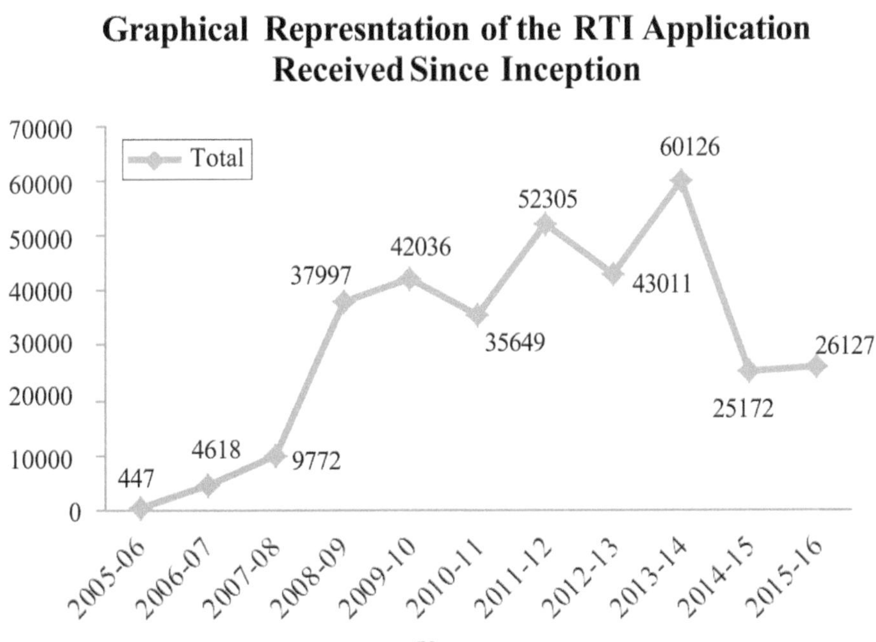

Figure 5.1 Graphical Representation of the RTI Application Received Since Inception (From 2005–2006 to 2015–2016). *Source*: Annual Reports, Orissa Information Commission, 2005–2006 to 2015–2016.

Public Authorities (PAs) that received RTI applications less than 200 include Governors Secretariat, PG and PA, and Textile and Handloom. The details of applications received by different departments as per the following trends (see figures 5.2 and 5.3).[5]

Number of Applications Filed

A total of 26,127 applications were filed during the year 2015–2016. The data indicate different trends.

Figures 5.2 and 5.3 explain the departmental status of the RTI applications and indicate two different trends.[6] Figure 5.2 explains the Secretariat Departments received more than 100 and less than 1,000 RTI applications and similarly figure 5.3 explains the Secretariat Department received less than 100 RTI applications. It clearly shows that the School and Mass Education Department received the highest RTI application of 790, whereas Revenue and Disaster Management Department received only 30 RTI applications in 2016.

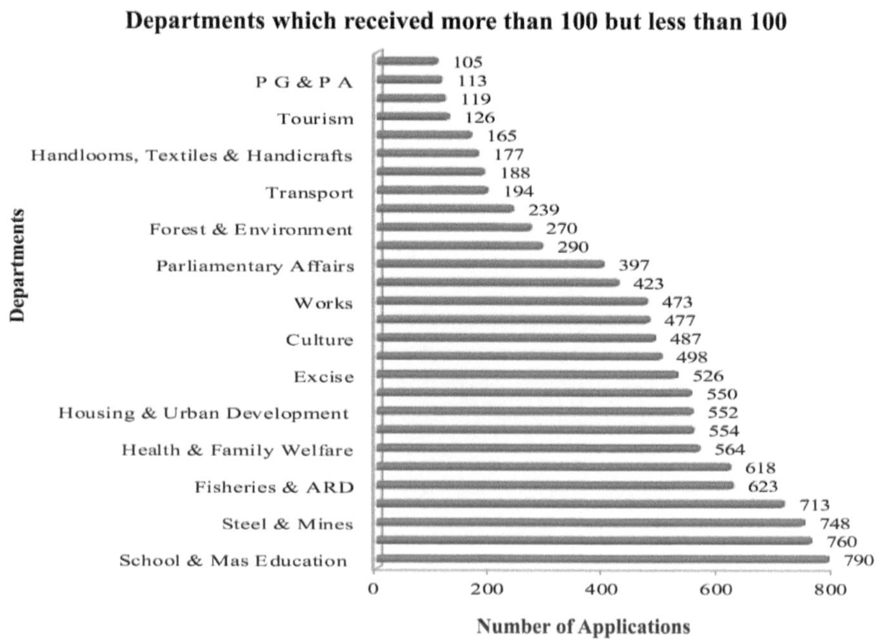

Figure 5.2 Secretariat Departments Which Received more than 100 and less than 1,000 RTI Applications. *Source*: Information and Public Relation Department, Government of Odisha.

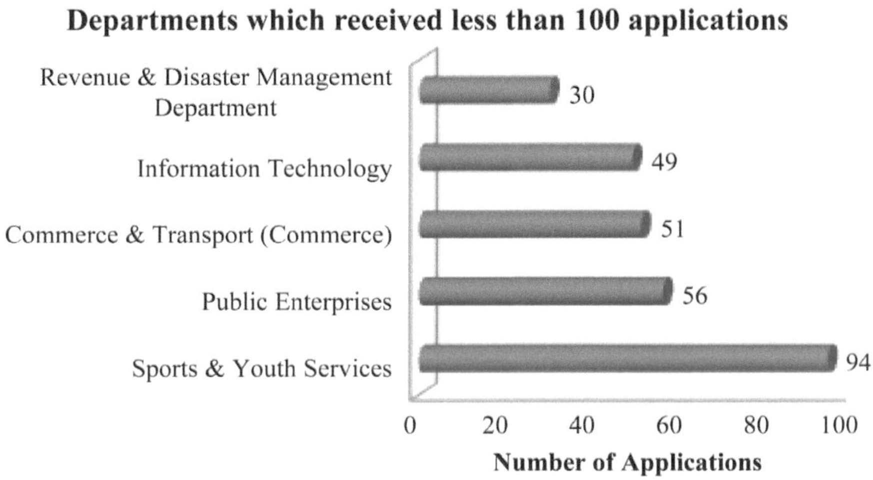

Figure 5.3 Secretariat Departments Which Received less than 100 RTI Applications. *Source*: Information and Public Relation Department, Government of Odisha.

Disposal of RTI Applications

At the beginning of the financial year 2015–2016, there was a pendency of 3,378 applications. During the period under reporting 26,127 applications were received. Thus, there were 29,505 applications for disposal out of which 27,256 applications have been disposed of. The rate of disposal was 92.38%. Out of the total 27,256 disposed RTI applications, information has been provided to the information-seekers in 19,875 cases. In 1,938 cases, requests for information have been rejected, and in 5,443 cases, applications have been transferred to other public authorities under Section 6(3) of the RTI Act, 2005. The public authorities under 21 departments have reported 100% disposal. Disposal of RTI applications in respect of public authorities under 9 departments was above 90%. The percentage of received and disposed RTI cases indicates that the grievance redressal of employees through the RTI Act plays a very crucial role for transparency and accountability in the society.[7] At the same time, opening balance cases are increasing, it creates an additional burden to the Indian judiciary.

The receipt and disposal of RTI applications during different years since inception is indicated in table 5.2.

Table 5.2 clearly indicates the receipt and disposal of RTI applications with percentages. The percentage of RTI applications was increasing till 2013–2014 at the same time disposal rate of RTI applications was also increasing. In 2014–2015, the percentage of the disposal rate of the RTI application was 95.41 and it was the highest.

Table 5.2 Number of Receipt and Disposal of RTI Applications with Percentage (2005–2006 to 2015–2016)

Years	*Opening Balance*	*Received*	*Total Application*	*Disposed*	*Percentage*
2005–2006	0	447	447	382	85.46
2006–2007	65	4,618	4,683	4,243	90.61
2007–2008	440	9,772	10,212	8,421	82.46
2008–2009	1,791	37,997	39,788	32,666	82.11
2009–2010	7,122	42,036	49,158	39,998	81.37
2010–2011	9,160	35,649	44,809	34,503	77.00
2011–2012	12,714	52,305	65,019	59,259	91.14
2012–2013	5,640	43,011	48,651	44,129	90.71
2013–2014	7,828	60,126	67,954	62,081	91.36
2014–2015	3,643	25,172	28,815	27,493	95.41
2015–2016	3,378	26,127	29,505	27,256	92.38

Source: Analysis is based on data received from Information and Public Relations Department, Government of Odisha (Nodal Department for RTI).

Receipt and Disposal of First Appeals

Similarly during the year 2015–2016, there were 1,992 (received 1,830+previous pendency 162) FAs for disposal, out of which 1,835 have been decided, registering a disposal rate of 92.11%. A comparative position since 2005 is shown in table 5.3 along with figures 5.4 and 5.5.[8]

Table 5.3 explains the number of receipt and disposal of FA RTI cases with percentages. It clearly indicates the comparative position of the FA RTI cases disposal rate with percentage in the different years. The highest percentage of the disposal of the FA cases in the year 2013–2014 was 92.54%. The lowest percentage of FA RTI cases disposal rate in the year 2008–2009 was 75.19%. The opening balance is gradually decreasing because of the fear of penalties for PIOs and APIOs. The opening balance of the different years indicates that PIOs and APIOs are more active in information sharing. The percentage of disposal rate in the different years is not highly satisfactory. The highest number of FA cases in the year 2011–2012 was 4,611 out of which 4,007 cases were disposed with information and the percentage was 86.90.

The number of receipt and disposal of FA RTI cases with percentage is better explained with the help of figure 5.4.

The statistical figure indicates the disposal of FA cases in figure 5.4 in the different years. The data was collected from the annual reports of the Odisha Information Commission. It clearly indicates that the disposal rate of FA cases was nearly about 90% during 2015–2016.

Figure 5.5 shows the disposal percentage of the FA cases in different years. The overall percentage of disposal of FA RTI cases in different years was more than 90%. The disposal percentages of the application are gradually increasing

Table 5.3 Number of Receipt and Disposal of First Appeals Cases with Percentage (2005–2006 to 2015–2016)

Years	*Opening Balance*	*Received*	*Total Applications*	*Disposal*	*% Disposal*
2005–2006	0	50	50	42	84
2006–2007	8	294	302	274	90.73
2007–2008	28	573	601	528	87.85
2008–2009	73	842	915	688	75.19
2009–2010	227	1,875	2,102	1,688	80.30
2010–2011	414	2,076	2,490	1,971	79.16
2011–2012	595	4,016	4,611	4,007	86.90
2012–2013	148	1,469	1,617	1,405	86.88
2013–2014	366	3,507	3,873	3,584	92.54
2014–2015	181	1,805	1,986	1,778	89.52
2015–2016	162	1,830	1,992	1,835	92.11

Source: Analysis is based on Annual Reports, Orissa Information Commission, 2005–2006 to 2015–2016.

but at the same time the number of FA applications also was highly increasing. That indicates the faith of the people in the RTI which plays an important role in the grievance redressal of the employees of Odisha Secretariat.

Receipt and Disposal of Complaint Cases and Second Appeals

During the year 2015–2016, the Commission received 560 Complaints and 3,209 SAs. Final orders have been passed by the Commission in 29 CC and

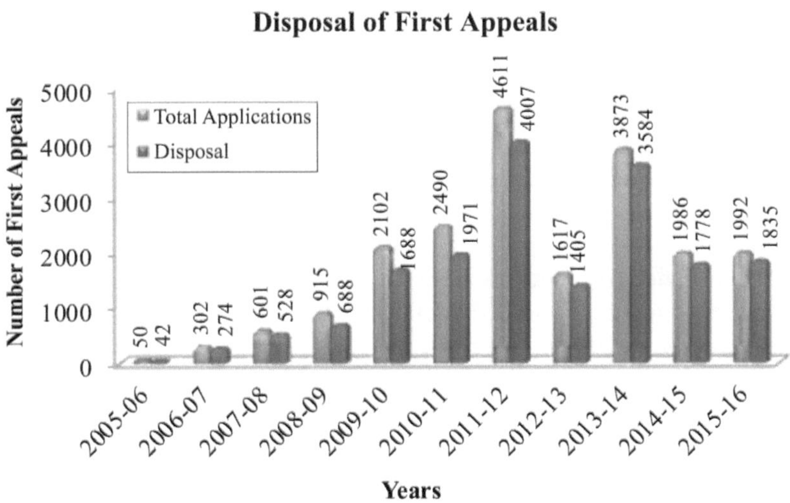

Figure 5.4 Disposal of First Appeals Cases (2005–2006 to 2015–2016). *Source*: Annual Reports, Orissa Information Commission, 2005–2006 to 2015–2016.

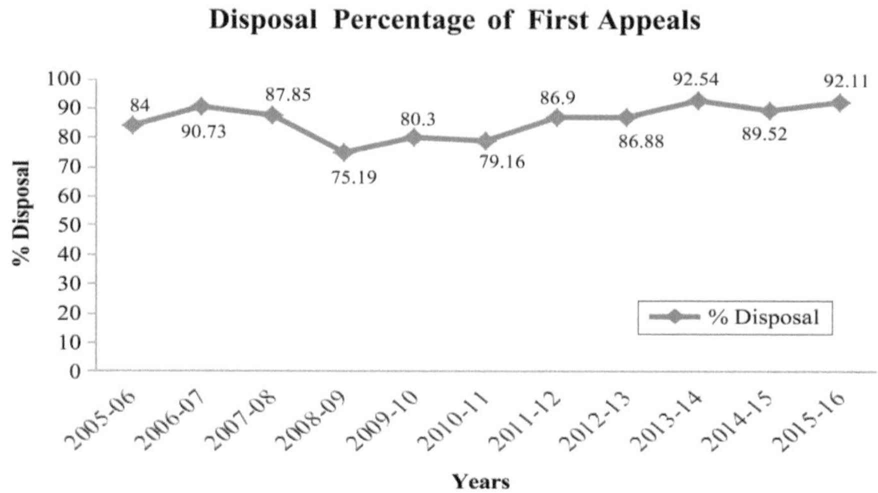

Figure 5.5 Disposal Percentage of First Appeals Cases (2005–2006 to 2015–2016). *Source*: Annual Reports, Orissa Information Commission (2005–2006 to 2015–2016).

491 SA during the period under report. The details of receipt, disposal, and cumulative pendency of CCs and SAs are given in table 5.4 and figure 5.6 along with representation of the position in table 5.5 and figure 5.7.

Table 5.4[9] explains the number of receipt and disposal of CCs with cumulative pendency from 2005–2006 to 2015–2016. It clearly indicates that cumulative pendency was increasing gradually due to the shortage of staff in the Odisha Information Commission and vacancies in the official position in the different public authorities. The opening balance also increases and disposal rate was decreasing which was one of the major problems of the grievance redressal of the employees of the Odisha Secretariat. The following statistical figure indicates the overall cumulative pendency of the different years. During the year 2015–2016 out of 560 received CCs only 29 cases were disposed and the cumulative pendency was 2,492.

Table 5.4 discusses the number of received and disposed CCs with cumulative pendency from 2005–2006 to 2015–2016, which indicate that the cumulative pendency was gradually increasing because of the PIO and APIO who have no much focus on the RTI cases which in turn indicates the inability of the PIOs of the different departments of the Odisha Secretariat. Figure 5.6 along with representation of the position in table 5.5 and figure 5.7 explains the number of SA cases received and disposed at Commission level with cumulative pendency during 2005–2006 to 2015–2016.[10]

Table 5.4 Number of Received and Disposed Complaint Cases with Cumulative Pendency from 2005–2006 to 2015–2016

Years	*Opening Balance*	*Received*	*Disposal*	*Cumulative Pendency*
2005–2006	0	0	0	0
2006–2007	0	1,012	367	645
2007–2008	645	2,051	463	2,233
2008–2009	2,233	2,029	597	3,665
2009–2010	3,665	2,662	1,103	5,224
2010–2011	5,224	3,658	1,706	7,176
2011–2012	7,176	3,197	5,047	5,326
2012–2013	5,326	2,555	5,197	2,684
2013–2014	2,684	1,482	1,948	2,218
2014–2015	2,218	518	775	1,961
2015–2016	1,961	560	29	2,492

Source: Annual Reports, Orissa Information Commission, 2005–2006 to 2015–2016).

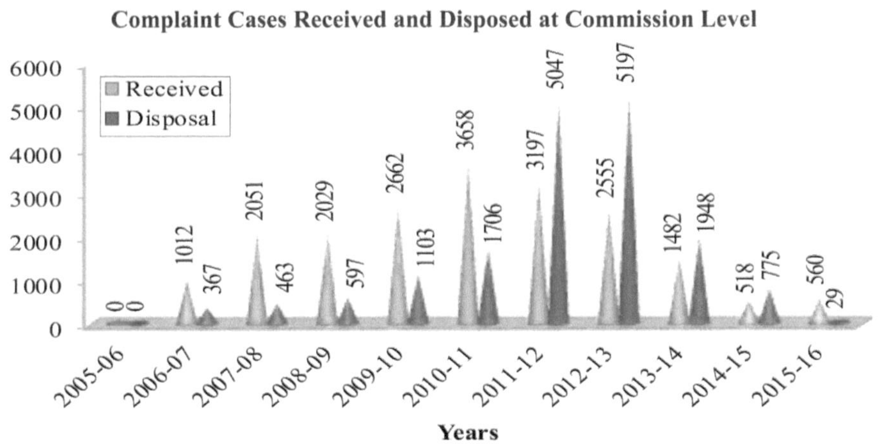

Figure 5.6 Number of Complaint Cases Received and Disposed at Commission Level during 2005–2006 to 2015–2016. *Source*: Graphical representation of the diagram based on the data submitted by Public Authorities at the Odisha Information Commission during 2005–2006 to 2015–2016.

Figure 5.6 highlights the number of CCs received and disposed at Commission level during 2005–2006 to 2015–2016. During the year 2012–2013, the Commission disposed the highest number of CCs at the Commission level which was 5,197. During the year 2015–2016, the Commission disposed 29 cases out of 560 CCs at Commission level. It's clearly reflecting that the percentage of disposal after 2012–2013 at the Commission level was gradually decreasing. The received CCs was also decreasing gradually at the Commission level.

Table 5.5 Number of Second Appeals Cases Received and Disposed at Commission Level with Cumulative Pendency during (2005–2006 to 2015–2016)

Years	*Opening Balance*	*Received*	*Disposal*	*Cumulative Pendency*
2005–2006	0	0	0	0
2006–2007	0	308	148	160
2007–2008	160	449	166	443
2008–2009	443	336	120	659
2009–2010	659	462	169	952
2010–2011	952	390	289	1,053
2011–2012	1,053	707	633	1,127
2012–2013	1,127	2,708	1,734	2,101
2013–2014	2,101	3,229	1,610	3,720
2014–2015	3,720	2,950	2,426	4,244
2015–2016	4,244	3,209	491	6,962

Source: Data are collected from Odisha Information Commission.

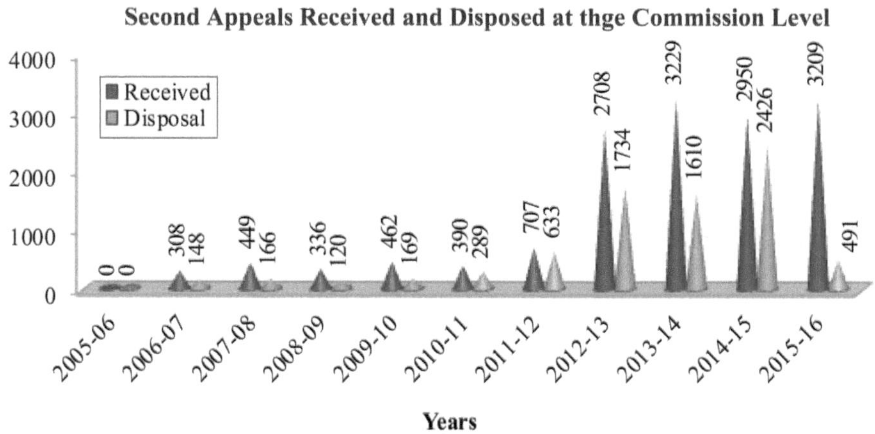

Figure 5.7 Number of Second Appeals Cases Received and Disposed at Commission Level during 2005–2006 to 2015–2016. *Source*: Data collected from Odisha Information Commission.

Table 5.5 highlights the number of SA cases received and disposed at Commission level with cumulative pendency during 2005–2006 to 2015–2016.[11] During the year 2014–2015 the Commission disposed the highest number of SAs cases at the Commission level which was 2,426. During the year 2008–2009 the Commission disposed 120 cases out of 336 SA cases at Commission level. It's clearly reflecting that the percentage of cumulative pendency at the Commission level was gradually increasing which creates over burden on judiciary which was already under pressure. The received SA cases are also increasing gradually at the Commission level.

Fgure 5.7 explains the number of SA cases received and disposed at Commission level with cumulative pendency during 2005–2006 to 2015–2016.[12] The graphical representations of SA cases clearly reflect that during 2014–2015 the Commission disposed 2,426 cases out of 2,950 at Commission level. The Commission received the highest number of SA cases during the year 2013–2014 which was 3,299 out of which 1,610 were disposed at Commission level.

Table 5.6 lists Odisha Secretariat with all the 40 department-wise disposal of applications (reporting period from April 1, 2015, to March 31, 2016). The opening balance request received under RTI was the highest which was 1,194 in the rural development department and the number of requests was also the highest which was 2,990 in this department during 2015–2016. The total number of request for RTI application received by the department of rural development was 3,884 which is the highest during 2015–2016. The opening balance was nil in the 13 departments of Odisha Secretariat. The request received by revenue and disaster management was the lowest which was only 30 during the year 2015–2016. The number of requests on which information provided by rural development department was the highest was 2,479 out of 3,884 applications and commerce and transport was the lowest which was 31 out of 51 applications during 2015–2016. The number of RTI case request transfer to other public authorities was the highest in Panchayati Raj Department which was 688 out of 1,766 RTI applications during 2015–2016. The number of RTI case request transfer to other public authorities was nil in the labor out of 104 applications and nil in the tourism department out of 194 applications. The decisions where applications for information were rejected was the highest in the water resource department which was 329 out of 553 RTI applications. The decisions where applications for information were rejected was nil in four departments these were higher education, public enterprises, science and technology, and InformationTtechnology departments. The total disposal of RTI application was the highest in the Women and Child Development Department which was 4,556 out of 5,111 applications during the year 2015–2016. The total disposal of RTI applications was the lowest in the Revenue and Disaster Management Department which was 30 out of 30 RTI applications during the year 2015–2016. The percentage of the disposal of RTI applications was 100% in 21 departments out of 40 Secretariat Departments. The remaining 19 department disposal rate of RTI applications was more than 90% during 2015–2016. It clearly reflects that the grievance redressal of employees of all the departments of Odisha Secretariat was overall 95% during 2015–2016.

Table 5.6 Department-Wise Disposal of Applications (Reporting Period from April 1, 2015 to March 31, 2016)

Sl. No.	*Name of the Public Authority*	*Opening Balance of Requests Received under RTI (as on April 1*	*No. of Requests Received during Year*	*Total no. of Requests (Column 3+4)*	*No. of Requests on which Information Provided*	*No. of Requests Transferred to other Public Authorities*	*Decisions where Applications for Information Rejected*	*Total Disposal 6+7+8*	*% of Disposal of Application*
1	2	3	4	5	6	7	8	9	10
1.	Agriculture	348	1,391	1,739	1,179	434	95	1708	98.22
2.	Co-operation	10	239	249	150	81	18	249	100.00
3.	Commerce and Transport (Commerce)	0	51	51	31	19	1	51	100.00
4.	Culture	28	487	515	365	137	13	515	100.00
5.	Employment and TE and T	0	119	119	52	65	2	119	100.00
6.	Energy	82	1,680	1,762	1,305	236	149	1690	95.91
7.	Excise	2	526	528	427	23	78	528	100.00
8.	Finance	21	1191	1212	997	99	104	1200	99.01
9.	Fisheries and ARD	6	623	629	498	103	28	629	100.00
10.	Food Supplies and Consumers Welfare	5	423	428	234	112	51	397	92.76

11.	Forest and Environment	0	270	270	208	52	10	270	100.00
12.	General Administration	0	1,090	1,090	737	326	27	1090	100.00
13.	Handlooms, Taxtiles and Handicrafts	1	177	178	107	40	17	164	92.13
14.	Health and Family Welfare	0	564	564	87	456	21	564	100.00
15.	Higher Education	0	761	761	714	47	0	761	100.00
16.	Home	0	618	618	345	239	34	618	100.00
17.	Housing and Urban Development	7	552	559	486	56	7	549	98.21
18.	Industries	101	477	578	398	42	33	473	81.83
19.	Information and Public Relations	14	498	512	117	236	68	421	82.23
20.	Information Technology	171	49	220	218	2	0	220	100.00
21.	Labor	0	105	105	105	0	51	105	100.00
22.	Law	109	713	822	675	35	54	761	92.58
23.	MS and ME	72	554	626	407	89	124	550	87.86
24.	Panchayati Raj	170	1,596	1,766	866	688	49	1678	95.02
25.	Parliamentary Affairs	0	397	397	116	232	6	397	100.00

(*Continued*)

Table 5.6 Continued

Sl. No.	*Name of the Public Authority*	*Opening Balance of Requests Received under RTI (as on April 1*	*No. of Requests Received during Year*	*Total no. of Requests (Column 3+4)*	*No. of Requests on which Informatio n Provided*	*No. of Requests Transferred to other Public Authorities*	*Decisions where Applications for Information Rejected*	*Total Disposal 6+7+8*	*% of Disposal of Application*
26.	Planning and Coordination	70	188	258	199	27	8	232	89.92
27.	Public Enterprises	0	56	56	35	13	0	56	100.00
28.	Public Grievances and Pension Administration	0	113	113	89	24	10	113	100.00
29.	Revenue and Disaster Management	0	30	30	5	15	314	30	100.00
30.	Rural Development	1194	2690	3884	2479	471	87	3264	84.04
31.	School and Mass Education	25	790	815	206	291	3	584	71.66
32.	Science and Technology	75	165	240	133	30	0	166	69.17

33.	Sports and Youth Services	54	94	148	125	3	6	128	86.49
34.	ST and SC Development	35	290	325	313	6	85	325	100.00
35.	Steel and Mines	38	748	786	509	72	9	666	84.73
36.	Tourism	0	126	126	117	0	10	126	100.00
37.	Transport	4	194	198	133	43	19	186	93.94
38.	Water Resources	3	550	553	449	85	329	553	100.00
39.	Women and Child Development	642	4,469	5,111	3,851	376	18	4,556	89.14
40.	Works	91	473	564	408	138		564	100.00
	Grand Total	3,378	26,127	29,505	19,875	5,443	1938	27,256	92.38

Source: Data submitted by 42 departments of Odisha Secretariat/different public authorities, Orissa.

Table 5.7 highlights the year-wise receipt and disposal of CCs from 2005 to 2018.[13] The CCs of RTI include both online and offline applications which was filed in the Odisha Information Commission. The highest number of CCs received by the Commission during 2010 was 3,344. After 2010 there was a gradual decrease in the CCs in the different years. The opening balance was highest in the year 2011 which was 6,817 and lowest in 2015 which was 291 out of 501 RTI received applications. The disposals of RTI CCs were highest in 2012 which was 6,265 and lowest in 2015 which was 69. The closing balances of the RTI CCs were highest during 2010 which was 6,817 and lowest in 2014 which was 291. The table clearly indicates closing balances were gradually increasing after 2015 and disposal rate of applications were gradually decreasing. The received CCs also gradually decreased.

Table 5.8[14] highlights the year-wise number of receipt and disposal of SA cases which were filed in Odisha Information Commission from 2006 to 2018. SAs opening balance was highest in the year 2018 which was 8,869 and the receipt of SA cases also highest in the year 2018 which was 3,395. The number of SA disposed cases was highest in the year 2014 which was 2,841 out of 3,182 SA applications. The closing balance of the SA RTI application was highest in the year 2018 which was 9,764 and lowest in the year 2006 which was only 94.

P.S. The hearing of CCs u/S 18 and SAs u/S 19(3)[15] of the RTI Act, 2005, started with effect from 02.04.2006, with the setting up of the Legal Wing of the SIC.

Table 5.7 Year-Wise Number of Receipt and Disposal of Complaint Cases (From 2005 to 2018)

Sl. No	*Year*	*As on*	*Opening Balance*	*Received*	*Disposed of*	*Closing balance*
1	2006	31-12-2006	–	644	309	335
2	2007	31-12-2007	335	1,972	381	1,926
3	**2008**	**31-12-2008**	**1,926**	**1,973**	**527**	**3,372**
4	2009	31-12-2009	3,372	2,557	886	5,043
5	2010	31-12-2010	5,043	3,344	1,570	6,817
6	2011	31-12-2011	6,817	3,310	5,163	4,964
7	2012	31-12-2012	4,964	2,781	6,265	1,480
8	2013	31-12-2013	1,480	1,733	2,168	1,045
9	2014	31-12-2014	1,045	709	1,463	291
10	2015	31-12-2015	291	501	69	723
11	2016	31-12-2016	723	600	136	1,187
12	2017	31-12-2017	1,187	643	277	1,553
13	2018	31-12-2018	1,543	867	422	1,998

Source: Data are collected from Odisha Information Commission.

Table 5.8 Year-Wise Number of Receipt and Disposal of Second Appeal Cases (From 2005 to 2018)

Sl. No	*Year*	*As on*	*Opening Balance*	*Received*	*Disposed of*	*Closing Balance*
1	2006	31-12-2006	–	202	108	94
2	2007	31-12-2007	94	437	152	379
3	**2008**	**31-12-2008**	**379**	**370**	**129**	**620**
4	2009	31-12-2009	620	373	132	861
5	2010	31-12-2010	861	421	273	1,009
6	2011	31-12-2011	1,009	605	456	1,158
7	2012	31-12-2012	1,158	2,197	1,274	2,081
8	2013	31-12-2013	2,081	3,111	2,003	3,189
9	2014	31-12-2014	3,189	3,182	2,841	3,530
10	2015	31-12-2015	3,530	3,229	657	6,102
11	2016	31-12-2016	6,102	3,121	1,240	7,983
12	2017	31-12-2017	7,983	3,484	2,598	8,869
13	2018	31-12-2018	8,869	3,395	2,500	9,764

Source: Odisha Information Commission.

Collection of Application Fees and cost of Information as per the Provisions of RTI Act and Rules

Table 5.9 supported by figure 5.8 indicates the amount collected toward application fees and cost of information under the provisions of the RTI Act and Rules framed there under in different years.

Table 5.9 supported by figure 5.8 highlights the collection of application fees and cost of information (amount in rupees) during 2005–2006 to 2015–2016. During the year 2010–2011, the collection of application fees and cost of information was highest which was ₹1,388,380/- and lowest during 2005–2006 which was ₹18,041. It indicates the cost of information was very high. The financially weak applicants do not get information due to this high cost of information. It creates a problem in grievance redressal of the employees of Odisha Secretariat.

The graphical representation in figure 5.8[16] clearly reflect that the collection of RTI Application fee and cost of information collected in form of rupee from the RTI applicants during 2005–2006 to 2015–2016. The collection of the cost of information and application fees was gradually decreasing after 2010–2011. During the year 2015–2016 the collection of application fees and cost of information was ₹653,242/-.

The Commission imposes a penalty on erring PIOs/referred PIOs under Section 20(1)[17] of the RTI Act, 2005, after giving them a reasonable opportunity of being heard. The numbers of cases in which penalties have been imposed and the penalty amount are given in table 5.10 and presented in figure 5.9.

Table 5.9 Collection of Application Fees and Cost of Information (Amount in Rupees) during (2005–2006 to 2015–2016)

Years	*Total Charges (Amount in Rupees)*
2005–2006	18,041
2006–2007	147,349
2007–2008	220,952
2008–2009	271,942
2009–2010	890,259
2010–2011	1,388,380
2011–2012	1,046,166
2012–2013	1,049,254
2013–2014	958,691
2014–2015	627,690
2015–2016	653,242

Source: Annual Reports of Odisha Information Commission during 2005–2006 to 2015–2016.

Table 5.10[18] supported by figure 5.9 highlights the number of penalty imposed cases, penalty imposed amount, and the number of cases of interim stay granted by High Court during 2006–2007 to 2015–2016. The highest number of cases penalty imposed during the year 2012–2013 which was 229 and the penalty amount was ₹3,224,999/-. The lowest number of cases of penalty during 2006–2007 which was ₹29,750/-. The number of RTI cases for which interim stay was granted by the High Court was highest during 2010–2011, which was 17. The number of RTI cases interim stay granted by the High Court is nil during the year 2006–2007 and 1 case during 2012–2013 and 2015–2016. The interim stay continuing amount was highest during 2010–2011 which was ₹ 339,000/- and nil during 2006–2007. Gradually the penalty amount was decreasing due to the mass consciousness about the RTI Act in the state.

Figure 5.9[19] indicates the number of RTI cases that imposed penalty in rupees during 2005–2006 to 2015–2016. The highest amount of penalty collected during 2012–2013 was ₹3,224,999/-. Gradually after 2012–2013 the penalty amount was decreasing which reflects that the PIOs, APIOs, and other public authorities were more active in the disposal of cases on time. At the same time, the percentage of grievance redressal of the employees of Odisha Secretariat was more than 90% during recent years.

Penalty

RTI Act is very clear about the imposition of penalty. Chapter V Section 20(1)[20] mentions that if the SIC fee that without any reasonable cause if the PAs refuse to receive an application for information or has not furnished information within the time specified under sub Section (1) of Section 7

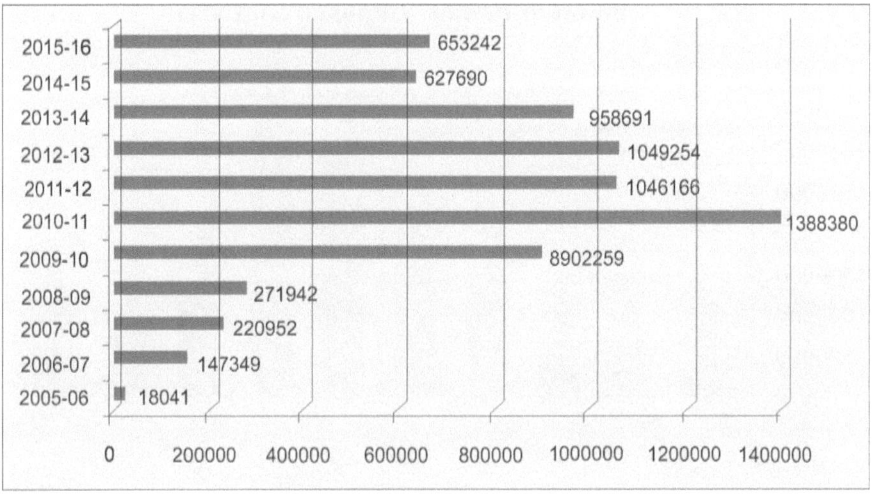

Figure 5.8 Collection of Application Fees and Cost of Information (Amount in Rupees) during (2005–2006 to 2015–2016). *Source*: The data are collected from the Annual Reports of Odisha Information Commission during 2005–2006 to 2015–2016.

Table 5.10 Collection of Application Fees and Cost of Information with Amount of Penalty Imposed during (2005–2006 to 2015–2016)

Years	*No. of Cases Penalty Imposed*	*Penalty Imposed Amount*	*No. of Cases Interim Stay Granted by High Court*	*Interim stay Continuing Amount*
1	2	3	4	5
2006–2007	4	29,750	0	0
2007–2008	46	550,750	7	235,000
2008–2009	66	547,250	6	94,750
2009–2010	89	1,094,750	9	171,000
2010–2011	102	1,518,250	17	339,000
2011–2012	203	3,007,750	12	255,250
2012–2013	229	3,224,999	1	25,000
2013–2014	94	1,026,760	7	135,000
2014–2015	57	766,250	2	35,000
2015–2016	21	444,000	1	25,000

Source: Annual Reports of Odisha Information Commission during 2005–2006 to 2015–2016.

or malafidely denied the request for information or knowingly given incorrect, incomplete or misleading information or destroyed information which was the subject of the request of obstructed in any manner in furnishing the information, it shall impose a penalty of ₹250/- each day till application is received and information is furnished, however, the total amount of penalty

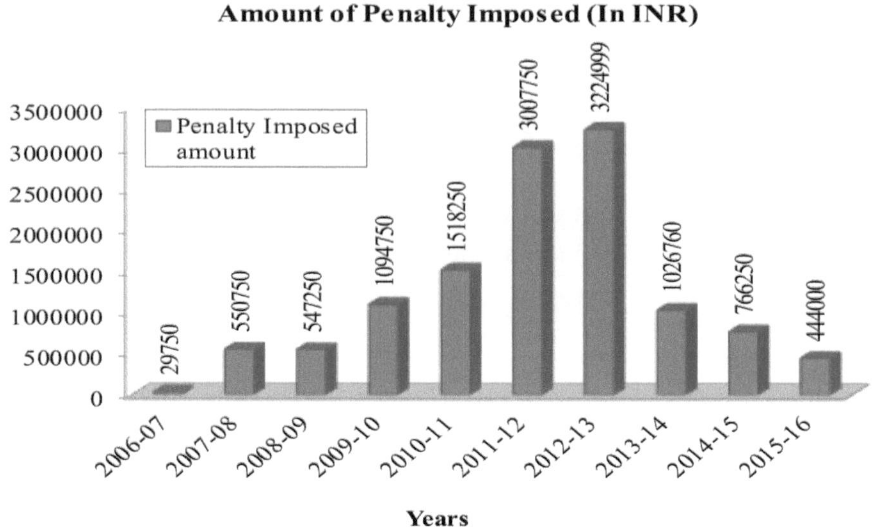

Figure 5.9 Amount of Penalty (in Rupees) Imposed during (2005–2006 to 2015–2016). *Source*: Annual Reports of Odisha Information Commission during 2005–2006 to 2015–2016.

shall not exceed ₹25,000. However, the designated authorities will be given a reasonable opportunity of being heard before any penalty is imposed on him.

With this provision, the study tried to find out the status of disciplinary action taken in different years, penalty imposed, reasons of penalty, appropriateness of the penalty, and changes observed in the functioning of RTI Act after the penalty is imposed. The study findings are analyzed according to public authorities and the qualitative perceptions of the PIOs and Head of Departments are also made.

Disciplinary Action

The data with respect to the disciplinary action taken against the violation of RTI Act was collected in different PAs from the Head of Departments. Head of Departments of 55 PAs were investigated. Not a single case of disciplinary action was reported during the year 2012–2013. In 2013–2014 only two such cases were reported in other PAs. In 2014–2015 similarly one case was reported in secretariat department and one case in other PAs, while in 2015–2016 one case each was reported in Secretariat Department and Heads of the Department. The Head of Departments viewed that disciplinary actions have been taken only in case of the deviants of the RTI Act, since it is the duty of the Head of Departments to ensure good environment for the implementation of the RTI Act in the PA. The details of the distribution of disciplinary cases taken in different PAs in different years are given in table 5.11.[21]

Imposition of Penalty by State Information Commission

The study attempted to find out the total number of cases imposed with penalty in different PAs. The data indicates that (table 5.12)[22] during 2012–2013 not a single case was penalized. In 2013–2014 only one case was reported penalized in other category of PA. In 2014–2015, 2 (40.00%) in Secretariat Departments, 1(20.00%) case in Heads of the Departments, and 2 (40.00%) cases in other PAs were reported. Thus, during the year five number of cases were penalized. In the year 2015–2016 the study reported that seven penalized cases of which four (57.14%) were reported in Secretariat Departments, two (28.57%) were reported in Heads of the Departments and one (14.28%) was reported in other PAs. Thus, in all the four years since the beginning of the RTI Act in Orissa the study shows that of the total 13 penalized cases, 4 (46.15%) were reported in Secretariat Departments, 3 (23.07%) were reported in Heads of the Departments, and 4 (30.76%) penalized cases were reported in other public authorities.

Major Reasons for Penalty Imposed by SIC

The reasons for the penalty imposed by SIC were also explored. The PIOs have given multiple reasons for the penalty out of the four penalized cases in Secretariat Departments—the reasons reported were delay in response (75.00%), shortage of staff (100%), and burden of work (50.00%). Of the three cases reported in Heads of the Departments delayed response is the major reason and difficulty in locating the files (66.66%) is the reason for the penalty. In other PAs out of four reported penalty cases non-supply of information in time and difficulty in locating files are the major reasons for the imposition of penalty. The details are given in table 5.13. The PIOs by and large strongly justified saying that in order to implement the RTI Act the state has to provide necessary conditions for employees to work. With shortage of work hands in each department and poor record management, it is difficult to provide information as demanded. The SIC is to also put pressure on the government to fulfill the logistic requirements in the government departments.

Appropriateness of Penalty by SIC

All the PIOs covered in different PAs were asked about the appropriateness of the penalty provision and imposition by SIC. In Secretariat

Table 5.11 Distribution of Cases of Disciplinary Action taken by Year for Deviation of RTI Act

Sl. No.	*Categories of PAs*	*Total no of PAs*	*No of Cases imposed disciplinary action*			
			2012–2013	*2013–2014*	*2014–2015*	*2015–2016*
1.	Secretariat Department	20	0	0	1	1
2.	Heads of the Department	18	0	0	0	1
3.	Other PAs	17	0	2	1	0
	Total	55	0	2	2	2

Source: Primary Survey, 2019 (figures in the bracket are percent of the total).

Table 5.12 Distribution of Cases Imposed with Penalty by SIC in Different Years

		No of Cases Penalized			
Sl. No.	*Years*	*Secretariat Departments (N-32)*	*Heads of the Departments (N-26)*	*Other PAs (N-62)*	*Total (N-13)*
1.	2012–2013	0	0	0	0
2.	2013–2014	0	0	1(100)	1(100)
3.	2014–2015	2(40.00)	1(20.00)	2(40.00)	5(100)
4.	2015–2016	4(57.14)	2(23.57)	1(14.28)	7(100)
	Total	6(46.15)	3(23.07)	4(30.86)	13(100)

Source: Primary Survey, 2019 (figures in the bracket are percent of the total).

Table 5.13 Distribution of Major Reasons for the Penalty Imposed by SIC

Sl. No.	*PAs/Reason*	*Responses in Number*	*In%*
A.	**Secretariat Department**	**4**	**100**
1.	Delay in response	3	75.00
2.	Complaint against the shortage of staff	4	100
3.	Due to heavy burden of work	2	50.00
B.	**Heads of the Department**	**3**	**100**
1.	Delay	3	100
2.	Difficult in locating files	3	66.66
C.	**Other PAs**	**4**	**100**
1.	Delay in response	3	75.00
2.	Non-supply of information in time	4	100
3.	Difficult in locating files	4	100

Source: Primary Survey, 2019 (figures in the bracket are percent of the total).

Departments out of 32 PIOs, only 15.63% agreed saying it as appropriate while 75 per cent did not give any view in this regard. In Heads of the Departments, similarly 23.08 per cent said it as appropriate while 19.23 per cent did not agree and 57.69 per cent did not give any view on it. Among the PIOs of other PAs, similarly, 11.29 per cent did not agree regarding the appropriateness while 24.19 per cent viewed that penalty is appropriate. Around 26.67 per cent agreed to the appropriateness of the penalty, 65.83 per cent did not give any view. The details of the responses are given in table 5.14.

Table 5.14 Responses of the PIOs on the Appropriateness of Penalty by SIC on PAs

Sl. No.	*PA category*	*Total PIO*	*Appropriateness of penalty*		
			Yes	*No*	*Can't say*
1.	Secretariat Department	32(100)	5(15.63)	3(9.38)	24(75.00)
2.	Heads of the Department	26(100)	6(23.08)	5(19.23)	15(57.69)
3.	Other PAs	62(100)	15(24.19)	7(11.29)	40(64.52)
	Total	120(100)	26(21.67)	15(12.50)	79(65.83)

Source: Primary Survey, 2019 (figures in the bracket are percent of the total).

The following common reasons were raised by the PIOs in all the PAs. They are as follows:

- The logistic support in PAs is to be strengthened. For example, the non-recruitment of different positions along with the increase of work pressure many times put pressure on the PIOs, and as a result they are unable to meet the timely requirement of the RTI Act.
- Since the RTI Act has a time binding with the provision of penalty, it should also provide some incentives to the RTI-designated persons.
- The record management systems of the PAs are to be developed. Infrastructure availability for proper record management is important. Special allotment is also required for the purpose.
- Many RTI-designated personnel do not know about the provisions of the Act. They have been designated to play the role but they have not been trained properly. Though four years have passed since the implementation of the RTI Act, state is yet to provide RTI-related training to all the designated RTI personnel.

Changes in RTI Functioning due to Penalty

In order to assess the changes in the functioning of RTI Act following the system of penalty, qualitative responses were collected from all the PIOs. The objective was to see whether penalty imposed by SIC on different designated RTI officials has any impact in bringing about changes in the quality of functioning of RTI Act in Orissa. Responses analyzed at three different levels of public authorities indicate that at Secretariat Departments five different types of responses were summarized. The awareness of RTI officials has increased (65.62%), followed by a decrease in ignorance of the government functionaries to the public (62.50%), adhering by the designated RTI personnel to the timeline of RTI Act (59.37%), psychological fear of the citizens has decreased (59.37%), and a lot of streamlining of information system (53.12%) has taken place.

The PIOs of Heads of the Departments were asked to provide their view on the probable changes they observe in RTI implementation due to penalty. More responses are observed in the increase of public access to government functioning (69.23%), followed by adherence to timeline by RTI officials (69.23%), decrease in the monopoly of the officials (61.53%), and so on.

The PIOs of other PAs also responded to the question seeking changes in the governance due to the imposition of penalty. They have pointed out a few qualitative processes which they feel have brought about changes in RTI functioning. They are improved governance (45.16%), increased sense of psychological fear in public authorities (59.37%), punctuality developed in the supply of RTI information, and so on. The details of responses of PIOs in different PAs are given in table 5.15.

Table 5.15[23] highlights the responses of PIOs analyzed at three different levels of public authorities indicating that at Secretariat Departments five

Table 5.15 Responses of the PIOs on the Changes Observed in the RTI Functioning after the Penalty Imposed on a Few PAs

Sl. No.	*Charges observed*	*Frequency*	*In %*
A.	**Secretariat Departments**	32	100
1.	Awareness Increased on RTI	21	0.03
2.	RTI personnel maintain Time line of RTI Act	19	0.03
3.	Information Supply system stream lined	17	0.03
4.	Ignorance to public decreased by Govt. officials	20	62.50
5.	Psycho-fear of people decreased to access PAs	19	59.37
B.	**Heads of the Departments**	**26**	**100**
1.	Government officials become alert	13	50.00
2.	Adhered to time line of RTI Act	18	69.23
3.	Maintenance of transparency in the governance	14	53.84
4.	Public access has increased to PAs	18	69.25
5.	Monopoly of bureaucrats has decreased	16	61.53
C.	**Other Public Authorities**	**62**	**100**
1.	Improved in grievances redressal	28	45.16
2.	Maintenance of transparency increased in the Governement	30	48.38
3.	Punctuality developed in supplying RTI	27	43.54
4.	Improvement in Record Management	19	30.64
5.	People's access into government has increased	26	41.93
6.	A sense of fear to the public has developed	29	46.77

Source: Primary Survey, 2019.

Table 5.16 Implementation of RTI by Various Public Authorities—2009–2010

		No. of application received up to March 31, 2010		*Total*	*Total No. of Requests disposed of*			*Appeals made before 1st Appellate Authority*		*Charges Collected under this Act*			
Sl. No	*Name of the Department/Public Authority*	*By PIO/ APIO*	*By Secretariat Information Cell (In Case of a Govt. Department Only*	*3+4*	*No. of Applicants Provided with Information*	*No of applicants Denied Access to Information*	*Total disposal 6+7*	*No. of Appeals Received*	*No. of Appeals Disposed of*	*Cash (₹)*	*Treasurey Challan (₹)*	*Court Fee (₹/ (I-P.O/ M.O./ D. D. etc.*	*Total*
1	2	3	4	5	6	7	8	9	10	11	12	13	14
1	Tourism Culture (Tourism)	2	37	39	26	13	39			240/-	40/-		280/-
2	Health and Family Welfare		424	424	303	14	317	30	30	240/-	660/-		900/-
3	Higher Education	1,436	260	1,696	1,584	111	1,695	145	145	37,825/-	4,530/-	2,035/-	44,390
4	Home	2,092	836	2,928	2,233	681	2,914	152	148	29,047/-	10,257/-	6,388/-	45,692/-
5	Industries	691	200	891	756	89	845	46	49	13,556/-	1,697/-	800/-	16,053/-
6	Labor and Employment	279	102	381	332	45	377	21	21	3,284/-	2,002/-	340/-	5,626/-
7	Planning and Coordination	111	138	249	212	24	236	12	10	3,082/-	90/-	220/-	3,392/-
8	Law	440	183	623	483	71	554	25	25	4,540/-	4,301/-	540/-	5,510-
9	Parliamentary Affairs	115	30	145	47	98	145	13	13	1,025/-	310/-	160/-	1,495/-
10	Works	677	785	1,462	1,261	83	1,344	36	31	41,179/-	2,287/-	320/-	43,786/-
11	Excise	405	52	457	417	14	431	1	1	9,152/-	2,598/-	95/-	11,845/-
12	Panchayati Raj	911	425	1,336	1,072	114	1,186	51	26	21,111/-	1,561/-	265/-	22,937/-

13	Agriculture	598	361	959	911	15	926	28	26	39,002/-	1,470/-	510/-	40,982/-
14	School and Mass Education	1,416	542	1,958	1,698	157	1,855	116	100	30,017/-	4,258/-	2,074/-	36,349/-
15	Housing and Urban Development	2,697	453	3,150	2,813	214	3,027	200	187/-	98,066/-	5,095/-	2,538/-	105,699/-
16	Sports and Youth Services	11	22	33	33		33	–	–	170/-	40	40	250/-
17	Co-operation	111	88	199	199	79	183	14	14	5,917/-	1,057/-	204/-	7,178/-
18	Public Enterprises	2	21	23	23	14	23	–	–	52/-	–	–	52/-
19	Textiles and Handloom	41	55	96	96	14	96	6	6	1,277/-	190/-	80/-	1,547/-
20	Commerce and Transport (Commerce)	54	79	133	133	18	128	7	7	3,088/-	260/-	140/-	3,488/-
21	Water Resources	748	436	1,184	1,184	199	1,124	84	62	26,684/-	2,844/-	1,300/-	30,828/-
22	Energy	160	73	233	233	27	226	22	21	9,589/-	170/-	280/-	10,039//-
23	W and CD	683	208	891	891	21	878	11	11	5,350/-	1,110/-	200	6,660
24	PG and PA	68	24	92	92	10	92	6	5	48/-	185/-	60/-	293/-
25	Finance	320	56	376	376	34	376	35	27	4882/-	220/-	640/-	5,742/-
26	It	36	–	36	36	11	36	–	-	325/-	70	–	395
27	Science and Tech.	20	22	42	42	–	33	11	-	318/-	30/-	–	348/-
28	Fisheries and ARD	78	102	180	180	4	176	14	12	4,339/-	310/-	260/-	4,909/-
29	RD	834	328	1,162	1,162	98	993	69	62	50,417/-	2,765/-	1,030/-	54,212/-
30	Forest and Environment	1,573	579	2,152	2,152	206	1,999	99	99	75,444/-	11,542/-	1,190/-	88,176/-
31	Orissa Legislative Assembly	57	–	57	57	13	57	9	9	766/-	395/-	140/-	1301/-
32	Police Comrnisionarate	230	54	284	284	46	274	23	23	2,596/-	1,040/-	405/-	4,041/-

(Continued)

Table 5.16 Continued

Sl. No	Name of the Department/Public Authority	No. of application received up to March 31, 2010		Total	Total No. of Requests disposed of			Appeals made before 1st Appellate Authority		Charges Collected under this Act			
		By PIO/ APIO	By Secretariat Information Cell (In Case of a Govt. Department Only	3+4	No. of Applicants Provided with Information	No of applicants Denied Access to Information	Total disposal 6+7	No. of Appeals Received	No. of Appeals Disposed of	Cash (₹)	Treasurey Challan (₹)	Court Fee (₹/ (I-P.O/ M.O./ D. D. etc.	Total
33	Governors Secretariat	97	–	97	97	–	97	11	11	2,198/-	390/-	220/-	2,808/-
34	I and PR	62	90	152	152	3	152	12	12	3,540/-	160/-	-	3,700/-
35	Revenue and Disaster Management	15,139	1,336	16,475	16,475	1,223	15,680	434	342	215,738/-	29,057/-	7,251/-	252,046/-
36	Food Supply and Consumer Welfare	61	39	100	100	1	100	7	7	2,307/-	100/-	140/-	2,547/-
37	Steel and Mines	85	76	161	161	–	161	17	17	1,442/-	–	–	1,442
38	General Administration	430	750	1180	1,180	372	1,183	129	129	20,322/-	1,838/-	2,493/-	24,653/-

Source: Information and Public Relation Department (Nodal Department for Monitoring RTI), Government of Odisha.

Table 5.17 Implementation of RTI by Various Public Authorities—2010–2011

		No. of Applications March 31, 2011			*No. of Requests disposed of*			*Appeal made before FAA*		*Charges Collected under this Act*			
Sl. No.	*Name of the Department/ Organization*	*By PIO/ API*	*Sectt. Cell*	*Total (3+4)*	*Pro vided inform ation*	*Denied Inform ation*	*Total Dis posed (6+7)*	*No. of Appeals Received*	*No. of Appeals Disposed*	*Cash /Mo*	*Try. Cha llan*	*Court fee*	*Total (in ₹)*
1	2	3	4	5	6	7	8	9	10	11	12	13	14
1	Agriculture	973	436	1,409	1,340	45	1,385	18	17	29,802	1,666	490	31,958
2	Comm. and Transport	22	33	55	43	12	55	6	6	1,152	0	120	1,272
3	Co-operation	334	88	422	298	93	391	33	32	7,379	1,780	380	9,539
4	Energy	210	89	299	268	31	299	15	15	3,957	290	160	4,407
5	Excise	38	43	81	78	3	81	3	3	4,222	90	60	4,372
6	Fisheries and ARD	100	200	300	289	7	296	14	13	5,420	330	260	6,010
7	Finance	177	236	413	399	14	413	18	12	8,564	1,130	360	10,054
8	Forest and Env.	1,349	598	1,947	1,508	263	1,771	81	70	44,570	9,438	895	54,907
9	FS and CW	891	412	1,303	1,095	194	1,289	59	54	7,827	2,442	480	10,749
10	Gen. Administration	1,315	740	2,058	1,496	562	2,058	184	184	28,818	1,902	3,460	34,180
11	Governor's Sect.	130	0	130	130	0	130	9	9	3,580	300	180	4,060
12	H and FW	389	793	1,182	1,091	43	1,134	75	75	8,254	1,297	580	10,131
13	H and UD	1,146	261	1,408	1,226	235	1,461	107	97	23,638	2,484	1,405	27,525
14	High Court	237	28	265	112	152	264	10	8	770	810	5,492	222
15	Higher Education	1,117	320	3,637	3,490	147	3,637	290	254	7,3500	5,350	3,500	82,350

(Continued)

Table 5.17 Continued

Sl. No.	Name of the Department/ Organization	No. of Applications March 31, 2011			No. of Requests disposed of			Appeal made before FAA		Charges Collected under this Act			
		By PIO/ API	Sectt. Cell	Total (3+4)	Pro vided inform ation	Denied Inform ation	Total Dis posed (6+7)	No. of Appeals Received	No. of Appeals Disposed	Cash /Mo	Try. Cha llan	Court fee	Total (in ₹)
16	Home	3,348	936	4,284	3,309	956	4,265	378	373	47,827	13,536	14,566	75,929
17	I and PR	95	73	168	163	5	168	9	9	2,737	70	10	2,817
18	Industries	1,155	205	1,360	1,137	208	1,345	63	64	21,869	1,790	1,145	24,804
19	IT	22	19	41	41	0	41	0	0	703	170	20	893
20	Labor and Employment	162	88	250	213	37	250	5	5	6,781	2,137	80	8,998
21	Law	542	123	665	519	48	630	54	54	6,237	630	1,090	7,957
22	OIC	432	0	432	180	40	432	17	17	670	290	260	1,220
23	OLA	83	0	83	68	15	83	3	3	11,810	293	110	12,213
24	Panchayati Raj	1,415	649	2,064	1,484	257	1,741	69	64	723,977	2,146	723	726,846
25	Parliamentary Affairs	139	62	201	57	144	201	15	15	730	330	240	1,300
26	PG and Pension Admn.	114	27	141	113	28	141	9	9	755	140	180	1,075
27	Planning and Coordination	162	198	360	306	48	350	2	2	5,647	360	60	6,067
28	Public Enterprises	32	54	76	76	0	76	4	4	920	0	0	920
29	Revenue and DM	595	0	595	552	11	536	32	28	14,360	0	0	14,360
30	Rural Development	841	897	1,738	1,376	183	1,559	42	41	32,453	2,837	560	35,850
31	Science and Technology	78	10	88	83	5	88	7	7	346	70	100	516

32	School and Mass Edn.	5,279	538	3,117	2,761	232	2,993	269	263	48,889	9,461	2,340	60,690
33	Sports and Youth	42	23	65	65	0	65	0	0	370	30	40	440
34	ST and SC Dev.	626		262	262		262	NA	NA				4,999
35	Steel and Mines	0	174	174	169	0	169	8	8	551	0	0	5,511
36	Taxtiles and Handloom	42	38	80	68	12	80	1	1	1,704	60	0	1,764
37	Tourism and Culture	237	24	261	240	21	261	3	3	709	220	60	989
38	W and CD	1,749	244	1,993	1,719	50	1,967	44	41	20,000	5,000	680	25,680
39	Water Resources	995	161	1,156	870	203	1,073	76	67	24,208	3,180	1,000	28,388
40	Works	624	462	1,086	984	48	1,032	44	44	41,140	2,718	560	44,418

Source: Information and Public Relation Department (Nodal Department for Monitoring RTI), Government of Odisha.

different types of responses were summarized. They are awareness of RTI officials has increased (65.62%), followed by a decrease in ignorance of the government functionaries to public (62.50%), adhering by the designated RTI personnel to timeline of RTI Act (59.37%), psychological fear of the citizens has decreased (59.37%), and a lot of streamlining of information system (53.12%) has taken place. The implementations of RTI by the 40 departments of Odisha Secretariat which reflect the status of number of application received and disposed by the PIOs and APIOs during 2009–2010 and 2010–2011.

Table 5.16[24] reflects the implementation of RTI by the Secretariat Departments during 2009–2010. The number of applications received up to March 31, 2010. The Revenue and Disaster Management Department received 16,435 RTI applications by the PIO and APIO which was the highest. The department like public enterprise receives only 23 RTI applications. The statistical figure indicates that the grievance redressal of the employees of Odisha Secretariat is more required in the Revenue and Disaster Management Department. The Revenue and Disaster Management Department received 1,336 RTI applications up to March 31, 2010, by PIO/APIO Secretariat Information Cell. In comparison, the Public Enterprise Department received only 21 RTI applications by PIO/APIO Secretariat Information Cell which was the lowest. The Housing and Urban Development disposes 2,813 RTI applications with information which was highest among the secretariat department and only 9 applications by the Public Enterprise Department which was the lowest. The following trend indicates the grievance redressal of the employees (RTI applicants) in the different departments of the Odisha Secretariat. The Housing and Urban Development received 200 FAs which highest among the Secretariat Departments. The departments like sports and youth services, public enterprise, and information technology did not receive single FAs during 2009–2010.

The grievance redressal of the employees of the Odisha Secretariat is better to explain with the help of the table 5.17.

Table 5.17[25] highlights the implementation of RTI by the Secretariat Departments during 2010–2011. The School and Mass Education Department received 5,279 RTI applications by the PIO and APIO which was the highest. The department like steel and mines don't receive any RTI applications during 2011. The statistical figure indicates the grievance redressal of the employees of Odisha Secretariat is more required in the School and Mass Education Department. The highest number of applications received by Home Department was 936 by PIO/APIO Secretariat Information Cell. In comparison, the Revenue and Disaster Management Department did not receive single RTI application by PIO/APIO Secretariat Information Cell which was the lowest during the year 2011. In total the Home department receives 4,284 RTI

Table 5.18 Department-Wise Disposal of Applications (Reporting Period from April 1, 2014 to March 31, 2015)

Sl. No.	*Name of the Public Authority*	*Opening balance of requests received under RTI (as on 1st April)*	*No. of requests received during year*	*Total no. of requests (3+4)*	*No. of requests on which information provided*	*No. of requests transferred to other public authorities*	*Decisions where applications for information rejected*	*Total Disposal (6+7+8)*	*% disposal of application*
1	Agriculture	270	1,287	1,557	1,066	430	61	1,557	100.00
2	Commerce and Transport (Commerce)	0	37	37	24	2	11	37	100.00
3	Co-operation	10	239	249	150	81	18	249	100.00
4	Culture	25	370	395	211	106	10	327	82.78
5	Employment and TE and T	0	132	132	58	70	4	132	100.00
6	Energy	78	1,166	1,244	935	309	32	1,276	100.00
7	Excise	2	630	632	463	35	134	632	100.00
8	Finance	40	1,252	1,292	1,090	105	97	1,292	100.00
9	Fisheries and ARD	41	496	537	431	65	41	537	100.00
10	Food Supplies and Consumers Welfare	76	966	1,042	624	295	109	1,028	98.66
11	Forest and Environment	0	194	194	166	28	0	194	100.00
12	General Administration	0	1,209	1,209	829	367	13	1,209	100.00

(*Continued*)

Table 5.18 Continued

Sl. No.	*Name of the Public Authority*	*Opening balance of requests received under RTI (as on 1st April)*	*No. of requests received during year*	*Total no. of requests (3+4)*	*No. of requests on which information provided*	*No. of requests transferred to other public authorities*	*Decisions where applications for information rejected*	*Total Disposal (6+7+8)*	*% disposal of application*
13	Handlooms, Textiles and handicrafts	2	187	189	120	29	31	180	95.24
14	Health and Family Welfare	0	557	557	64	456	37	557	100.00
15	Higher Education	0	808	808	777	31	0	808	100.00
16	Home	0	683	683	394	247	42	683	100.00
17	Housing and Urban Development	8	528	536	449	71	9	529	98.69
18	Industries	68	519	587	443	48	42	533	90.80
19	Information and Public Relations	10	512	522	174	262	83	519	99.42
20	Information Technology	145	39	184	181	3	0	184	100.00
21	Labor and ESI	1	211	212	119	45	48	212	100.00
22	LAW	4	425	429	391	26	11	428	99.77
23	MS and ME	65	556	621	424	80	55	559	90.02
24	Panchayati Raj	64	1,497	1,561	682	704	113	1,499	96.03
25	Parliamentary Affairs	0	294	294	105	146	43	294	100.00

26	Planning and Coordination	71	277	348	287	21	19	327	93.97
27	Public Enterprises	0	54	54	25	18	11	54	100.00
28	Public Grievances and Pension and Administration	0	89	89	68	21	0	89	100.00
29	Revenue and Disaster Management	34	461	495	331	145	19	495	100.00
30	Rural Development	941	2,034	2,975	2,069	291	233	2,593	87.16
31	School and Mass Education	1	102	103	25	13	12	50	47.57
32	Science and Technology	52	115	167	109	34	22	165	98.80
33	Sports and Youth Services	32	85	117	98	5	0	103	88.03
34	ST and SC Development	31	322	353	351	1	1	353	100.00
35	Steel and Mines	27	930	957	729	76	130	935	97.70
36	Tourism	0	112	112	108	1	3	112	100.00
37	Transport	6	243	249	187	52	5	244	97.99
38	Water Resources	14	527	541	450	73	18	541	100.00
39	Women and Child Development	1,031	4,131	5,162	3,844	377	311	4,532	87.80
40	Works	494	1,107	1,601	970	352	122	1,444	90.19
	Grand Total	3,643	25,175	28,818	20,021	5,523	1,949	27,493	95.41

Source: Odisha Information Commission and Secretariat Information Cell.

applications in the form of FAs and SAs which was highest during 2011. That reflects more grievance redressal of employees required in Home Department. In total Information Technology department receives only 41 RTI applications which lowest in 2011. The higher education department disposed 3,490 RTI applications request provided with information which was highest in 2011. It highlights higher education department redressed more grievances of the employees of the Odisha Secretariat. The IT department disposed 41 RTI applications request provided with information which was lowest during 2011. The Home department also denied giving information to 956 RTI applications. It's one of the major problems in the grievance redressal of the employees of the Odisha Secretariat. In total the highest number of RTI request disposed by Home department which was 4,265 and only 41 by IT department which was lowest during 2011. The departments like information technology, public enterprise, and steel and mines had not denied single RTI request. The grievance redressal of the employees of Odisha Secretariat is based on the RTI request provided with information to the employees of the entire Secretariat Departments.

Table 5.18 reflects the status of the department-wise disposal of RTI applications. It highlights a total number of request received by various departments of the Odisha Secretariat during 2014–2015. It's a good basis for the comparative analysis of the grievance redressal of thee employees of the Odisha Secretariat. The table also provides overall picture of the number of request provided with information and number of RTI rejection applications with percentage.

Table 5.18[26] highlights the department-wise disposal status of RTI applications during 2014–2015. The Women and Child Development Department opening balance cases during the year 2014–2015 was the highest which was 1,031. It indicates that the grievance redressal of the employees of Odisha Secretariat was comparatively less in the Women and Child Development Department. The highest number of RTI applications received by the Women and Child Development Department which was 5,162 during 2014–2015. Commerce and Transport department received only 37 RTI applications which lowest during the year 2014–2015. In total the highest number of RTI cases received by Women and Child Development Department 5,162 and Commerce and Transport Department received only 37 RTI applications which was lowest during the year 2014–2015. The Women and Child Development Department provided 3,844 RTI cases with information which was highest, and only 24 applications provided with information by the commerce and transport department which was lowest during 2014–2015. It highlights the overall grievance redressal procedure of the employees of Odisha Secretariat. The 704 RTI request transfer to other public authorities out of 1,561 RTI cases by the Panchayati Raj Department which was highest and department like Tourism and SC and ST Departments only 1 request transfer to other public authorities which was lowest during the year 2014–2015. The highest number of application for the information rejected by the women and child development was 311 and the department like forest and environment, higher education, information technology, public grievances and pension administration, sports and youth affairs had not rejected a single application for information during 2014–2015. In total 4,532 applications disposed by the Women and Child Development Department was highest and only 37 applications disposed by the commerce and transport department was lowest during 2014–2015. Finally out of 40 Secretariat Departments, 22 departments disposal rate was 100% and other 18 departments' RTI applications disposal rate was within 80 to 99 percentages. Percentage of disposal was lowest in culture department that is 82.78. The percentage figure indicates the lowest grievance redressed by culture department during 2014–2015.

Table 5.19[27] highlights the implementation of RTI by various public authorities 2014–2015 (reporting period from April 1, 2014, to March 31, 2015).The highest number of PIOs appointed by the water resource department was 761 out of the total PIOs appointed by the secretariat department that is 2,425. The opening balance cases are highest in the Women and Child Development Department that is 1,031 out of the total 3,643 opening balance cases during 2014–2015. The trend indicates that the grievance redressal procedure in the Women and Child Development Department was very slow. The Women and Child Development Department received 4,131 opening balance request out of the total RTI opening balance request 25,172 during 2014–2015. The total number of RTI request was highest in the Women and Child Development Department was 5,162 out of the total request of 28,815. This statistical figure indicates that the grievance redressal was more required in the Women and Child Development Department. The Women and Child Development Department provided 3,844 request with information that was highest in the secretariat department. Only 25 RTI request provided with information by the commerce and transport department during 2014–2015 was lowest. The total number of request provided with information by all the department of Odisha Secretariat 20,021. The total number of RTI request transfer to other public authorities was highest in the Panchayati Raj that is 704 and lowest in the commerce and transport department that is 02. The total RTI request transfer to other public authorities in the entire secretariat department was 5,523 during 2014–2015. The decision where application for information rejected was highest in the Women and Child Development Department that is 311. The departments like forest and environment, higher education,

Table 5.19 Implementation of RTI by Various Public Authorities 2014–2015 (Reporting Period from April 1, 2014 to March 31, 2015)

Sl. No.	*Name of the Department/ Organization*	*No of PIOs Appointed*	*Opening Balance of Requests Received under RTI (as on April1)*	*No. of Requests Received during Year*	*Total no. of Requests (Column 4+5)*	*No. of Requests on which Information Provided*	*No. of Requests Transferred to Other Public Authorities*	*Decisions Where Applications for Information Rejected*	*Opening Balance of First Appeals Received under RTI (as on April1)*	*No. of First Appeals Received during Year*	*No. of Appeals Disposed Off*	*No. of eases where disciplinary action taken against any officer in request of administration of RTI Act*	*Disclosure made u/s 4(1)(b) of the Act*	*Total amount (fee+ addl. Charges+ penalty) (in ₹)*
1	2	3	4	5	6	7	8	9	10	11	12	13	14	15
1	Agriculture	112	270	1,287	1,557	1,066	432	61	22	113	135	0	Yes	47,272
2	Commerce and Transport (Commerce)	33	10	239	249	150	81	18	1	16	17	0	Yes	6,507
3	Co-operation	1	0	37	37	24	2	11	0	1	1	0	Yes	515
4	Culture	55	25	370	395	211	106	10	7	22	29	0	Yes	3,166
5	Employment and TE and T	1	0	132	132	58	70	4	0	3	3	0	Yes	2,630
6	Energy	106	78	1,166	1,244	935	309	32	17	120	133	0	Yes	18,684
7	Excise	28	2	630	632	463	35	134	0	8	8	0	Yes	14,868
8	Finance	127	40	1,252	1,292	1,090	105	97	0	80	78	0	Yes	24,317
9	Fisheries and ARD	136	41	496	537	431	65	41	2	54	54	0	Yes	7,752
10	Food Supplies and Consumers Welfare	60	76	966	1,042	624	295	109	9	56	64	0	Yes	13,947

11	Forest and Environment	21	0	194	194	166	28	0	3	17	15	8	Yes	8,390
12	General Administration	9	0	1,209	1,209	829	367	13	0	167	167	0	Yes	20,047
13	Handlooms, Textiles and handicrafts	45	2	187	189	120	29	31	4	35	25	0	Yes	2,084
14	Health and Family 3Welfare	29	0	557	557	64	456	37	0	82	82	0	Yes	2,771
15	Higher Education	3	0	808	808	777	31	0	0	130	130	0	Yes	6,162
16	Home	2	0	683	683	394	247	42	0	51	51	0	Yes	6,171
17	Housing and Urban Development	9	8	528	536	449	71	9	0	13	10	0	Yes	5,548
18	Industries	10	68	519	587	443	48	42	1	42	43	0	Yes	17,285
19	Information and Public Relations	18	10	512	522	174	262	83	1	14	15	0	Yes	5,157
20	Information Technology	2	145	39	184	181	3	0	1	4	5	0	Yes	13,228
21	Labor and ESI	1	1	211	212	119	45	48	18	0	8	8	Yes	0
22	LAW	14	4	425	429	391	26	11	3	26	28	0	Yes	8,743
23	MS and ME	65	65	556	621	424	80	55	3	28	28	0	Yes	16,089
24	Panchayati Raj	64	64	1,497	1,561	682	704	113	7	56	56	0	Yes	24,882
25	Parliamentary Affairs	1	0	294	294	105	146	43	0	17	17	0	Yes	2,579
26	Planning and Coordination	31	71	277	348	287	21	19	0	12	11	0	Yes	10,075
27	Public Enterprises	1	0	54	54	25	18	11	0	0	0	0	Yes	186
28	Public Grievances and	1	0	89	89	68	21	0	0	7	7	0	Yes	330

(Continued)

Table 5.19 Continued

Sl. No.	Name of the Department/ Organization	No of PIOs Appointed	Opening Balance of Requests Received under RTI (as on April1)	No. of Requests Received during Year	Total no. of Requests (Column 4+5)	No. of Requests on which Information Provided	No. of Requests Transferred to Other Public Authorities	Decisions Where Applications for Information Rejected	Opening Balance of First Appeals Received under RTI (as on April1)	No. of First Appeals Received during Year	No. of Appeals Disposed Off	No. of eases where disciplinary action taken against any officer in request of administration of RTI Act	Disclosure made u/s 4(1)(b) of the Act	Total amount (fee+ addl. Charges+ penalty) (in ₹)
	Pension and Administration													
29	Revenue and Disaster Management	1	34	461	495	331	145	19	3	19	16	0	Yes	24643
30	Rural Development	136	941	2,034	2,975	2,069	291	233	21	184	122	0	Yes	68114
31	School and Mass Education	6	1	102	103	25	13	11	0	4	4	0	Yes	1884
32	Science and Technology	7	52	115	167	109	34	22	5	9	11	0	Yes	1710
33	Sports and Youth Services	16	32	85	117	98	5	0	2	15	15	0	Yes	968
34	ST and SC Development	23	31	322	353	351	1	1	0	9	9	0	Yes	3460
35	Steel and Mines	30	27	930	957	729	76	130	3	75	78	0	Yes	34814

36	Tourism	27	0	112	112	108	1	3	0	0	0	1	Yes	2152
37	Transport	27	6	243	249	187	52	5	0	13	11	0	Yes	3283
38	Water Resources	761	14	527	541	450	73	18	0	12	12	0	Yes	12771
39	Women and Child Development	353	1,031	4,131	5,162	3,844	377	311	40	214	199	0	Yes	108679
40	Works	63	494	1,107	1,601	970	352	122	5	77	81	0	Yes	75649
	Grand Total	2,425	3,643	25,172	28,815	20,021	5,523	1,949	181	1,805	1,778	17	Yes	627690

Source: Odisha Information Commission and Secretariat Information Cell.

information technology, public grievances and pension administration, and sports and youth services had not rejected single RTI request during 2014–2015. The entire Secretariat Departments rejected 1,949 RTI request for the information during 2014–2015. Out of the total 1,805 RTI FA cases received by the entire Secretariat Departments, the Women and Child Development Department received 214 applications and disposed 199 applications which highest during the year 2014–2015. The above trends indicate the grievance redressal of the employees of the Odisha Secretariat is comparatively slow so more and more PIOs and APIOs are necessary to bring transformation in the Odisha Secretariat grievance redressal system. To better analysis of grievance redressal of employees of Odisha Secretariat, it is important to know the trends of registration of public authorities.

Trends in Registration and Return Submission of Public Authorities

Table 5.20 and figure 5.10 give the trend of registration of public authorities during the last 13 years. The number of public authorities undergo change for various reasons, namely, creation/identification/deletion of public authorities, directions of the Commission or superior courts, and so on.

As per Section 25 of the RTI Act, there is a legal requirement for the public authorities to submit Annual Returns to the Commission. Due to efforts made

Table 5.20 Number of Public Authorities Registered and Percentage Compliance in Last 13 Years

Sl. No.	*Year*	*Total PAs Registered (No.)*	*PAs who Submitted Returns (No.)*	*PAs Who Did not Submit Returns (No.)*	*Percentage Compliance*
1.	2005–2006	938	837	101	89.23
2.	2006–2007	1,412	1,168	244	82.72
3.	2007–2008	1,597	1,382	215	86.54
4.	2008–2009	1,770	1,528	242	86.33
5.	2009–2010	1,847	1,427	420	77.26
6.	2010–2011	2,149	1,452	697	67.57
7.	2011–2012	2,314	1,593	721	68.84
8.	2012–2013	2,333	1,864	469	79.9
9.	2013–2014	2,276	1,651	625	72.54
10.	2014–2015	2,030	1,528	502	75.27
11.	2015–2016	2,023	1,903	120	94.07
12.	2016–2017	2,092	1,964	128	93.88
13.	2017–2018	2,079	2,079	0	100.00

Source: Central Information Commission Annual Report (2017–2018).

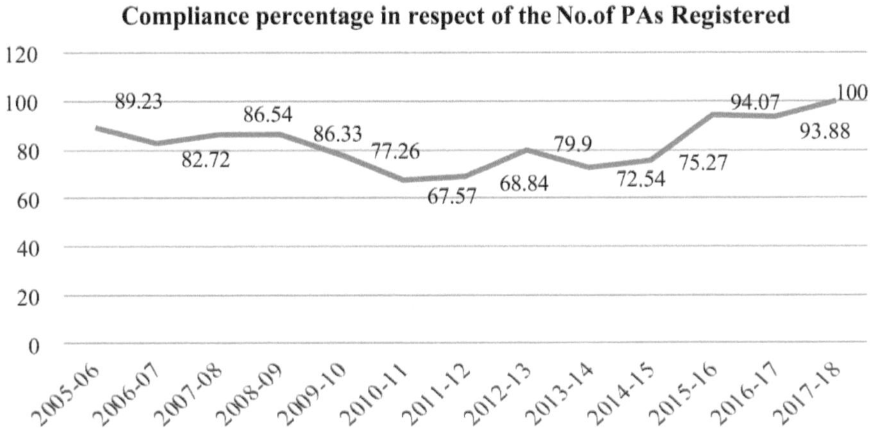

Figure 5.10 Compliance Percentage in respect of the Number of PAs Registered. *Source*: Central Information Commission Annual Report (2017–2018).

by the Commission, 100% of public authorities submitted returns during the reporting year 2017–2018. The graph depicts the performance of the public authorities in respect of their statutory obligation to submit annual returns.

Table 5.20[28] highlighted the number of public authorities registered and percentage compliance in the last 13 years. During the year 2013–2014, the total number of registered public authorities, 2,314 that was highest, and the number of public authorities who submitted returns was highest during the year 2017–2018, that is 2,079. The percentage of compliance was highest during the year 2015–2016, that is 94.07%, and lowest during the year 2010–2011, that is 67.67%. The following trends indicate gradual increase in the public authorities which leads to an increase in the percentage of compliance and grievance redressal of the employees in the different years. The graphical representation of figure 5.10[29] clearly explains the compliance percentage in the last 13 years.

Figure 5.10 clearly explains the compliance percentage in the last 13 years. The following trends reflect that the compliance percentage was gradually increasing after 2015–2016. It indicates that the more grievances from the different sections of the society with regard to the various public authorities. There is a need for a strong redressal mechanism to overcome the compliance percentage and smooth management of the administrative setup.

Table 5.21 supported by figure 5.11 highlights the disposal of RTI applications with percentage by the public authorities from 2005–2016 to 2017–2018.

Table 5.21[30] clearly explains the opening balance RTI request gradually increasing after 2015–2016. It indicates the public authorities are not disposing the RTI cases within the stipulated period so the opening balance cases are highly increasing day by day. At the same time, the number of RTI requests speedily is increasing due to the increasing consciousness among the people.

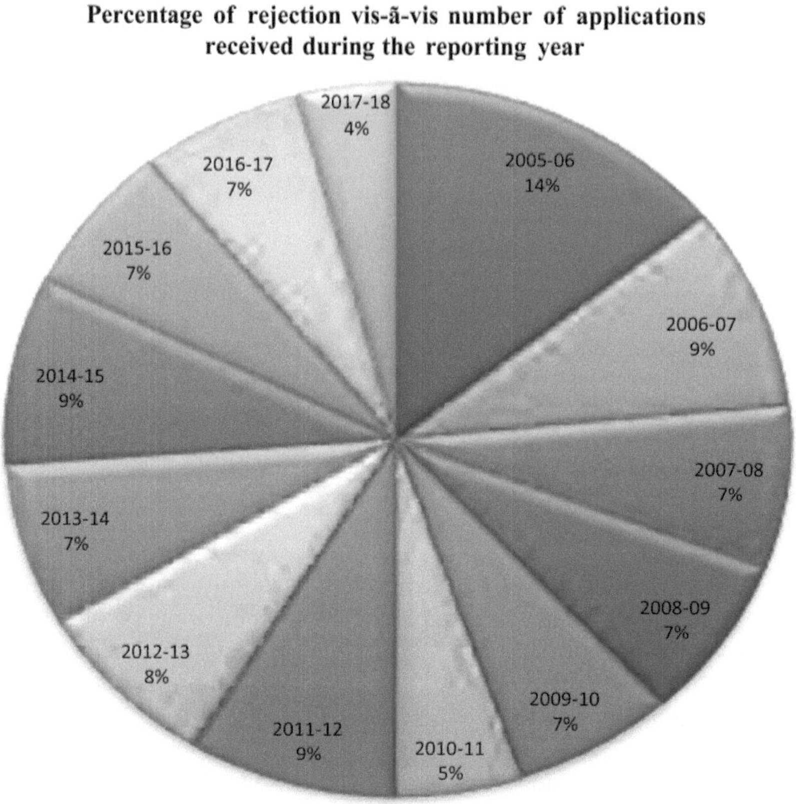

Figure 5.11 Percentage of Rejection vis-à-vis Number of Applications Received during the Reporting Year. *Source*: Central Information Commission Annual Report (2017–2018).

The total number of RTI opening balance request was 1,448,673 during the year 2017–2018. The number of requests rejected for the information was 63,206 during the year 2017–2018. The highest percentage of rejection for the information during the year 2005–2006, that is 13.9 percentages, followed by 8.39 percentage during the year 2014–2015. The table also explains the increasing number of applications and disposal of RTI requests in the different year and status of the opening balance cases are not satisfactory.

Figure 5.11[31] focuses on the percentage of the rejection of applications for the information during the last 13 years.

The percentage of the rejection of applications for the information was highest during 2005–2006, that is 14%, and lowest during 2017–2018, that is 4 percent. The following tends of the rejection of the RTI request for the information is gradually decreasing due to the level of consciousness among the people of the different sections of the society.

Table 5.21 Disposal of RTI Applications by Public Authorities during 2005–2006 to 2017–2018

Sl. No.	*Year / Key Aspects*	*Number of Public Authorities Registered with the Commission*	*Opening Balance of RTI Requests*	*No. Of RTI Requests Received*	*Total Number of RTI Requests = Opening Balance of RTI Request + No. of RTI Requests Received*	*Number of Requests for Information Rejected*	*Percentage of rejection vis-à-vis Number of Applications Received during the Reporting Year*
1.	2005–2006	938	0	24,436	24,436	3,387	13.9
2.	2006–2007	1,412	12,026	171,398	183,424	15,388	9
3.	2007–2008	1,597	23,926	263,261	287,187	18,966	7.20
4.	2008–2009	1,770	32,792	329,728	362,520	32,954	7.26
5.	2009–2010	1,847	97,474	529,274	626,748	34,057	6.43
6.	2010–2011	2,149	137,771	417,955	555,726	21,413	5.1
7.	2011–2012	2,314	76,016	629,960	705,976	52,313	8.3
8.	2012–2013	2,333	75,331	811,350	886,681	62,231	7.70
9.	2013–2014	2,276	128,447	814,183	962,630	60,127	7.21
10.	2014–2015	2,030	89,785	755,247	845,032	63,351	8.39
11.	2015–2016	2,024	188,538	976,679	1,165,217	64,666	6.62
12.	2016–2017	2,092	212,430	915749	112,8179	60,428	6.59
13.	2017–2018	2,079	215,466	123,3207	144,8673	63,206	4

Source: Central Information Commission Annual Report (2017–2018).

CONCLUSION

In spite of all the analysis of the grievance redressal of the employees of Odisha Secretariat the more and more consciousness is required among the employees of the different departments of the Odisha Secretariat. Most of the departments redresses the grievance of the employees and disposes the RTI cases with 100% information. In very few departments, the number of PIOs and APIOs are very less and it's a problem in the grievance redressal procedure of the employees of Odisha Secretariat. RTI applications received increased by 34.67% during the reporting year in comparison to previous year 2016–2017. A decrease of 6.1% was observed in 2016–2017 in comparison to 2015–2016. An increase of 5.48% was observed in 2015–2016 in comparison to 2014–2015 there was a decrease of 9.46% in 2014–2015, whereas an increase of 2.18 % was observed in 2013–2014 in comparison to respective previous years. Thus a fluctuating trend is seen in the receipt of RTI applications during last five years. The RTI plays a crucial role in employees' grievance redressal in the different departments of Odisha Secretariat and maintains transparency and accountability in the administration.

NOTES

1. Julio, Faundz. (1997), *Good Governance and Law: Legal Constitutional Reforms in Developing Country.* Macmillan, London.
2. See Section 29 (1) of the Right to Information Act – 2005 also see Orissa Right to Information Rules, 2005 published by Orissa Information Commission, Government Press, Cuttack.
3. See the Annual Reports of Odisha Information Commission of the different years (2005–2006 to 2015–2016). Also see www.orissasoochanacommission.nic.in.
4. See Annual Reports of the Odisha Information Commission of different years, based on the data submitted 40 by Government Department and other Public Authorities.
5. Odisha Secretariat Information Cell also see record of Information and Public Relation Department, Government of Odisha.
6. The analysis is based on the data submitted by Information and Public Relation Department (Nodal Department) supplied by Public Authorities and Odisha Secretariat Information Cell.
7. See Annual Reports of the Odisha Information Commission of different years from 2005-06 to 2015-16. Also see www.orissasoochanacommission.nic.in.
8. See Annual Reports of the Odisha Information Commission of different years from 2005-06 to 2015-16. Also see www.orissasoochanacommission.nic.in.
9. The analysis is based on the Annual Reports of the Odisha Information Commission in the different year's data supplied by Public Authorities.
10. The analysis is based on the Annual Reports of the Odisha Information Commission in the different years (2005–2006 to 2015–2016) also see the database of Information and Public Relation Department, Government of Odisha.

11. The analysis is based on the secondary data collected from Odisha Information commission also see www.orissasoochanacommission.nic.in.

12. Compilation of data based on the secondary sources and Annual Reports of Orissa Information Commission (2005–2006 to 2015–2016).

13. The analysis is based on the Annual Reports of the Odisha Information Commission in the different years (2005–2006 to 2015–2016) also see the database of Information and Public Relation Department, Government of Odisha.

14. The analysis is based on the Annual Reports of the Odisha Information Commission in the different years (2005–2006 to 2015–2016) also see the database of Information and Public Relation Department, Government of Odisha.

15. See Section 19 (3) of the Right to Information Act – 2005 also see Orissa Right to Information Rules, 2005 published by Orissa Information Commission, Government Press, Cuttack.

16. Compilation of data based on the secondary sources and Annual Reports of Orissa Information Commission during different years (2005–2006 to 2015–2016).

17. Section 21(1) of the Right to Information Act – 2005 also see Orissa Right to Information Rules, 2005 published by Orissa Information Commission, Government Press, Cuttack.

18. Analysis of data based on the secondary sources and Annual Reports of Orissa Information Commission during different years (2005–2006 to 2015–2016).

19. The data collected from the Annual Reports of Orissa Information Commission during different years (2005–2006 to 2015–2016).

20. See Chapter- V, Section 21(1) of the Right to Information Act – 2005 also see Orissa Right to Information Rules, 2005 published by Orissa Information Commission, Government Press, Cuttack.

21. The data collected from Secretariat Departments and Information and Public Relation Department, Government of Odisha (Primary Survey, 2019).

22. The data collected from Secretariat Departments and Information and Public Relation Department, Government of Odisha (Primary Survey, 2019).

23. The data collected from Secretariat Departments and Information and Public Relation Department, Government of Odisha (Primary Survey, 2019).

24. The data received from the different public authorities and Information and Public Relation Department, Government of Odisha.

25. Data collected from Information and Public Relation Department, Government of Odisha also see the Annual Report of the Odisha Information commission, 2010–2011.

26. Data collected from Information and Public Relation Department, Government of Odisha also see the Annual Report of the Odisha Information commission, 2014–2015.

27. Ibid.

28. Data collected from Central Information Commission, Government of India also see the Annual Report of the Central Information Commission, 2017–2018.

29. Ibid.

30. The data analysis is based on the Annual Report of the Central Information Commission, 2017–2018.

31. Ibid.

Conclusion

The study attempted to gather a wide range of information from the PIOs, First Appellate Authority (FAAs), Heads of Departments of PAs, and employees of Odisha Secretariat with respect to the implementation of RTI Act, operational constraints, and grievance redressal of employees of different sections of the Odisha Secretariat. The study tries to identify a certain area for recommendations to strengthen the functioning of RTI in the state and more particularly in Odisha Secretariat. It is the two-way communication between government and citizens. Thereafter, the study of "Right to Information and Grievance Redressal of Employees: A Study of Odisha Secretariat" becomes important for appreciating the process of good governance.

The RTI Act 2005 is one of the monumental accomplishments of our countries' democratic governance in the recent years. The significance of RTI Act and its expanding use to redress the grievances of the employees in the different departments is that the government must take bold step to strengthen the policy making institutions in India.

It is important to analyze whether this Act has been able to actually result in citizen's empowerment by ensuring accountability. While a lot has been said in praise and appreciation of the Act, it is important to examine whether the Act has actually been able to deliver all that it promised. It is a common critique of this Act that it has lead to an additional burden on a bureaucracy which is already crumbling under pressure. Also, this research initiates analysis into the debate of whether the Act leads to an actual redressal of grievances or is it merely an attempt to gather innocuous information which may not have further use; which leads this research into the third most important question, i.e. whether the absence of an inbuilt redressal mechanism defeats the core purpose with which the Act was promulgated.

A quasi judicial system of addressing complaints regarding the denial of information has sprung up from the genesis of this Act. However, it seems that instead of reducing the burden on the judicial system of India, the Act has resulted in increasing the cases related to denial of information from public offices that have reached the courts of law.

MAJOR ISSUES

Delivery of Services

The delivery of services by the RTI-designated persons is influenced by various factors. Financial factor is one among them. PIOs when asked in this respect in Secretariat Departments 62.55% opined that charges collected toward xerox are less than the actual cost. The application submission cost is also very nominal. It is observed that few professionals like journalists, advocates, activists, and so on misuse the Act more in a commercial manner. The information supply to such applications is very much time-consuming. It affects the normal work of the departments. In Heads of the Departments around 62% PIOs were of a similar view. In other public authorities, 79.60% PIOs also equally viewed that time invested for the preparation of information should be charged from the applicants.

Shortage of Staff/Working Hands in PAs.

Shortage of staffs/working hands in PAs is a common complaint by the PIOs. This tunes to 53.50% in Secretariat Departments, 43% in Heads of the Department, and 39% in other public authorities. They viewed that we might be spending a few days on RTI assignments but departmental works are increasing day by day. By and large there is no recruitment in public authorities, which pressurizes the old staffs. Searching the old records within a limited time sometimes become difficult for us. On an average 22–29% FAAs also hold such types of views.

Time Management

PIOs are unable to manage their time distribution while accomplishing RTI demand in time. Around 58% in Heads of the Department, 32% in Secretariat Department, and 49% in other PAs pointed out that the training on RTI Act and specifically on time and work management issues are to be provided.

They are unable to solve the time-management-related problems. Work burden with little knowledge along with the shortage of staff pressurizes them.

Poor Record Management

Availability and accessibility to old records while compiling information is a major problem for the PIOs observed in all types of public authorities. The overall record management is poor in government departments. Records are not properly maintained and preserved. Lack of specific responsibility and accountability in operations with the government employees results in a non-enabling environment as per the demand of the RTI Act. Many times, the records are also incomplete to provide the multiple demand and information of a few RTI applications.

Poor Inter- and Intra-Departmental Coordination

Lack of inter- and intra-departmental coordination in the collection of information as sought by the RTI applicants sometimes creates problem to adhere to the timeline of the Act. The PIO is not getting adequate assistance in tracing the information. As a result, PIOs not only face work stress but also sometimes are unable to meet the timeline of the Act.

Question Pattern by the RTI Applicant

The RTI applicants many times do not put the question in the right form. The structure and spirit of the question do not go together. The confusing questions sometimes delay the process. Multiple questions raised by the applicants in one RTI application also burden the PIO. Sometimes the habitual RTI applicants in order to meet the interest of others also apply and intentionally burden the PIO for RTI work. In Secretariat Department, 21.40% of PIOs gave such opinion, while the Heads of the Department 36.50% PIOs also similarly complained.

Non-response of RTI Applicants

Sometimes it is observed that the RTI applicants under the RTI Act apply for the information, but few of them do not turn to collect the xerox materials or deposit the amount for the xerox. In such cases, the time invested by the PIO in search of the information and compiling them become useless. This is commented by 28.50% of PIOs in Secretariat Departments, 19% in Heads of Departments, and 30% in the case of other PAs. In the case of non-collection of information by the applicants, it demotivates the PIOs in the subsequent period. There is no such provision in the Act to punish such abuse of the Act.

Lack of Required Support to PIO

In a few public authorities, it was reported the authorities did not cooperate with the PIO to supply information to the RTI applicants. As a result of this, the PIOs in a few cases could not adhere to the timeline. This creates confusion for the PIOs whether to adhere to the timeline or to respond to the constraints of the PA and the authority.

Lack of Role Clarity of RTI Cell

The RTI cells in all Secretariat Departments are not functioning as it was expected. Specific roles and responsibilities are yet to be formulated and delivered in a practical sense. The Heads of the Departments are yet to give adequate operational importance to such RTI cells. As a result, these cells are not provided with the basic infrastructural support required for operation in day-to-day functioning. The role of the Nodal Department in streamlining and strengthening the RTI cells in each Secretariat Department and Heads of the Departments is very important and needs to be proactive.

Lack of Review and Monitoring of RTI Activities

By and large, the PIOs in each PA viewed that the authorities of the PAs very rarely review the RTI activities. As a result, the heads of the authorities are not getting opportunities to appreciate various issues linked to compilation of information as required by RTI applicants. The Nodal Departments also do not monitor the progress of RTI operations in public authorities in a routine manner. The lack of such monitoring inputs on a regular basis from the Nodal Department has directly affected the quality of implementation of the Act in public authorities.

Lack of Incentives to designated RTI Officers

The PIOs and FAAs by and large strongly feel that since there is a clause of financial punishment in the RTI Act and a few of the designated officials have been punished even due to none of their faults, they should be compensated with allowances. Lack of allowances to the designated RTI personnel many times influences them and their work performance.

Incomplete Staffing of State Information Commission

The cases/appeals at SIC are pending due to less number of State Information Commissioners which leads to delayed information. Delayed justice is popularly known as denied justice. It can be considered as no information or not useful for RTI applicants unless the applicant gets information in time. They viewed that if the RTI applicants are to wait one to two years for the disposal of their applications at SIC, then it is sometimes equal to the state judiciary system. The lack of circuit courts at three RDC headquarters or regions also either increases the non-disposal of cases or not creating interest in the minds of the people to use RTI Act and or to seek justice from SIC which is located at Bhubaneswar.

Lack of Adequate Training

Section 26(2) provides training provisions of PIOs and FAAs to be carried out by the Nodal Department of the State Government. In fact quite a sizeable number of PIOs are hot given basic training on the RTI Act. Refresher training in such cases does not arise. As a result, many PIOs are either ignorant of various provisions of the Act or not sensitized properly to play their role effectively in the implementation of the Act.

UPDATION OF PROACTIVE DISCLOSURE

Many of the public authorities do not have their website under Section 4(1)(b) and 4(1)(c) for giving detailed information under 17 items. The Secretariat Department though have website but updation on regular time intervals are not done. The Nodal Information and Public Relations Department through close monitoring and review is yet to establish a close and participatory proactive disclosure mechanism in all the PAs. The Nodal Information and Public Relations Department is not making any analysis of the data made by the public authorities under proactive disclosure which would have been impacted in streamlining the qualitative maintenance of the data under this section.

SELECTION OF PIO AND FAA

Selection of PIO is very important. In many cases, the PAs have not taken the consent and willingness of the PIOs while appointing them. There should be some criteria to designate an official as PIO and FAA. People without any selective criteria become a burden in the smooth functioning of the RTI Act in a public authority. Non-consideration of these aspects while designating a person has affected in many cases the quality of implementation of various provisions of the RTI Act. The study indicates that persons with higher qualifications and higher positions in the PA having positive attitudes are not designated as RTI authorities.

POOR OR NO AWARENESS PROGRAM

Various educational programs generate awareness among the people of the RTI Act. The awareness programs carried out by SIC and Information and Public Relations Department are not adequate and yet need to be contextual in many tribal regions and communities. As a result, the RTI knowledge among the public authorities is not yet sufficient and not reaching the people. Public awareness programs based on audio-video and print media are yet to be adopted.

MAJOR SUGGESTIONS

- The time required for compiling the information by PIO against RTI applications may be nominally charged to the RTI applicants. This will restrict the fake RTI applications to misuse the RTI Act.
- The workload of each staff to be assessed in the government and if required government may need to fill up the vacant post. High vacancy of staff should not be an excuse for RTI-designated officers to delay and deviate from compliance of the applications.
- Adequate basic training on RTI Act may be provided to all staff. Similarly, refresher training on RTI Act may be provided every second year so as to understand the operational importance of the Act.
- RT-designated officers should be provided with basic training on time, work, and record management. This will streamline their work processes and yield higher productivity.
- Government to improve the old record manual. Special investment to be made in each department for modernization of infrastructure, record storage, and presentation. Incomplete and old records should be reviewed before considering for preservation.
- Provision of RTI cell in each Secretariat Department and Heads of the Departments with senior RTI Nodal Officers in charge may be established and strengthened within a stipulated time period.

- In the Secretariat and Heads of the Departments, there should be an RTI application receipt counter with e-documentation provision. This will reduce the long-time consumption and harassment of the RTI applicants.
- RTI cell of each department is to coordinate the sections within the department and with other departments. Intra- and inter-departmental coordination is to be encouraged and willful deviations should be punished. Information and Public Relations has to play a proactive role in maintaining the inter- and intra-departmental coordination for smooth implementation of the Act.
- Massive awareness program at block levels through various audio-visual aids may be carried out in specific periods of the year. The local NGOs/CBOs should be involved in this campaign process. Various JEC programs contextual to different regions may be devised and implemented by taking into account the folk culture. This may be adopted to popularize various provisions of the RTI Act.
- The RTI Act and the RTI Rule may be translated into tribal languages. This will help the dissemination processes of the Act and will help for a wider presentation of the message in tribal communities of the state.
- The authorities if found influencing the PIO/FAA for noncompliance or noncooperation with the RTI applicants should be strongly punished in an exemplary manner. This will give a moral boosting to PIOs/FAAs to adhere to RTI Act.
- Information and Public Relations the Nodal Department of the Government to implement RTI Act in the state needs to have a quarterly review of all Nodal Officers of the public authorities on the functioning of the RTI Act in public authorities. They are also to find out various problems encountered by them and provide feedback for smooth implementation of the Act. This will streamline the process of accountability of the PIO/FAA and the public authorities.
- As per the RTI Act, the PIOs/FAAs are to be punished if they do not follow the time-line. They have to meet the RTI applicants in supplying information. Since there is a provision of cash punishment to PIO/FAAs in case of noncompliance, therefore, they should be provided with all technical supports like staff, e-services, and cooperation to furnish the information in time.
- The FAA should be endowed with necessary powers to render his services more effectively in supplying information. He should have the power to call PIO, RTI applicants, files, and records for timely disposal of RTI cases.
- The Law Department should give legal assistance, clarifications on various related doubts of FAAs within a short time on RTI-related issues. This will reduce the movement of complaint cases to the SIC.

- The important decisions of SIC should be compiled, published in manual form by the SIC, and supplied to all departments for enhancement of knowledge and clarifications of doubts.
- Adequate funding from the Government of India for training and awareness building may be provided since the State Government is implementing many Government of India-sponsored programs and the Sstate does not have much funding provision for software activities in this regard.
- A few aggressive administrative reform mechanisms may be devised by the state and be implemented so as to support the implementation processes for the progressive policies like RTI Act, NREGS Act, R & R Act, and special programs like NRHM, SSA, and so on.

PROPOSED AMENDMENT TO THE RTI RULES

Amendment to the RTI Rules may be taken into account with respect to the following aspects:

- The demand of the identity proof for the RTI applicants should be waived out.
- Form-A of the RTI Act should be simplified so as to make the applicants more friendly to the Act. It violates Section 6(2) since the applicant has to first submit 13 items of the information before he gets the information. The name of the father/spouse should not be demanded and permanent address is not required, present address is sufficient.
- The modes of fee/charges collection can be expanded. It may include postal money order, and so on.

The SIC in its present structure is unable to meet the timely needs of the RTI applicants who are deprived of public authorities and come to SIC to get justice. Practically, at SIC they also face problems. The following aspects of SIC may be taken into account.

- The number of State Information Commissioner should be increased so as to make the disposal of appeals speedier.
- Regular trained staffs should be appointed to SIC in order to make it more vibrant and effective.
- The SIC should be assigned with contempt power. By this, habitual offenders of the decisions of the SIC under the Act will be punished.
- In order to reduce the long-time and pendency of RTI cases at SIC, prehearing processes at the registrar level of SIC may be made. The RTI

appeals may be scrutinized and reviewed in a time-bound manner for all required information before it is placed for final hearing in one date only.
- There should be a time limit for the SIC for the disposal of RTI appeals/ complaint cases.

As a part of the infrastructure preparation in public authorities, Government of India should provide budgetary support to the State Government. This will help and motivate the people to a high extent.

- The detailed guidelines are to be prepared for *suo motu* discloser in public authorities.
- In each PA, particularly Secretariat Departments and Heads of the Departments, the Nodal Officers to RTI should be declared. These Nodal Officers should act as Central Coordinating Officers to the RTI Act both inside and outside Public Authority.
- Administrative actions should be taken if a designated RTI person is not taking up RTI matters seriously and are not complying RTI applications in time.
- The Nodal Department should develop an RTI Performance Index consisting of different indices for use in the assessment of each Public Authority with respect to the role performance while providing the information sought by the applicants.
- According to Form C of Rule 5 (1) and (2) of RTI Rules, PIO can reject an application that violates the Act. Only in the case of exempted information applied for can be legitimately denied by the PIO under Section 8 or 11 or 24.
- Requests which cannot be dubbed as "information U/S (f)" can also be denied. The fact that RTI Act provides for the denial of information and not for rejection of the RTI application or rectification of defects of the application.
- In case the RTI application is incomplete, the PIO can ask to rectify the application or file a revised application once the fees are paid. Rejection of an RTI application leads to loss of time and denial of justice to the applicant.
- Lack of identity proof cannot be a cause for the rejection of RTI application. Again Section 6(2) of the Act does not require the applicant to give any detail other than the contact address.
- Rejection of RTI application on the ground of "for any other reason," "matter on sub-judice information sought for is not specific," and so on over-empowers the PIO at an operational level. This is a clear-cut violation of the RTI Act. A Rule made by the state cannot question the Act rather it can strengthen the Act.

- The RTI Act does not empower the PIO to reject an application on the ground that non-deposit of cost for information not made within the prescribed time of 15 days under Rule 4 (3). Odisha rule thus empowering PIO is illegal and questions the Act.

POLICY PRESCRIPTIONS

Awareness among citizens holds the key to making RTI a success. The massive awareness campaigns by the government in collaboration with civil society and media are essential for improving the awareness of citizens relating to various provisions of the Act. Advertisements in major national and regional newspapers and TV channels can help in a big way in making people aware of the benefits of the Act. Conducting street plays in remote areas and organizing workshops for citizens on RTI Act would definitely improve the awareness level of citizens. Besides improving the awareness, people need to be educated about not to misuse the Act or file frivolous applications under the RTI Act. This move will not only lessen the burden on public authorities but also make the use of the Act more impactful.

With a view to promptly supplying quality information, the process of digitalization of official records is mandatory for the successful implementation of the Act and the quality of information largely depends on it. The compliance with Section 4 of the Act should be regularly monitored. Needless to mention that records are well maintained and easily accessible, relevant, precise, and intelligent information can be provided to information seekers in an expeditious manner. The PIOs and public authorities need to be more vigilant and careful in this regard. The use of Information and Communication Technology (ICT) in managing the records deserves special mention. The use of ICT will make the record-keeping exercise more efficient. The provision of additional funds and basic infrastructure will harness the capacity of public authorities in records management.

Change in mindset and attitude of officials (employees of Odisha Secretariat) involved in the implementation of the Act holds the key to foster transparency and openness in the working of the public authorities. Capacity building of officials through sustained training efforts is necessary for bringing desirable changes in the mindset of the officials. The process of seeking information under RTI needs to be made more citizens friendly. Ensuring the availability of user guides can help citizens a long way to know about the process of seeking information under the Act. When a citizen visits PIO office for filing an RTI application, the placement of display boards containing details of PIO and other relevant details such as procedure to file an appeal will facilitate the citizens in seeking information. The creation of Citizen

Service Centres to provide assistance in filing an application will significantly aid the citizens in reaping the benefits under the Act. Making available more options for fee deposit preferably like payment through credit/debit cards will simplify the fee deposit mechanism and citizens will not have to shed more money from their pockets.

Compliance with various provisions of the Act like active disclosure under Section 4, adoption of management information system, and sending of annual returns under Section 25(2) by public authorities play a pivotal role in success of the Act and need to be implemented expeditiously. Many people have sacrificed their lives for unearthing the cases of corruption. The government is yet to implement Whistleblower Protection Law. A strong law is needed to protect the whistleblowers that are utilizing the tool of RTI for highlighting issues of corruption.

An effective monitoring mechanism is a prerequisite for ensuring successful implementation of the Act. The Second Administrative Reforms Commission recommended that Information Commissions should be entrusted with this responsibility. The recommendation has been accepted by the government. Information Commissions should play a proactive role through regular monitoring for ensuring the compliance of the Act by the public authorities.

The institutions of civil society and media have positively participated in the formulation of the Act. Their role in the implementation needs to be strengthened by appointing persons of eminence and integrity as information commissioners from civil society organizations and media. This move will encourage these institutions to be more proactive toward the implementations of the Act. Moreover, the move will make the composition of the Information Commissions more broad-based.

MAJOR RECOMMENDATIONS

- All PIOs should be provided with special training on RTI Act. The FAAs should be provided with special training separately at Bhubaneswar, the state headquarter, where the role of Odisha Information Commission (OIC) and Information and Public Relations in giving training to them is important.
- The funds placed by OIC toward organizing training programs on RTI Act should be used within the time period. Information and Public Relations functionaries be involved in monitoring the progress of such training programs at various levels to ensure the quality and timely completion of the programs.
- Training programs be organized for the RTI-designated personnel at regular intervals.

- Information and Public Relations should monitor and review from time to time to see the preparation, maintenance, and updation of information under 4(I) B self-disclosure. All the PIOs should have a hard copy of the information prepared under *suo motu* disclosure.
- Sign boards in each PAs as per the RTI Act should be written in Oriya language with complete basic information.
- In order to create mass awareness among the PAs, NGOs should bound to make all preparatory works to implement RTI Act.
- The number of questions asked by each RTI applicants should be limited in number and refer to a specific time period.
- A special budget may be placed to each PA to improve the quality of office infrastructure and computerization of RTI cells in the Secretariat offices.
- In order to create awareness among all employees of the PAs, training camps should be organized at all the levels of Odisha Secretariat.
- The responsibility of PIO should be given to an employee for a specific time period. This will increase the functional efficiency of the RTI-designated personnel and delivery of equal responsibilities among all government employees.
- Regular review of progress on RTI matters may be made at various levels and specific guidelines may be circulated by Information and Public Relations and progress in this regard may be maintained and consolidated for each department on a quarterly basis.
- Data reporting on a monthly, quarterly, half-yearly, and annual bases may be made and this should be the prime responsibility of Information and Public Relations Department.
- Special training programs may be funded by OIC for the legal professionals and staffs of the judicial services on the RTI Act.
- Legal Literacy Camps made by the judiciary may also be used as a platform to disseminate information on RTI Act.
- Government is to improve the old record manual. Special investments may be made in each department to modernize the record storage room. Incomplete and old records may be reconsidered for preservation properly.
- The RTI Act and RTI Rule need to be translated in tribal dialects which will help the dissemination processes more closely to people.
- Adequate funding by Government of India may be made to popularize RTI Act in tribal-dominated districts where the people and the region are much behind in many respects.
- FAs should be made compulsory before the FAA by the RTI applicants before one goes to OIC for lodging a direct complaint.
- At OIC there should be some time limit for the disposal of SAs and Complainant Cases under the RTI Act.

- The PIO may ask the applicants to comply if their application is found incomplete in some respect.
- To reduce the time at OIC for the disposal of RTI applications only serious lapses should be examined.
- Corporate Sectors, Business Houses, and NGOs in general should be covered under the purview of the RTI Act.
- Protection to RTI workers/RTI applicants should be provided by the state on a priority basis.
- The Commission should be empowered to review the recovery status of the penalty imposed by them on the deviants of the RIT Act.
- A strong mechanism at the state level and OIC level is to be developed to check the misuse of the Act by a few groups.
- Very busy persons and official positions should not be entrusted with RTI assignments. The RTI-assigned persons should not be entrusted with the charges of other departments.
- Senior officials of a PA are declared as the RTI authorities who will help them in better understanding of the Act and in implementing the Act more qualitatively.

Appendix A

Preamble of Right to Information Act, 2005

THE RIGHT TO INFORMATION ACT, 2005

No. 22 of 2005

[15th June, 2005]

An Act to provide for setting out the practical regime of right to information for citizens to secure access to information under the control of public authorities, in order to promote transparency and accountability in the working of every public authority, the constitution of a Central Information Commission and State Information Commissions and for matters connected therewith or incidental thereto.

Whereas the Constitution of India has established democratic Republic;

And whereas democracy requires an informed citizenry and transparency of information which are vital to its functioning and also to contain corruption and to hold Governments and their instrumentalities accountable to the governed;

And whereas revelation of information in actual practice is likely to conflict with other public interests including efficient operations of the Governments, optimum use of limited fiscal resources and the preservation of confidentiality of sensitive information;

And whereas it is necessary to harmonise these conflicting interests while preserving the paramount of the democratic ideal;

Now, therefore, it is expedient to provide for furnishing certain information to citizens who desire to have it. Be it enacted by Parliament in the Fifty-sixth Year of the Republic of India

Interview Schedule for RTI Applicants (Employees of Odisha Secretariat)

1. Name of the Applicant (Optional):____________________
2. Address______________________________________
3. Gender (a) Male ☐ (b) Female ☐
4. Information Sought:
   (a) Yes (b) No
5. In which Department did you file RTI:
6. Date of Filing RTI:
7. Date of receiving RTI:
8. Did you file First Appeal? If yes, give reasons
   (a) Yes (b) No
9. Date of filing First Appeal:
10. Date of hearing First Appeal:
11. Did you get complete information after First Appeal?
    (a) Yes (b) No
12. Did you file second appeal/ Complaint? If yes, please mention the reason
    (a) Yes (b) No
13. Date of filing second appeal/Complaint:
14 Date of hearing of second appeal/ Complaint:
15. Are you satisfied with the order of SIC?
    (a) Yes (b) No
16. If no, please state the reason
17. Do you belong to BPL category?
    (a) Yes (b) No
18. Did you have to face any pressure/threat from anyone due to filing of RTI? If yes, please explain
    (a) Yes (b) No
19. Did you have to face any difficulty while using RTI?
    (a) Yes (b) No
20. Please explain your experience in dealing with PIO
21. Please explain your experience in dealing with appellate authorities
22. Please share your experience dealing with Information Commissioner
23. Was your purpose achieved for which the RTI was filed?
    (a) Yes ☐ (b) No ☐
24. Do you think that you got your work done by using RTI otherwise the same was not happening
    (a) Yes ☐ (b) No ☐
25. Did you ever encourage any other person to file RTI?
    (a) Yes ☐ (b) No ☐
26. Have you ever participated in any workshops or training on RTI?
27. Would you consider using RTI in the future for similar or other cases
    (a) Yes (b) No
28. What according to you should be changed in order to make the RTI stronger and effective?

Interview Schedule for (Public Information Officers)

---

1. Name of Public Information Officer:

2. Designation of PIO:

3. Do you know the provisions of the RTI act?

4. (a) Yes ☐ (b) No ☐ Don't know

5. How long have you been PIO for your Department?
(a) 2-3 years ☐ (b) 1-2 years ☐ (3) Less than one year ☐

6. Have you been a PIO in any other department before this assignment?
(a) Yes ☐ (b) No ☐

7. Did you want to be a PIO?
(a) Yes ☐ (b) No ☐ (c) Don't know ☐

8. (If Yes) Why did you want to be PIO?
(a) To support RTI
(b) Gives power
(c) Gives recognition
(d) Others (please specify)_______

9. (If No) Why you did not want to be PIO?
(a) Additional Work
(b) Fear of Penalty
(c) Lack of Cooperation from colleagues
(d) No financial/or other incentives
(e) Poor record management and retrieval of information difficult
(f) Lack of support system
(g) Others (Specify)____________

9. Have you received any training on RTI?
Yes ☐ (b) No ☐

10. (If Yes) How many times?
(a) Once (b) Twice (c) Thrice

11. What about your experience of the training?

12. What about your experience of the training?
(a) Helpful (b) Not helpful (c) No opinion

12. (If not Helpful) What is the reason?
(a) Training too short
(b) Trainer not clear
(c) Trainer not knowledgeable
(d) Poor training materials/ documentation
(e) No training on the practical aspects of effectively addressing an information request
(f) No refresher course
(g) Other (Specify) ________

13. How many RTI applications have you received since you became a PIO? (Record number per year and code total applications)

14. How many applications have you transferred to other PIOs/public authorities?

15. Do you have any limits /constraints for financial provisions/approvals to cover the cost of servicing RTI applications?
(a) Yes ☐ (b) No ☐ (c) Can't Say ☐

16. (If Yes) What are the constraints?
(a) Postage
(b) Photocopy
(c) Others (Specify) ___________

17. On an average, how much time do you spend per week on the RTI related work?
(a) Less than 1 hour
(b) Between 1 and 2 hours
(c) Between 2 and 5 hours
(d) Between 5 and 10 hours

(e) More than 10 hours

18. How much time do you spend appearing before the Information Commission every month?

(a) Less than 1 day
(b) Between 1 and 3 days
(c) Between 3 and 6 days
(d) More than 6 days

19. Have you/ your department made any changes in RTI related office management systems?

(a) Yes
(b) No
(c) Can't Say

20. (If Yes) Please tell what changes have been made:

(a) Improving record maintenance
(b) Digitization of information
(c) Putting records on website
(d) Changing procedures of functioning and decision making for maintaining records for RTI
(e) Others (Specify)______________

21. In responding to information requests what difficulties do you generally face?

(a) Incomplete application
(b) Unclear applications
(c) Requests for voluminous information
(d) Need to make repeated internal follow- ups
(e) Difficulty in getting information from colleagues/superiors
(f) Inadequate & incomplete internal record-keeping and filing system
(g) Information pertaining to the query does not exist within Department
(h) Compiling information from disparate sources
(i) Reducing available information into the format in which it is asked
(j) Others (Specify)

22. What other constraints, if any, do you face in implementing the RTI?

(a) Lack of awareness of provisions of law/ procedures/rules
(b) Lack of training
(c) Lack of guides/manuals/materials
(d) Deficiencies in RTI applications
(e) Too many applications
(f) Others (Specify)

23. Do you have a copy of the RTI Act with you?

Yes ☐ (b) No ☐

24. Would you like to suggest any improvements in the RTI law/rules and/or procedures for processing RTI applications (Please specify)

Yes ☐ (b) No ☐

Appendix B

Year-wise Receipt and Disposal of Cases (Complaint Cases)

Sl. No	*Year*	*As on*	*Opening Balance*	*Received*	*Disposed of*	*Closing balance*
1	2006	31-12-2006	–	644	309	335
2	2007	31-12-2007	335	1972	381	1926
3	**2008**	**31-12-2008**	**1,926**	**1,973**	**527**	**3,372**
4	2009	31-12-2009	3,372	2,557	886	5,043
5	2010	31-12-2010	5,043	3,344	1,570	6,817
6	2011	31-12-2011	6,817	3,310	5,163	4,964
7	2012	31-12-2012	4,964	2,781	6,265	1,480
8	2013	31-12-2013	1,480	1,733	2,168	1,045
9	2014	31-12-2014	1,045	709	1,463	291
10	2015	31-12-2015	291	501	69	723
11	2016	31-12-2016	723	600	136	1,187
12	2017	31-12-2017	1,187	643	277	1,553
13	2018	31-12-2018	1,543	867	422	1,998

Year-wise Receipt and Disposal of Cases (Second Appeal)

Sl. No	*Year*	*As on*	*Opening Balance*	*Received*	*Disposed of*	*Closing balance*
1	2006	31-12-2006	–	202	108	94
2	2007	31-12-2007	94	437	152	379
3	**2008**	**31-12-2008**	**379**	**370**	**129**	**620**
4	2009	31-12-2009	620	373	132	861
5	2010	31-12-2010	861	421	273	1,009
6	2011	31-12-2011	1,009	605	456	1,158

Sl. No	Year	As on	Opening Balance	Received	Disposed of	Closing balance
7	2012	31-12-2012	1,158	2,197	1,274	2,081
8	2013	31-12-2013	2,081	3,111	2,003	3,189
9	2014	31-12-2014	3,189	3,182	2,841	3,530
10	2015	31-12-2015	3,530	3,229	657	6,102
11	2016	31-12-2016	6,102	3,121	1,240	7,983
12	2017	31-12-2017	7,983	3,484	2,598	8,869
13	2018	31-12-2018	8,869	3,395	2,500	9,764

Source: Odisha Information Commission.

P.S. The hearing of Complaint Cases u/s 18 and Second Appeals u/s 19(3) of the RTI Act, 2005, started with effect from 02.04.2006, with the setting up of the Legal Wing of the State Information Commission.

Public Information Officers (PIOs) in Secretariat Departments

Sl. No.	Name	Department
1.	Mr. Debi Prasad Panda	Textile and Handloom Department
2.	Mr. Priyadarshi Mahapatra	Information Technology
3.	Mr. Bansidhar Mahapatra	Fisheries and A.R.D Deptt
4.	Mr. Narayan Hansdah	P.R. Dept Orissa
5.	Smt. Indumati Mishra	Department of Tourism
6.	Mr. Suresh Chandra Panigrahi	Excise Dept.
7.	Mr. Padma Lochan Sethi	T&C Culture Department
8.	Mr. Duryodhan Mohanty	Home Deptt
9.	Mr. Satyanarayan Das	Law
10.	Mr. Ganesh Chandra Patra	Excise Department, Orissa Secretariat
11.	Mr. Sarat Chandra Mohapatra	Sports & Youth Deptt
12.	Mr. Lingaraj Nayak	Works Deptt
13.	Mr. Mahendra Kumar Rath	P.E Deptt
14.	Mr. Bamadev Nanda	PG & PA Department, Orissa Secretariat, Bhubaneswar
15.	Mr. Gopabandhu Satapathy	Co-operation
16.	Mr. Shyam Sundar Singh	School and Mass Education Deptt.
17.	Mr. Muralidhar Das	Rural Development Department
18.	Mr. Mahendra Naik	Works Dep.t Government of Orissa
19.	Mr. Sibashis Dhal	Works Deptt
20.	Mr. Sarat Chandra Mohapatra	Higher Education Deptt
21.	Smt. Manjulata Swain	Food Supplies and Consumer Welfare Department
22.	Mr. Dilip Kumar Bihara	W&CD Deptt
23.	Mr. Dolamani Kandher	H & U.D Department
24.	Mrs. Subhasree Nanda	Deputy Secretary

Sl. No.	Name	Department
25.	Mrs. Akshaya Kumar	General Administration Deptt.
26.	Mr. Pradipta Kumar Sahani	R and DM
27.	Mr. Prafulla Kumar Rout	Finance Deptt, Govt. of Orissa
28.	Mr. Khatua Mallick	Dept. of Energy
29.	Mr. Pravat Kumar Das	ST & SC RTI
30.	Mr. Padmanav Choudhury	Finance Deptt, Govt. of Orissa
31.	Mr. Yudhistar Sethi	Planning Coordination Deptt.

Receipt and Disposal of RTI Applications by Government Departments up till the End of 2018

Sl. No.	*Name of the Departments*	*No of Applications received up to 31st March 2018*			*Total of applications disposed off*			*Appeals made before 1st Appellate Authority*		*Charges Collected under this act (in Rs)*			
		By PIO/ APIO	*By secretariat information cell (in case of a government department only)*	*Total (3+4)*	*No of applicants provided with information*	*No of Applicants denied access to information*	*Total Disposal (6+7)*	*No of Appeals received*	*No of appeals disposed off*	*Cash*	*Treasury Challan*	*Court fee*	*Total*
1	**2**	**3**	**4**	**5**	**6**	**7**	**8**	**9**	**10**	**11**	**12**	**13**	**14**
1	Finance	278	472	750	494	175	669	71	68	12,703	1,146	1,440	15,289
2	P & E	5	134	139	47	87	134	56	56	1,669	300	80	2,049
3	P. A	230	115	345	75	267	342	20	20	2,067	920	240	3,227
4	PG & PA	6	53	59	38	29	61	0	0	197	0	0	197
5	Industries	175	377	552	543	9	552	45	45	7,824	730	860	9,414
6	F & ARD	179	110	289	270	9	279	22	21	12,002	330	460	12,792
7	Energy	40	377	417	388	27	415	45	43	6,672	682	812	8,166
8	SC & ST	294	178	472	400	48	448	23	22	8,618	480	470	9,562
9	I & PR	477	368	845	793	44	837	19	6	12,099	280	1,019	13,398
10	Agriculture	1694	502	2196	2,045	62	2107	89	81	73,085	2,574	1,230	76,889
11	Works Deptt	14	75	89	83	4	87	3	3	1369	110	60	1539
12	Tourism & Culture (Tourism)	52	46	96	86	1	87	9	9	2342	1128	190	3642
13	T & H	0	36	36	34	2	36	4	4	838	300	48	1,186
14	Excise	259	53	312	301	4	305	2	2	5,643	2904	40	8,587
15	IT	16	4	20	18	3	21	4	1	9,961	60	40	10,061
16	H & UD	724	48	772	802	50	852	93	94	4,382	1,094	1,765	46,687
17	Planning & Co-ordination	177	144	321	264	50	314	9	9	6,740	408	160	7,308
18	H & FW	725	1345	2079	1,742	114	1,856	144	138	23,137	3178	1,670	27,985
19	LAW	348	167	515	370	70	440	30	30	50	30	340	60,06,060

20	Home	3,087	1161	4247	2,937	1381	4,318	201	201	55,000	20636	7,147	82,782
21	Labor and Emp	261	95	359	298	58	356	25	25	3,564	2,402	460	6,462
22	Steel and Mines	0	126	126	126	0	126	13	13	5,645	0	260	5,905
23	ST & SC Development	582	316	898	783	70	853	757	52	23,749	1,001	1,240	25,990
24	FS & CW	399	75	474	394	39	433	25	18	6,951	1,819	490	9,260
25	Commerce & Transport	44	63	107	86	21	107	110	11	8,107	261	240	8,608
26	Cooperation	38	161	199	122	14	136	19	19	9,893	355	400	1,648
27	Forest & Environment	1,140	471	1,644	1,307	241	1,548	154	132	62,307	5,066	2,890	70,263
28	Sports & Youth Services	48	36	84	72	7	59	1	1	3483	60	1,102	4,645
29	Science & Technology	21	17	38	37	1	38	1	1	2,313	30	20	2,362
30	Water Resources	880	458	1338	1,128	170	1,298	128	119	50,676	5215	2,330	58,221
31	GA	575	1,198	1773	1,290	206	1469	168	165	23,004	6230	3,410	29,034
32	School & Mass Education	3	34	37	13	2	15	5	3	484	60	200	745
33	Women and Child Development	56	238	288	258	30	288	31	31	3933	0	4700	8,633
34	Revenue & Disaster Management	566	300	866	769	66	835	31	19	12,475	980	310	13,765
35	Works Dept.	487	310	788	678	76	754	44	39	33,814	1,915	636	36,365
	Grand Total	13,879	9657	23,536	19,019	3431	22,522	1,701	1,501	541,204	59,474	37,018	637,696

Distribution of RTI Applications Received by Different Authorities from 201 to 2018

Sl.No.	Name of the Departments	Applications Received by		
		PIO/ APIO	Secretariat Information Cell	Total (3+4)
1	2	3	4	5
1	Finance	37.07	62.93	100.00
2	P & E	3.60	96.40	100.00
3	P.A	66.67	33.33	100.00
4	PG & AP	10.17	89.83	100.00
5	Industries	31.70	68.30	100.00
6	F & ARD	61.94	38.06	100.00
7	Energy	9.59	90.41	100.00
8	SC & ST	62.29	37.71	100.00
9	I & PR	56.45	43.55	100.00
10	Agriculture	77.14	22.86	100.00
11	Works Deptt	15.73	46.9	100.00
12	Tourism & Culture (tourism)	53.06	46.94	100.00
13	T & H	0.00	100.00	100.00
14	Excise	83.01	16.99	100.00
15	I.T	80.00	20.00	100.00
16	H & U.D	93.78	6.22	100.00
17	Planning & Co-ordination	55.14	44.86	100.00
18	H & F.W	34.87	65.13	100.00
19	LAW	67.57	32.43	100.00
20	Home	72.66	27.34	100.00
21	Labour and Emp.	73.31	26.69	100.00
22	Steel and Mines	0.00	100.00	100.00
23	ST & SC Development	64.81	35.19	100.00
24	FS & CW	84.18	35.19	100.00
25	Commerce & Transport	41.12	58.88	100.00
26	Cooperation	19.10	80.90	100.00
27	Forest & Environment	70.76	29.24	100.00
28	Sports & Youth Services	57.14	42.86	100.00
29	Science & Technology	55.26	44.74	100.00
30	Water Resources	65.77	34.23	100.00
31	GA	32.43	67.57	100.00
32	School & Mass Education	8.11	91.89	100.00
33	Women and Child Development	19.44	80.56	100.00
34	Revenue & Disaster Management	65.36	34.64	100.00
35	Works Department	61.80	38.20	100.00
	Grand Total	58.97	41.03	100.00

Source: Annual Reports, Orissa Information Commission, 2014–2015, 2015–2016, 2016–2017, and 2017–2018.

Distribution of Disposal of RTI Aapplications in Five Years from 2014–2015 to 2017–2018

		Applications Received by		
Sl. No.	*Name of the Departments*	*With Information*	*Denied Application*	*Total*
1	**2**	**3**	**4**	**5**
1	Finance	73.84	26.16	100.00
2	P & E	35.07	64.93	100.00
3	P.A	21.93	78.07	100.00
4	PG & AP	62.30	37.70	100.00
5	Industries	98.37	1.63	100.00
6	F & ARD	96.77	3.23	100.00
7	Energy	93.49	6.51	100.00
8	SC & ST	89.29	10.71	100.00
9	I & PR	94.74	5.26	100.00
10	Agriculture	97.06	2.94	100.00
11	Works Deptt	95.40	4.60	100.00
12	Tourism & Culture (tourism)	98.85	1.15	100.00
13	T & H	94.44	5.56	100.00
14	Excise	98.69	1.31	100.00
15	I.T	85.71	14.29	100.00
16	H & U.D	94.13	5.87	100.00
17	Planning & Co-ordination	84.08	15.92	100.00
18	H & F.W	93.86	6.14	100.00
19	LAW	84.08	15.91	100.00
20	Home	68.02	31.98	100.00
21	Labour and Emp.	83.71	16.29	100.00
22	Steel and Mines	100.00	0.00	100.00
23	ST & SC Development	91.79	8.21	100.00
24	FS & CW	90.99	9.01	100.00
25	Commerce & Transport	80.37	19.63	100.00
26	Cooperation	89.71	10.29	100.00
27	Forest & Environment	84.43	15.57	100.00
28	Sports & Youth Services	91.14	8.86	100.00
29	Science & Technology	97.37	2.63	100.00
30	Water Resources	86.90	13.10	100.00
31	GA	86.23	13.17	100.00
32	School & Mass Education	86.67	13.33	100.00
33	Women and Child Development	89.58	10.42	100.00
34	Revenue & Disaster Management	92.10	7.90	100.00
35	Works Department	89.92	10.08	100.00
	Grand Total	84.77	15.23	100.00

Source: Annual Reports, Orissa Information Commission, 2014–2015, 2015–2016, 2016–2017, and 2017–2018.

Disposal of First Appeals Received by Government Departments in Four Years from 2015–2016 to 2017–2018

			1st Appeals Received		*Applications Received to Total Application (in %)*	
Sl. No.	*Name of the Departments*	*Total Application*	*No of Appeals Received*	*No of Appeals Disposed off*	*No of Appeals Received*	*No of Appeals Disposed off*
1.	Finance	750	71	68	9.47	95.77
2.	P & E	139	56	56	40.29	100
3.	P.A	345	20	20	5.80	100
4.	PG & AP	59	0	0	0.00	00
5.	Industries	552	45	45	8.15	45
6.	F & ARD	289	22	21	7.61	95.45
7.	Energy	417	45	43	10.79	95.55
8.	SC & ST	472	23	22	4.87	95.67
9.	I & PR	845	19	6	2.25	31.57
10.	Agriculture	2196	89	81	4.05	91.9
11.	Works Deptt	89	3	3	3.37	100
12.	Tourism & Culture (tourism)	98	9	9	9.18	100
13.	T & H	36	4	4	11.11	100
14.	Excise	312	4	2	0.64	100
15.	I.T	20	4	1	20.00	25.00
16.	H & U.D	772	93	94	12.05	199
17.	Planning & Co-ordination	321	9	9	2.80	100
18.	H & F.W	2079	144	138	6.93	95.82
19.	LAW	515	30	30	5.83	100
20.	Home	4247	201	201	4.73	100
21.	Labour and Emp.	356	25	25	7.02	100
22.	Steel and Mines	126	13	13	10.32	100
23.	ST & SC Development	898	57	52	6.35	91.22
24.	FS & CW	474	25	18	5.27	72.00
25.	Commerce & Transport	107	107	11	100	10.28
26.	Cooperation	199	19	19	9.55	100
27.	Forest & Environment	1611	154	132	91.56	85.71
28.	Sports & Youth Services	84	1	1	1.19	100

Sl. No.	Name of the Departments	Total Application	1st Appeals Received		Applications Received to Total Application (in %)	
			No of Appeals Received	No of Appeals Disposed off	No of Appeals Received	No of Appeals Disposed off
29.	Science & Technology	38	1	1	2.63	100
30.	Water Resources	1338	128	119	9.57	92.96
31.	GA	1773	168	165	9.48	98.21
32.	School & Mass Education	37	5	5	13.61	60.00
33.	Women and Child Development	288	31	31	10.76	100
34.	Revenue & Disaster Management	866	31	19	3.38	61.29
35.	Works Department	788	44	39	5.58	88.63
	Grand Total	23,536	1701	1501	7.23	88.24

Source: Annual Reports, Orissa Information Commission, 2014–2015, 2015–2016, 2016-17, and 2017–2018.

Department-wise Distribution of Penalty Cases Who Have Not Adhered to RTI Act and Imposed by SIC in Different Years (Penalty in Rs)

Sl. No.	List of Government Departments and other PAs Odisha	Years						
		2015–2016		2016–2017		2017–2018		
		No. of Cases	Average Penalty	No. of Cases	Average Penalty	No. of Cases	Average Penalty	Total no of Cases
1.	H & F. W. Department			3	3,417	10	4,550	13
2.	Home Department							
3.	Housing & Urban Department	1	15,500	5	9,650	5	11,550	11
4.	Higher Education Department	2	7,250	8	6,375	5	3,950	15
5.	Agriculture Department					1	4,000	1
6.	School & Mass Education Department	1	1,500	6	6,250	5	10,750	12
7.	Energy Department							
8.	Finance Department			1	19,250			1
9.	Forest & Environment Department			3	9,833	4	9,125	7
10.	Industries Department					2	3,857	2
11.	Law Department	1	250	2	13,625			3
12.	Panchayati Raj Department					9	5,056	9
13.	Revenue Department and Disaster Management			21	17,417	22	13,705	43
14.	Rural Development Department					8	9,656	8
15.	Steel & Mines Department			1	2,750	1	11,500	2

Sl. No.	List of Government Departments and other PAs Odisha	Years						
		2015–2016		2016--2017		2017–2018		
		No. of Cases	Average Penalty	No. of Cases	Average Penalty	No. of Cases	Average Penalty	Total no of Cases
16.	S.T. & S.C. Development Department and Minorities & Backward Classes Welfare Department					1	2,250	1
17.	Water Resources Department			1	25,000		9,750	2
18.	Works Department			3	11,500	1	25,000	4

Source: Annual Reports, Orissa Information Commission, 2015–2016, 2016–2017, and 2017–2018.

Department-wise Distribution of Penalty Cases Who Have Not Adhered to RTI Act and Imposed by SIC in Different Years

		Charges Collected under this act (in Rs)				*Forms of Collection in %*		
Sl. No	*Name of Departments*	*Cash*	*Treasure Challan*	*Court fee*	*Total Collected (in Rs)*	*Cash*	*Treasury Challan*	*Court fee*
1	Finance	12,703	1,146	1,440	15,289	83.08	7.49	9.41
2	P & E	1,669	300	80	2,049	81.45	14.64	3.90
3	P.A	2,067	920	240	3,227	64.05	28.50	7.43
4	PG & PA	197	0	0	197	100.00	0.00	0.00
5	Industries	1,824	730	860	9,414	83.11	7.75	9.13
6	F & ARD	12,002	330	460	12,792	93.82	2.58	3.59
7	Energy	6,672	682	812	8,166	81.70	8.35	9.94
8	SC & ST	8,618	480	470	9,568	90.07	5.01	4.91
9	I & PR	12,099	280	1,019	13,398	90.30	2.09	7.60
10	Agriculture	73,085	2,574	1,230	76,889	75.05	3.34	1.60
11	Works Deptt	1,369	110	60	1,539	88.95	7.14	3.89
12	Tourism & culture (Tourism)	2,324	1,128	190	3,642	63.81	30.97	5.21
13	T & H	838	300	48	1,186	70.65	25.29	4.04
14	Excise	5,643	2,904	40	8,587	65.71	33.81	0.46
15	I.T	9,961	60	40	10,061	99.00	0.59	0.39
16	H & U.D	43,827	1,094	1,765	46,686	93.876	2.343	3.78
17	Planning & Coordination	6,740	408	160	7,308	92.228	5.583	2.18
18	H & F.W	23,137	3,178	1,670	27,985	82.676	11.356	5.96
19	Law	5,030	430	600	6,060	83.003	7.096	9.90
20	Home	55,000	20,636	7,146	82,782	66.440	24.928	8.63
21	Labour and Emp.	3,564	2,402	460	6,426	55.462	37.379	7.15
22	Steel and Mines	5,645	0	260	5,905	95.597	0.000	4.40

23	ST & SC Development	23,749	1,001	1,240	25,990	91.377	3.851	4.77
24	FS & CW	6,951	1,819	490	9,260	75.065	19.644	5.29
25	Commerce & Transport	8,107	261	240	8,608	94.180	3.032	2.78
26	Cooperation	9,893	355	400	10,648	92.909	3.334	3.75
27	Forest & Environment	62,307	5,066	2,890	70,263	88.677	7.210	4.11
28	Sports & Youth Services	3,483	60	1,102	4,645	74.984	1.292	23.72
29	Science & Technology	2,313	30	20	2,363	97.884	1.270	0.84
30	Water Resources	50,676	5,215	2,330	85,221	87.0414	8.957	4.00
31	GA	23,004	2,620	3,410	29,034	79.231	9.024	11.74
32	School & Mass Education	485	60	200	745	65.101	8.054	26.84
33	Women and Child Development	3,933	0	4,700	8,633	90.628	7.120	2.25
34	Revenue & Disaster Management	12,475	980	310	13,765	90.628	7.120	2.25
35	Works Department	33,814	1,915	636	36,365	92.985	5.266	1.74
	Grand Total	541,204	59,474	37,018	63,769 6	84.869	9.326	5.80

Source: Annual Reports, Orissa Information Commission, 2014–2015, 2015–2016, 2016–2017, and 2017–2018.

Implementation of RTI by Various Public Authorities—2015–2016

Sl. No.	Name of Deptt./ Organisation	No. of Applications 31st March 2016			No. of Requests disposed of			Appeal made before FAA			Charges Collected under this Act		
		By PIO/ API	Sectt. Cell	Total (3+4)	Pro vided inform ation	Denied Inform ation	Total Dis posed (6+7)	No. of App eals Receiv ed	No. of App eals Dispos ed	Cash/Mo	Try. Cha llan	Court fee	Total (in Rs.)
1	2	3	4	5	6	7	8	9	10	11	12	13	14
1	Agriculture	973	436	1,409	1,340	45	1,385	18	17	29,802	1,666	490	31,958
2	Comm. & Transport	22	33	55	43	12	55	6	6	1,152	0	120	1,272
3	Co-operation	334	88	422	298	93	391	33	32	7,379	1,780	380	9,539
4	Energy	210	89	299	268	31	299	15	15	3,957	290	160	4,407
5	Excise	38	43	81	78	3	81	3	3	4,222	90	60	4,372
6	Fisheries & ARD	100	200	300	289	7	296	14	13	5,420	330	260	6,010
7	Finance	177	236	413	399	14	413	18	12	8,564	1,130	360	10,054
8	Forest & Env.	134 9	598	1947	1508	263	1771	81	70	44,570	9,438	895	54,907
9	FS & CW	891	412	1303	1,095	194	1,289	59	54	7,827	2,442	480	10,749
10	Gen. Administration	1,315	740	2,058	1,496	562	2,058	184	184	2,8818	1,902	3,460	34,180
11	Governor's Sect.	130	0	130	130	0	130	9	9	3,580	300	180	4,060
12	H & FW	389	793	1,182	1,091	43	1,134	75	75	8,254	1297	580	10,131
13	H & UD	1,146	261	1,408	1,226	235	1,461	107	97	23,638	2,484	1,405	27,525

14	High Court	237	28	265	112	152	264	10	8	770	810	5,492	222
15	Higher Education	1,117	320	3,637	3,490	147	3,637	290	254	73,500	5,350	3,500	82,350
16	Home	3,348	936	4,284	3,309	956	4,265	378	373	47,827	13,536	14,566	75,929
17	I & PR	95	73	168	163	5	168	9	9	2,737	70	10	2817
18	Industries	1,155	205	1,360	1137	208	1,345	63	64	2,1869	1790	1,145	24,804
19	IT	22	19	41	41	0	41	0	0	703	170	20	893
20	Labour & Employment	162	88	250	213	37	250	5	5	6,781	2137	80	8,998
21	Law	542	123	665	519	48	630	54	54	6,237	630	1090	7,957
22	OIC	432	0	432	180	40	432	17	17	670	290	260	1,220
23	OLA	83	0	83	68	15	83	3	3	11,810	293	110	12,213
24	Panchatati Raj	1415	649	2064	1,484	257	1741	69	64	723,977	2,146	723	726,846
25	Parliamentary Affairs	139	62	201	57	144	201	15	15	730	330	240	1,300
26	PG & Pension Admn.	114	27	141	113	28	141	9	9	755	140	180	1,075
27	Planning & Co-ordn.	162	198	360	306	48	350	2	2	5,647	360	60	6,067
28	Public Enterprises	32	54	76	76	0	76	4	4	920	0	0	920
29	Revenue & DM	595	0	595	552	11	536	32	28	14,360	0	0	14,360
30	Rural Development	841	897	1,738	1,376	183	1,559	42	41	32,453	2,837	560	35,850
31	Science & Technology	78	10	88	83	5	88	7	7	346	70	100	516

(Continued)

		No. of Applications 31st March 2016			No. of Requests disposed of			Appeal made before FAA			Charges Collected under this Act		
Sl. No.	Name of Deptt./ Organisation	By PIO/ API	Sectt. Cell	Total (3+4)	Pro vided inform ation	Denied Inform ation	Total Dis posed (6+7)	No. of App eals Receiv ed	No. of App eals Dispos ed	Cash/Mo	Try. Cha llan	Court fee	Total (in Rs.)
32	School & Mass Edn.	5279	538	3117	2761	232	2,993	269	263	48,889	9461	2,340	60,690
33	Sports & Youth	42	23	65	65	0	65	0	0	370	30	40	440
34	ST & SC Dev.	626		262	262		262	NA	NA				4,999
35	Steel & Mines	0	174	174	169	0	169	8	8	551	0	0	5,511
36	Taxtiles & Handloom	42	38	80	68	12	80	1	1	1704	60	0	1,764
37	Tourism & Culture	237	24	261	240	21	261	3	3	709	220	60	989
38	W & CD	1749	244	1,993	1719	50	1,967	44	41	20,000	5,000	680	25,680
39	Water Resources	995	161	1,156	870	203	1,073	76	67	24,208	3,180	1,000	28,388
40	Works	624	462	1,086	984	48	1,032	44	44	41,140	2,718	560	44,418

Source: Annual Reports, Orissa Information Commission, 2015–2016

Appendix C

RTI ACT: MAIN SECTIONS AT A GLANCE

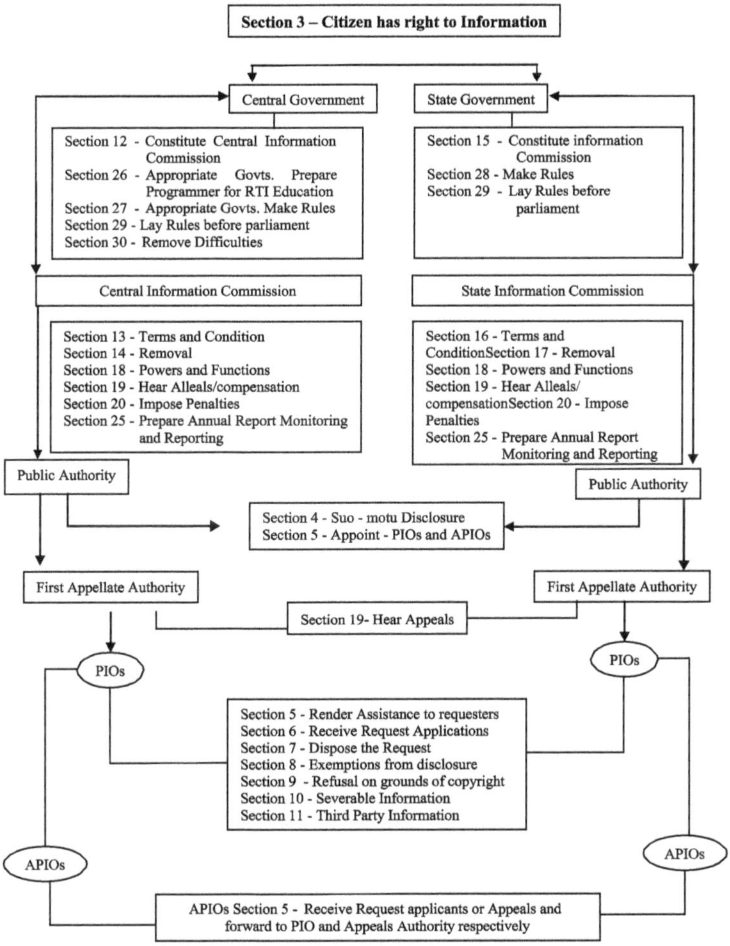

Some other sections
Extent and commencement of the Act -1
Definitions: Appropriate Government-2a; Competent Authority -2e; Information - 2f; PublicAuthority 2h; Records -2i; Right to information -2j; Third Party -2n;
Protection of action taken and good faith for PIO-21; Act has overriding effect -22; Bar on Jurisdiction of court -23;and doesn't apply to listed agencies -24
Source: Handbook on Right to Information Act, 2005, Yashada, Pune

FLOW CHART OF APPEAL/COMPLAINT

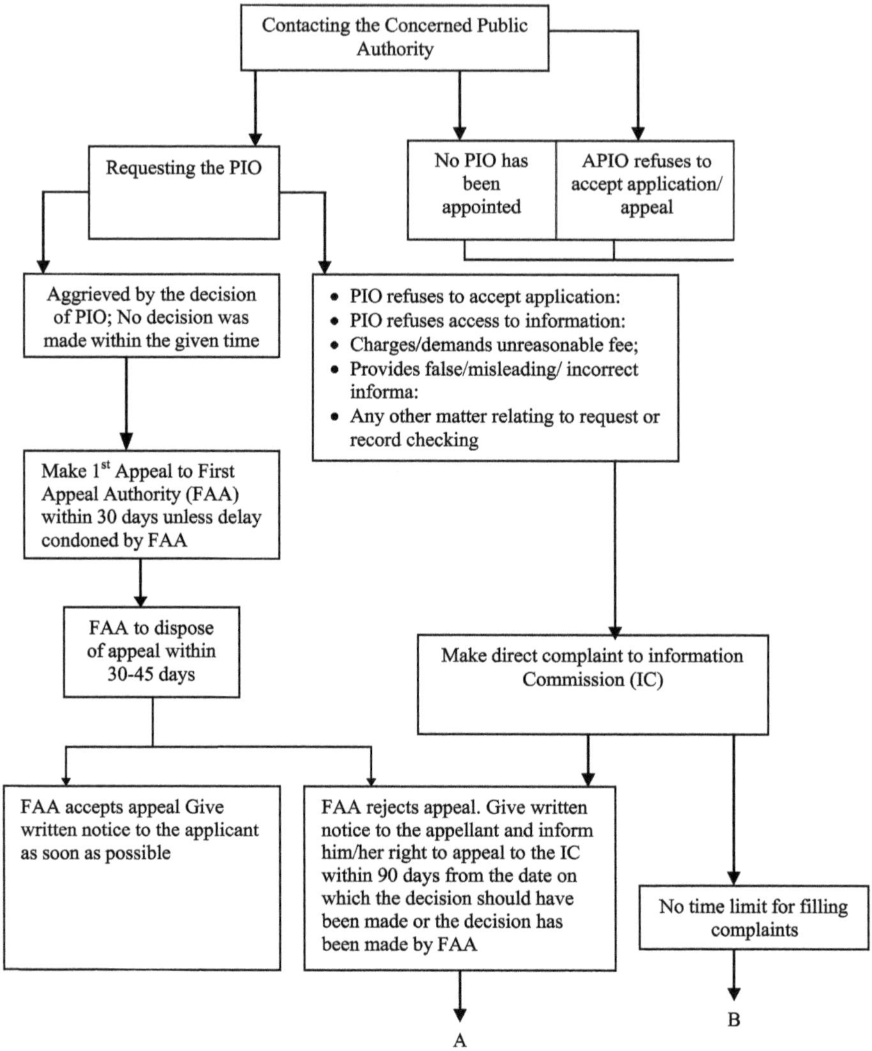

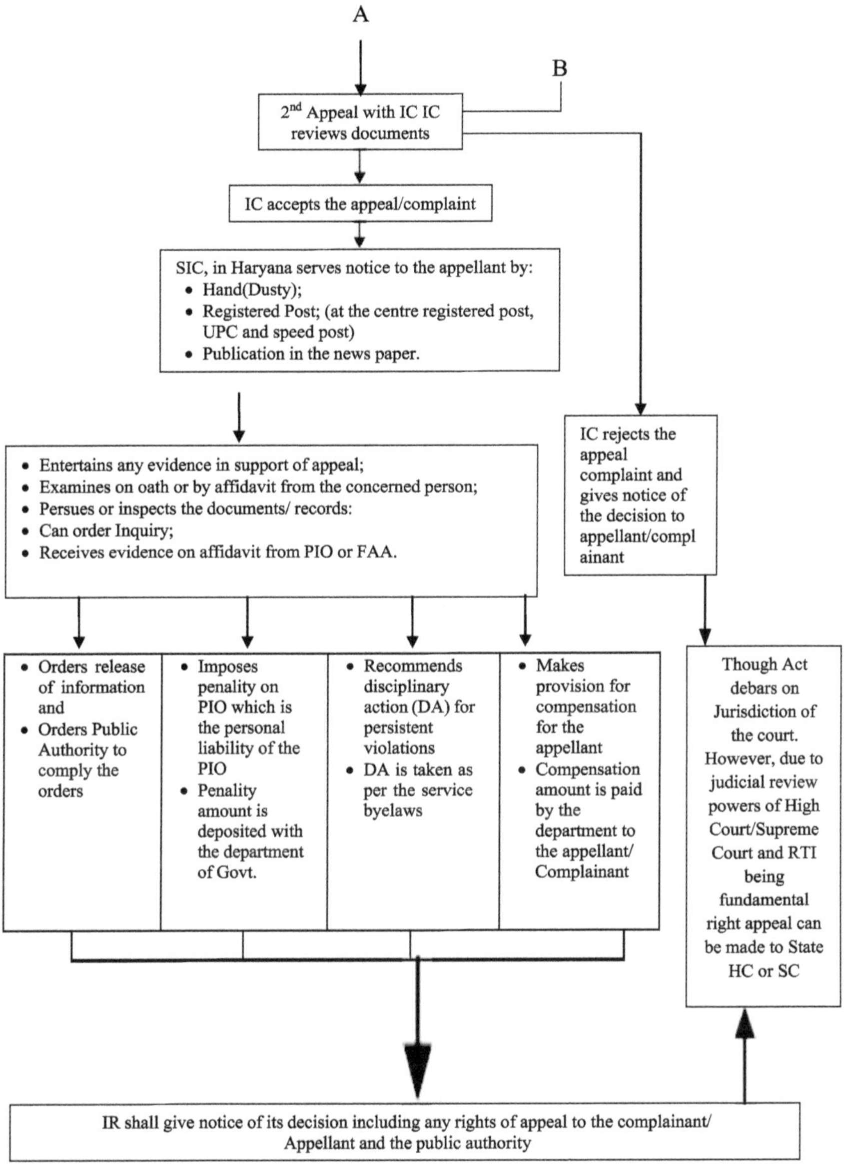

Source: Handbook on Right to Information Act, 2005, Yashada, Pune

FLOW CHART OF APIO'S DUTIES AND RESPONSIBILITIES

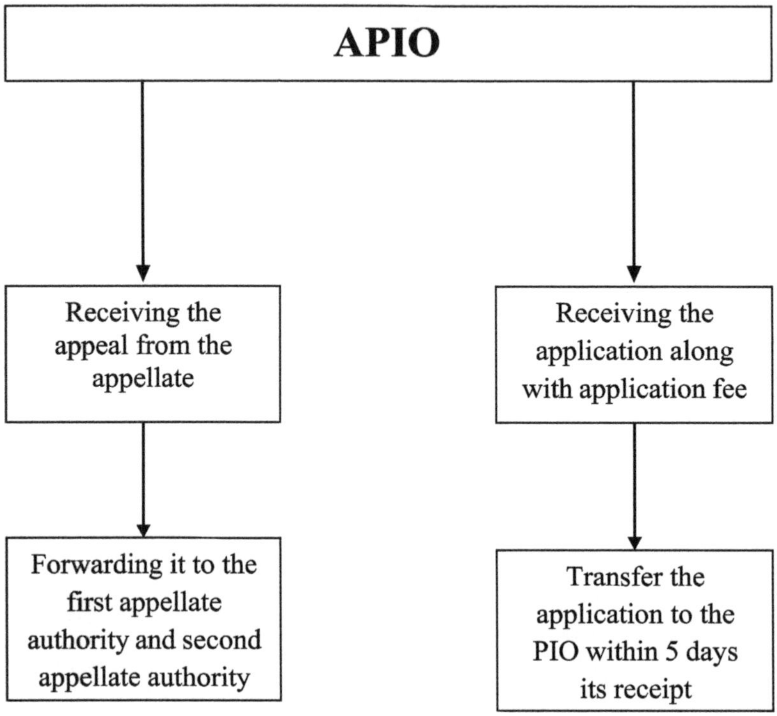

Source: Odisha Information Commission, Odisha, India, 2005.

SET UP OF PUBLIC AUTHORITIES

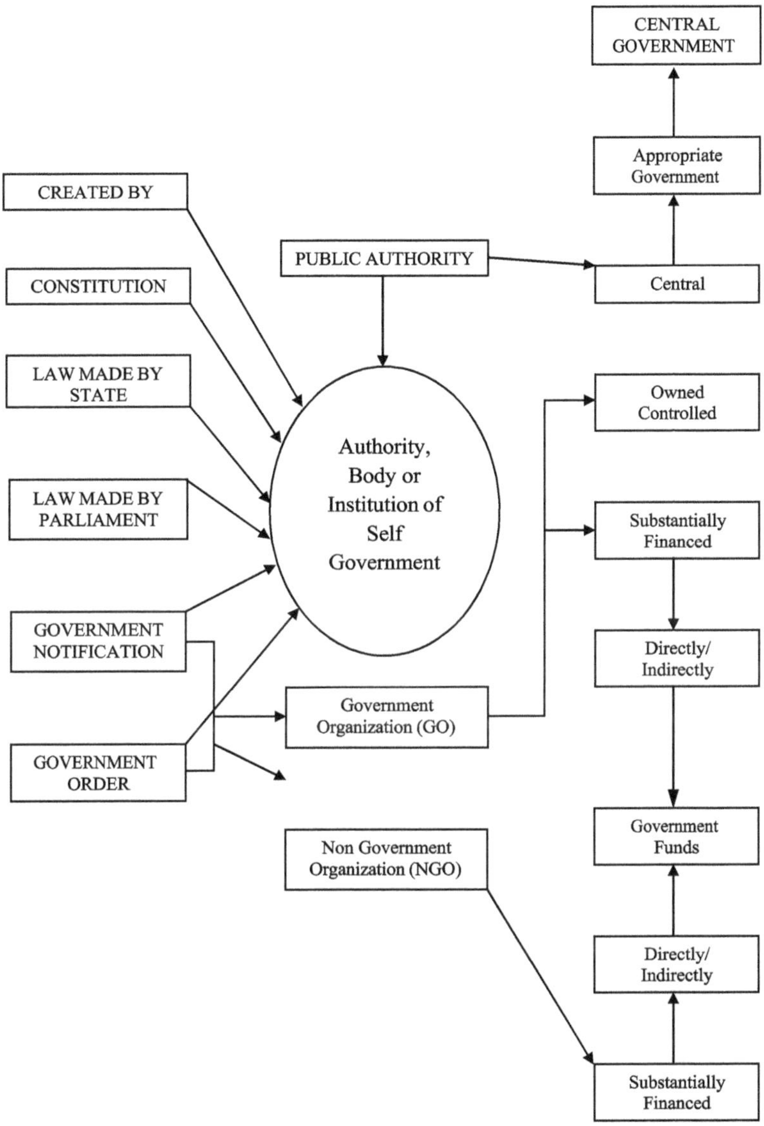

Source: Handbook on Right to Information Act, 2005 Yashada, Pune.

ORGANIZATION CHART OF THE COMMISSION

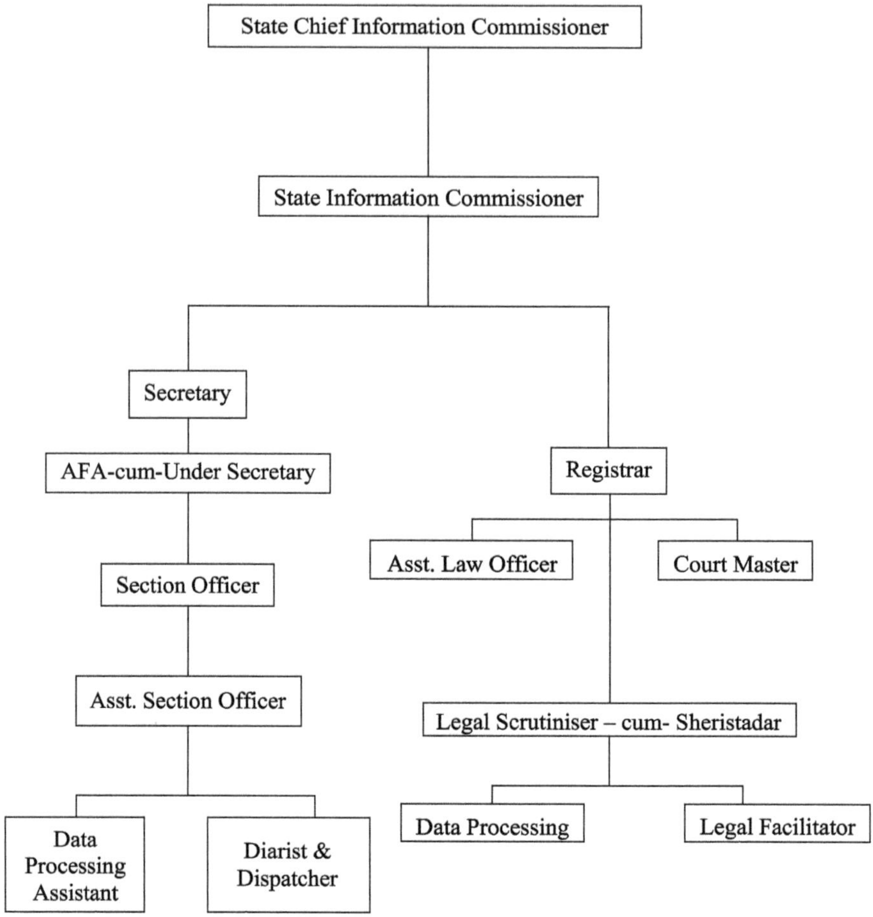

Bibliography

SELECTED BOOKS

Advani, Rani. (1995). *Judicial Pronouncements on Access to Information.* Consumer Education and Research Centre, Ahmadabad.

Anam, Shaheen. (2011). "Evolution of the RTI Act in Bangladesh". In Shekhar Singh et al. (ed.), *Transparent Governance in South Asia.* Indian Institute of Public Administration, New Delhi.

Athan G., Theoharis. (ed) (1998). *A Culture of Secrecy: The Government versus the People's Right to Know.* University Press of Kansas, Kansas.

Banisar, D. (2006). *Freedom of Information around the World 2006: A Global Survey of Access to Government Information Laws.* Privacy International, London.

Barowalia, J.N. (2006). *Commentary on the Right to Information Act.* Universal Law Publishing Co.

Beetham, D. (1999). *Democracy and Human Rights.* Cambridge Polity Press, Cambridge.

Bellver, Ana, Marcos, Mendiburu & Maria, Poli. (2008). *Strengthening Transparency and Accountability through Access to Information.* World Bank, Washington DC.

Blau, Peter. (1956). *Bureaucracy in Modern Society.* Crown Publishing Group, New York.

Bury, John B. (1975). *A History of Freedom of Thought.* Greenwood Press.

Caiden, G.E. (1988). "The Problem of Ensuring the Public Accountability of Public Officials". In J.G. Jabbra, and O.P. Dwivedi (eds.), *Public Service Accountability: A Comparative Study.* Kumarian Press, West Hartford.

Calland, Richard & Tilley, Allison. (ed.) (2000). *The Right to Know: The Right to Live, Access to Information and Socio-Economic Justice.* ODAC, Cape Town.

Calland, Richard & Tilley, Allison. (2002). *The Right to Know: The Right to Live.* ODAC, Cape Town.

Center for Civil Society Publications. (2003). *State of Governance: Delhi Citizen's Handbook.* New Delhi.

Chandhoke, N. (2003). *The Conceits of Civil Society.* Oxford University Press, New Delhi.

Chaturvedi, T.N. (ed.) (1980). *Open Government in India.* Indian Institute of Public Administration, New Delhi.

Cohen, Jean & Arato, Andrew. (1992). *Civil Society and Political Theory.* Mass MIT Press, Cambridge.

Darbishire, H. (2010). *Proactive Transparency: The Future of the Right to Information? A Review of Standards, Challenges, and Opportunities.* World Bank Institute, Washington DC.

Das, S.K. (1998). *Civil Service Reform and Structural Adjustment.* Oxford University Press, New Delhi.

Das, S.K. (2001). *Public Office, Private Interest: Bureaucracy and Corruption in India.* Oxford University Press, New Delhi.

Day, P. & Klein, R. (1987). *Accountabilities: Five Public Services.* Tavistock, London.

Dreze, Jean & Sen, Amartya. (1995). *India: Economic Development and Social Opportunity.* Oxford University Press, New Delhi.

Ebrahim, Alnoor & Weisband, Edward. (ed.) (2007). *Global Accountabilities: Participation, Pluralism and Public Ethics.* Cambridge University Press, New York.

Finnis, John. (1980). *Natural law and Natural Rights.* Oxford University Press, New York.

Florini, Ann. (ed.) (2007). *The Right to Know.* Columbia University Press, New York.

Foerstel, Herbert N. (1999). *Freedom of Information and The Right to Know.* Greenwood Press, London.

Fox, J. & Brown, L.D. (ed.) (1998). *The Struggle for Accountability: The World Bank, NGOs and Grassroots Movements.* Mass MIT Press, Cambridge.

Freedom House. (2011). *Freedom in the World Report 2010.* Freedom House, Washington DC.

Fung, Archon, Mary, Graham & David, Weil. (2007). *Full Disclosure: The Perils and Promise of Transparency.* Cambridge University Press, New York.

Goetz, A.M. & Jenkins, R. (2005). *Reinventing Accountability: Making Democracy Work for Human Development.* Palgrave Macmillan, Basingstoke.

Gujral, I.K. (2007). *Democracy: A View from India.* In Jorge I. Dominguez. & Anthony, Jones (eds.), *An Essay in the Construction of Democracy: Lessons from Practice and Research.* John Hopkins University Press.

Gutmann, Amy & Dennis, Thompson. (2004). *Why Deliberative Democracy?* Princeton University Press, Princeton?.

Habermas, Jurgen. (1996). *Between Facts and Norms: Contributions to a Discourse Theory of Law and Democracy.* Mass MIT Press, Cambridge.

Held, David & Koenig-Archibugi, Mathais. (2005). *Global Governance and Public Accountability.* Blackwell Publishers.

Heller, P. (2000). *Degrees of Democracy: Some Comparative Lessons from India.* World Politics.

Institute of Public Administration. (1998). *Governance and Accountability: Power and Responsibility in Public Service.* Institute of Public Administration, New Delhi.

Jasper, James M. (1997). *The Art of Moral Protest: Culture, Biography and Creativity in Social Movements.* Chicago University Press, Chicago.

Jayal, Niraja Gopal & Mehta, Pratap Bhanu. (ed.) (2010). *The Oxford Companion to Politics in India.* Oxford University Press, New Delhi.

Jenkins, R. (1999). *Democratic Politics and Economic Reforms in India.* Cambridge University Press, Cambridge.

Jenkins, R. (2002). "The Emergence of the Governance Agenda: Sovereignty, Neoliberal Bias and the Politics of International Development." In Desai, V. & Potter, Robert (eds.), *The Companion to Development Studies.* Oxford University Press, New York.

Katzenstein, Mary, Smitu, Kothari & Mehta, Uday. (2002). "Social Movement Politics in India: Institutions, Interests and Identities". In Kohli, Atul. (ed.), *The Success of India's Democracy.* Foundation Books, New Delhi.

Kaviraj, S. (ed.) (1997). *Politics in India.* Oxford University Press, New Delhi.

Kaviraj, S. (2010). *The Imaginary Institution of India: Politics and Ideas.* Columbia University Press, New York.

Kohli, Atul. (1991). *Democracy and Discontent: India's Growing Crisis of Governability.* Cambridge University Press.

Kothari, Rajni. (1970). *Politics in India.* Orient Longman, New Delhi.

Lindberg, S.I. (2009). *Accountability: The Core Concept and its Subtypes.* Overseas Development Institute, London.

Pollit, C. & Bouckaert, G. (2000). Public *Management Reform.* Oxford University Press.

Putnam, Robert D. (1993). *Making Democracy Work.* Princeton University Press, Princeton.

Maheshwari, S.R. (1980). *Secrecy in Government in India.* In Chaturvedi, T.N. (ed.), *Secrecy in Government.* Indian Institute of Public Administration, New Delhi.

Maheshwari, S.R. (1981). *Open Government in India.* Indian Institute of Public Administration, New Delhi.

Maheshwari, S.R. (1993). *Administrative Reform in India.* Jawahar Publishers & Distributors, New Delhi.

Maheshwari, S.R. (1994), *Indian Administration - An Historical Account.* Jawahar Publishers and Distributors, New Delhi.

Maheshwari, S.R. (2005). *Public Administration in India: The Higher Civil Service.* Oxford University Press, New Delhi.

Marshall, T.H. (1950). *Citizenship and Social Class.* Cambridge University Press, Cambridge.

McClure, Charles R. (1980). *Information for Academic Library Decision Making: The Case for Organizational Informational Management.* Greenwood Press, Westport.

Mehra, Achal. (1986). *Free flow of Information- A New Paradigm*. Greenwood Press.
Mendel, T. (2008). *Freedom of Information: A Comparative Legal Survey*. UNESCO, Paris.
Mills, C. Wright. (2000). *The Power Elite*. Oxford University Press, New York.
Mustonen, Juha. (ed.) (2006). *The World's First Freedom of Information Act: Anders Chydenius' Legacy Today*. Anders Chydenius Foundation, Kokkola.
Newell, P. & Joanna, Wheeler. (ed.) (2006). *Taking Accountability into Account: The Debate So Far*. *Zed* Books, London.
Nigam, Raj K. (ed.) (1998). *Public Accountability in Indian Polity*. Blackwell Publications, New Delhi.
Noorani, A.G. (2002). *Citizens Rights, Judges and State Accountability*. Oxford University Press.
Normanton, E. L. (1966). *The Accountability and Audit of Governments*. Manchester University Press, Manchester.
Piotrowski, Suzanne. (2010). *Transparency and Secrecy: A Reader Linking Literature and Contemporary Debate*. Lexington Books, Plymouth.
Potter, David (1986). *India's Political Administrators 1919-1983*. Clarendon Press, Oxford.
Rawls, J. (1971). *A Theory of Justice*. Mass MIT Press, Cambridge.
Rawls, J. (1993). *Political Liberalism*. Columbia University Press, New York.
Richard, D. Brown. (1996). *The Strength of a People: The Idea of an Informed Citizenry in America*. University of North Carolina Press.
Roberts, A. (2006). *Blacked Out: Government Secrecy in the Information Age*. Cambridge University Press, New York.
Ronald, Sims R. (ed.) (1998). *Accountability and Radical Change in Public Organisations*. Quorum books.
Rose-Ackerman, Susan. (1999). *Corruption and Government*. Cambridge University Press, New York.
Rowat, D.C. & Holm, Niels E. (ed.) (1979). *Denmark Administrative Secrecy in Developed Countries*. Columbia University Press, New York.
Schedler, Andreas. (1999). "Conceptualizing Accountability." In Andreas, Schedler, Larry, Diamond & Marc F, Plattner (eds.), *The Self-Restraining State: Power and Accountability in New Democracies*. Lynne Rienner, Boulder.
Seligman, Adam. (1992). *The Idea of Civil Society*. The Free Press, New York.
Sen, Amartya. (1981). *Poverty and Famines: An Essay on Entitlement and Deprivation*. Oxford University Press, New York.
Sen, Amartya. (1999). *Development as Freedom*. Alfred A. Knopf, New York.
Shah, Ghanshyam. (2004). *Social Movements in India: A Review of Literature*. Sage Publications, New Delhi.
Shapiro, Ian. (ed.) (1994). *The Rule of Law*. York University Press, New York.
Singh, Shekhar. (2007). "India: Grassroots Initiatives". In Ann, Florini (ed.), *The Right to Know*. Columbia University Press, New York.
Singh, Shekhar. (2011). "The Genesis and Evolution of the Right to Information Regime in India". In Singh, Shekhar et al (ed.), *Transparent Governance in South Asia*. Indian Institute of Public Administration, New Delhi.

Singh, Shekhar, Sharma, Prashant, Chand, Vikram . Chassy, Stephanie de. Mendiburu, Marcos. Nayak, Venkatesh. Benerji, Pranab. Munjoo, Munshi. & Dutt, Sunil. (ed.) (2011), *Transparent Governance in South Asia,* Indian Institute of Public Administration, New Delhi

Srivastava, K.M. (2009). *The Right to Information: A Global Perspective.* Lancer Publishers and Distributors, New Delhi.

Szekely, I. (2007). "Central and Eastern Europe: Starting from Scratch". In Ann, Florini (ed.), *The Right to Know.* Columbia University Press, New York.

United Nations Development Programme. (1997). *Governance for Sustainable Human Development.* UNDP, New York.

Van Doren, Mark. (1954). *Man's Right to Knowledge and the Free Use Thereof - with an Introduction* by Richard R, Powell. Columbia University, New York.

Watkins, John. (1976). The Freedom of Information Act and Special treatment for the Press. In Anderson, D. (ed.), *Privacy and Public Disclosure under the Freedom of Information Act.* University of Texas.

Wide, David. (1973). *Politics of Lying, Government Deception, Secrecy and Power.* Random House, New York.

World Bank. (1992). *Governance and Development.* World Bank, Washington, DC.

World Bank. (1997). *World Development Report 1997: The State in a Changing World.* Oxford University Press, New York.

SELECTED ARTICLES

Ackerman, J. (2004). "Co-Governance for Accountability: Beyond "Exit" and "Voice"". *World Development*, 32(3): 447–463.

Ackerman, J.M. & Sandoval-Ballesteros, I.E. (2006). "The Global Explosion of Freedom of Information Laws". *Administrative Law Review*, 58(1): 85–130.

Ala'i, P. (2008). "From the Periphery to the Centre: The Evolving WTO Jurisprudence on Transparency and Good Governance". *Journal of International Economic Law*, 11(4): 779–802.

Amulya, Gopal Krishnan. (2003). "Information by Right". *Frontline*, 20(01): 18–31.

Andersson, S. & Heywoo, P.M. (2009). "The Politics of Perception: Use and Abuse of Transparency International's Approach to Measuring Corruption". *Political Studies*, 57(4): 746–767.

Banisar, D. (2005). "The Irresistible Rise of a Right". *Index on Censorship*, 34(3): 79–84.

Barton, Allan D. (2006). "Public Sector Accountability and Commercial-in-Confidence Outsourcing Contracts". *Accounting, Auditing & Accountability Journal*, 19(2): 256–271.

Bell, Robin and Watchirs, Helen. (1988). Freedom of Information: The Commonwealth Experience. *Australian Journal of Public Administration*, XLVII(4).

Bennett, Colin J. (1997). "Understanding Ripple Effects: The Cross National Adoption of Policy Instruments for Bureaucratic Accountability". *Governance: An International Journal of Policy and Administration*, 10(3): 213–233.

Bhaduri, Amit. (2005). "Guarantee Employment and the Right to Information". *Economic and Political Weekly*, 40(4): 267–269.

Birchall, C. (2011). "Introduction to 'Secrecy and Transparency': The Politics of Opacity and Openness". *Theory, Culture and Society*, 28: 7–25.

Blanton, T. (2002a). "The Openness Revolution: The Rise of a Global Movement for Freedom of Information". *Development Dialogue*, 1: 7–21.

Blanton, T. (2002b). "The World's Right to Know". *Foreign Policy*, 131: 50–58.

Bovens, Mark. (2010). "Two Concepts of Accountability: Accountability as a Virtue and as a Mechanism". *West European Politics*, 33(5): 946–967.

Cheung, Anthony B.L. (2005). "The Politics of Administrative Reforms in Asia: Paradigms and Legacies, Paths and Diversities". *Governance: An International Journal of Policy, Administration, and Institutions*, 18(2): 257–282.

Das, S.K. (1995). "Disempowerment of Indian Bureaucracy: A Class Analysis". *Economic and Political Weekly*, 30(2): 119–122.

Dogra, Bharat. (1997). "Right to Information: Hope and Despair". *Economic and Political Weekly*, 32(29): 1794.

Doornbos, M. (2001). "'Good Governance': The Rise and Decline of a Policy Metaphor?" *Journal of Development Studies*, 37(6): 93–108.

Editorial. (2005). "Power to the People". *Economic and Political Weekly*, 40(21): 2115–2116.

Editorial (2008a). "Auditing the Right to Information Act". *Economic and Political Weekly*, 43(18): 6.

Editorial (2009). "The Right to Know". *Economic and Political Weekly*, 44(48): 6.

Foley, Michael W. & Bob, Edwards. (1996). "The Paradox of Civil Society". *Journal of Democracy*, 7(3): 38–52.

Fox, Jonathan. (2007). "The Uncertain Relationship between Transparency and Accountability". *Development in Practice*, 17(4): 663–671.

Fukuyama, F. (2001). "Social Capital, Civil Society and Development". *Third World Quarterly*, 22(1): 7–20.

Ghosh, Arun. (1997). "Advice without Accountability". *Economic and Political Weekly*, 32(41): 2574–2577.

Goel, S.L. (ed.) (2009). "Right to Information: Present Status and Issues". Special number of the *Indian Journal of Public Administration*, 55(3).

Goetz, A.M. & R. Jenkins. (2001). "Hybrid Forms of Accountability: Citizen Engagement in Institutions of Public Sector Oversight in India". *Public Management Review*, 3(3): 363–383.

Gothoskar, Sujata & Kanhere, Vijay. (1992). "Asserting Right to Information". *Economic and Political Weekly*, 27(26): 1324.

Hanus, J.J. & Relyea, Harold. (1976). "A Policy Assessment of the Privacy Act of 1974". *The American University Law Review*, 25(3).

Haque, M.S. (2008). "Global Rise of Neoliberal State and its Impact on Citizenship: Experiences in Developing Nations". *Asian Journal of Social Science*, 36: 11–34.

Hood, Christopher. (2010). "Accountability and Transparency: Siamese Twins, Matching Parts, Awkward Couple?" *West European Politics*, 33(5): 989–1009.

Huque, S.H. (1994). "Public Administration in India: Evolution, Change, and Reform". *Asian Journal of Public Administration*, 16(2): 249–259.

Huque, A.S. (2001). "Governance and Public Management: The South Asian Context". *International Journal of Public Administration*, 24(12): 1289–1297.

Jain, R.B. (2001)."Towards Good Governance: A Half Century of India's Administrative Development". *International Journal of Public Administration*, 24(12): 1299–1334.

Jayal, N.G. (2008). "New Directions in Theorising Social Accountability". *IDS Bulletin*, Institute of Development Studies, 38(6): 105–110.

Jenkins, J. Craig. (1983). "Resource Mobilization Theory and the Study of Social Movements". *Annual Review of Sociology*, 9: 527–553.

Jenkins, R. (2004). "Introduction". *India Review*, 3(4): 257–268.

Jenkins, R. (2006). "Democracy, Development and India's Struggle Against Corruption". *Public Policy Research*, 13(3): 147–155.

Jenkins, R. (2007). "Civil Society Versus Corruption". *Journal of Democracy*, 18(2): 55–69.

Jenkins, Rob & Anne, Marie Goetz. (1999). "Accounts and Accountability: Theoretical Implications of the Right-to-Information Movement in India". *Third World Quarterly*, 20(3): 603–622.

Joseph, K.P. (1987)."Public Accountability and Audit in India". *Economic and Political Weekly*, 22(22): M67–M75.

Khera, Reetika. (2005). "Bringing Grassroots Democracy back to life, MKSS campaign in *Rajasthan*". *Economic and Political Weekly,* February 19.

Kulkarni, Ashwini. (2008). "Governance and the Right to Information in Maharashtra". *Economic and Political Weekly*, 43(35): 15–17.

Lamble, S. (2003). "United States FoI laws are a Poor Model for Statutes in Other Nations". *Freedom of Information Review*, (106): 51–55.

Maloney, Arthur. (1979). The Ombudsman Idea, United States: Senate, Hearings Before the Sub-Committee on Administrative Practice and Procedure of the Committee on the Judiciary: Oversight of the Freedom of Information Act. *University of British Columbia Review,* Vol. 13.

Mc Clean, Tom. (2010). "Who Pays the Piper? The Political Economy of Freedom of Information". *Government Information Quarterly*, 27: 392–400.

Mcmillan, John. (1977). "Freedom of Information in Australia: Issue closed". *Federal Law Review,* 8(4): 379–434.

McMillan, John. (1977). "Making Government Accountable: A Comparative Analysis of Freedom of Information Statutes". *New Zealand law Journal*, 1: 248–256.

Mikecz, Robert. (2012). "Interviewing Elites: Addressing Methodological Issues". *Qualitative Inquiry*, 18(6): 482–493.

Mulgan, Richard. (2000). "'Accountability': An Ever Expanding Concept". *Public Administration*, 78(3): 555–573.

Niranjan, Oulac. (2005). "Right to Information and the Road to Heaven". *Economic and Political Weekly*, 40(47): 4870–4872.

Noorani, A.G. (1982). "The Right to Know". *Economic and Political Weekly*, 17(46–47): 1859–1860.
Noorani, A.G. (1985). "Ban on Information". *Economic and Political Weekly*, 20(34): 1416.
Noorani, A.G. (1986). "Right to Know or Freedom of Information". *Economic and Political Weekly*, 21(31): 1337.
Noorani, A.G. (1996). "The Press Council's Bill on Right to Information". *Economic and Political Weekly*, 31(51): 3283.
Noorani, A.G. (1998). "Law on Right to Information". *Economic and Political Weekly*, 33(45): 2826.
Noorani, A.G. (2001). "Stifling the NGOs". *Economic and Political weekly*, 2731–2732.
Noronha, Frederick. (2001). "Perils of Knowing: Right to Information Act, 1997". *Economic and Political Weekly*, 36(32): 3021–3023.
O'Donnell, Guillermo. (1998). "Horizontal Accountability in New Democracies". *Journal of Democracy*, 9(3): 112–126.
O'Loughlin, M.G. (1990). "What is Bureaucratic Accountability and How Can We Measure it?" *Administration and Society*, 22(3): 275–302.
Olson, J.P. (2008). "The Ups and Downs of Bureaucratic Organization". *Annual Review of Political Science*, 11: 13–37.
Ostry, S. (1998). "China and the WTO: The Transparency Issue". *UCLA Journal of International Law and Foreign Affairs*, 1–22.
Pedersen, J.D. (1992). "State, Bureaucracy and Change in India". *Journal of Development Studies*, 28(4): 616–639.
Peters, B. Guy & Pierre, John. (1998). "Governance Without Government? Rethinking Public Administration". *Journal of Public Administration Research and Theory*, 8(2): 223–243.
Priya, Deepti. (1996). "People's Knowledge, People's Power: Campaign for Citizens' Right to Information". *Economic and Political Weekly*, 31(2–3): 83–85.
Relyea, H. (1977). "The Freedom of Information Act: Its Evolution and Operational Status", *Journalism Quarterly*, 54(3): 538–544.
Roberts, A. (2010). "A Great and Revolutionary Law? The First Four Years of India's Right to Information Act". *Public Administration Review*, 70(6): 925–933.
Romzek, Barbara S., & Dubnick, Melvin J. (1987). "Accountability in the Public Sector: Lessons from the Challenger Tragedy". *Public Administration Review*, 47(3): 227–238.
Roy, Aruna & Dey, Nikhil (2002). "Fighting for the Right to Know in India". *Development Dialogue*, 1: 77–90.
Roy, Bunker. (1996). "Right to Information: Profile of a Grass Roots Struggle". *Economic and Political Weekly*, 31(19): 1120–1121.
Roy, Bunker. (1997a). "Transparency in the Voluntary Sector: A First Step". *Economic and Political Weekly*, 32(48): 3055–3056.
Roy, Bunker. (1997b). "Where Does All the Money Go? People's Struggle for Information". *Economic and Political Weekly*, 32(28): 1688–1689.

Roy, Jaytilak Guha. (2006), "Administrative Reform Initiatives for Excellence in Public Services", *Indian Journal of Public Administration*, Special Number on Excellence in Public Service, LII (3) July-September.

Roy, Jaytilak Guha. (2007). "Second Administrative Reforms Commission on Right to Information: Critical Review". *Indian Journal of Public Administration*, 53(3): 558–570.

Roy, Peled & Yoram, Rabin. (2011). "The Constitutional Right to Information". *Columbia Human Rights Law Review*, 42(2): 357–401.

Santiso, Carlos. (2001). "Good Governance and Aid Effectiveness: The World Bank and Conditionality". *The Georgetown Public Policy Review*, 7(1): 1–22.

Saxena, N.C. (2010). "The IAS Officer - Predator or Victim?" *Commonwealth & Comparative Politics*, 48(4): 445–456.

Saxena, Prabodh. (2009). "Public Authority and the RTI". *Economic and Political Weekly*, 44(16): 13–16.

Shah, Ghanshyam. (2011). "Social Movements in India". *Economic and Political Weekly*, 46(21): 33–35.

Sharma, Pradeep. (2004). "Civil Society and Right to Information: A Perspective on India's Experience". Governance Centre, UNDP.

Singh, Kavaljit. (1990). "Peoples' Struggle for Information" (Letter to the Editor), *Economic and Political Weekly*, March 24, 578.

Varshney, Ashutosh. (2000). "Is India Becoming More Democratic?" *Journal of Asian Studies*, 59(1): 3–25.

Venkatesan, V. (2002). "The Voter's Right to Know". *Frontline*, 19(12): 8–21.

Wagle, S.S. (2003). "Quiet Burial of Right to *Information*". *Economic and Political Weekly,* 2017–2019.

Webb, M. (2010). "Success Stories: Rhetoric, Authenticity, and the Right to Information Movement in North India". *Contemporary South Asia*, 18(3): 293–304.

Weiss, Thomas G. (2000). "Governance, Good Governance and Global Governance: Conceptual and Actual Challenges". *Third World Quarterly*, 21(5): 795–814.

Welch, E.W. & W. Wong. (2001). "Effects of Global Pressures on Public Bureaucracy: Modeling a New Theoretical Framework". *Administration & Society*, 33(4): 371–402.

Wennergren, B. (1970). "Civic Information- Administrative Publicity". *International Review of Administrative Science*, 36(3): 243–250.

Whitton, J.B. (1949). "The United Nations Conference on Freedom of Information and the Movement against International Propaganda". *The American Journal of International Law*, 43: 73–87.

Wolfe, R. (2003). "Regulatory Transparency, Developing Countries and the WTO". *World Trade Review*, 2(2): 157–182.

Wood, E.M. (1990). "The Uses and Abuses of 'Civil Society'". *The Socialist Register*, 26: 60–84.

Woods, Ngaire. (2000). "The Challenge of Good Governance for the IMF and the World Bank Themselves". *World Development*, 28(5): 823–841.

GOVERNMENT DOCUMENTS AND REPORTS

Accessing Information in South Asia (1999), A Conference Report, CHRI, July 5–7, Article 19, Freedom of Expression Manual, Article 19- www.articlel9.org

Article 19, Centre for Policy Alternatives, Commonwealth Human Rights Initiative and Human Rights Commission of Pakistan (2001), "Global Trends on the Right to Information: A Survey of South Asia", Article 19, CHRI, CPA and HRCP, London, Colombo, New Delhi and Lahore. 316.

Australian Law Reform Commission (1995), Open Government: A Review of the Federal freedom of Information 1982, Report 77.

Canada, Task Force on Government Information, To Know and Be Known: The Report of the Task Force on Government Information, Volume IIOttawa. Queen's Printer, 1969.

Canada Standing Committee (1974), Report of the Standing Senate Committee on National Finance on Information Canada, Queen's Printer.

Canadian Information Commissioner's Report (2000), Report-1.

Central Information Commission (2006), *Annual Report 2005-06*, New Delhi: Ministry of Personnel, Public Grievances and Pensions.

Centre for Policy Research (1990), "Report of the Workshop on Freedom of Information and Official Secrecy held at the Centre for Policy Research, New Delhi on March 21–22, 1990" Centre for Policy Research, New Delhi.

Commonwealth Human Rights Initiative (2004), "Detailed Analysis of the Indian Right to Information Bill 2004 & Recommendations for Amendments", Commonwealth Human Rights Initiative, New Delhi.

Commonwealth Human Rights Initiative (2012), "A Rapid Study of Information Commissions Established Under the Right to Information Laws in India", Commonwealth Human Rights Initiative, New Delhi.

Global Corruption Report 2003: Special Focus on Access to Information, *Transparency International,* www.globalcorruptionreport.org

Government of India (1961), "Complete Transaction of Business Rules up to Amendment Series No. 62", Cabinet Secretariat, New Delhi.

Government of India (1997), "Report of the Working Group on Right to Information and Promotion of Open and Transparent Government", New Delhi: Ministry of Personnel, Public Grievances and Pensions.

Government of India (1997), "Right to Information Bill, 1997 (Press Council - NIRD Bill of 1997)", Hyderabad: National Institute of Rural Development.

Government of India (2005), "Right to Information Act 2005", *The Gazette of India, Extraordinary*, Part II, Section 1, No. 25, June 21, 2005.

Government of India (2006), "Right to Information: Master Key to Good Governance", First report of the Second Administrative Reforms Commission, New Delhi: Second Administrative Reforms Commission.

Government of India (2010), "Civil Services Survey - A Report", New Delhi: Ministry of Personnel, Public Grievances and Pensions, Department of Administrative Reforms & Public Grievances.

Government of India (2011), *Handbook on writing Cabinet notes*, New Delhi: Cabinet Secretariat.

Lal Bahadur Shastri National Academy of Administration (1995), "Right to Information: A preliminary set of readings", Workshop on Right to Information, 7th and 8th October 1995, Mussoorie: Lal Bahadur Shastri National Academy of Administration.

Lal Bahadur Shastri National Academy of Administration (2011), "Profile of the Officer Trainees of the 86th Foundation Course", Mussoorie: Lal Bahadur Shastri National Academy of Administration.

Lok Sabha Secretariat (1989), "Constituent Assembly Debates", Vol. VII (4 Nov. 1948– 8 Jan. 1949), Reprint, New Delhi: Lok Sabha Secretariat.

Lok Sabha Secretariat (2009), "Demarcation of Responsibilities in Government of India", New Delhi: Lok Sabha Secretariat.

Mazdoor Kisan Shakti Sangathan (2001), "Dossier on Right to Information", Developing Source Material on Human Rights Education Series, Karnataka Women's Information and Resource Centre, Bangalore.

Mendel, T. (2004), "Parliament and Access to Information: Working for Transparent Governance", Conclusions of a Commonwealth Parliamentary Association - World Bank Institute Study Group on Access to Information, held in partnership with the Parliament of Ghana, 5–9 July,World Bank Institute, Washington, DC.

Price water house Coopers (2009), "Final Report: Understanding the "Key Issues and Constraints" in implementing the RTI Act", Report Commissioned by the Department of Personnel and Training, Ministry of Personnel, Public Grievances and Pensions, Government of India, New Delhi.

Rajya Sabha Secretariat (2001), "Seventy Eighth Report on Freedom of Information Bill, 2000 (Presented to the Rajya Sabha on 25 July, 2001)", Department Related Parliamentary Standing Committee on Home Affairs, New Delhi: Parliament of India, Rajya Sabha Secretariat.

Rajya Sabha Secretariat (2005), "Third Report on the Right to Information Bill, 2004 (Presented to the Rajya Sabha on 21 March, 2005)", Department Related Parliamentary Standing Committee on Personnel, Public Grievances, Law and Justice, New Delhi: Parliament of India, Rajya Sabha Secretariat.

RTI Assessment & Analysis Group (RAAG) and National Campaign for People's Right to Information (NCPRI) (2009), "Safeguarding the Right to Information: Report of the People's RTI Assessment 2008: Revised Executive Summary & Draft Agenda for Action", RAAG and NCPRI, New Delhi.

Second Administrative Reforms Commission (2006), First Report on Right to Information, Master Key to good governance, Government of India.

Shankari, Dabashish. (2000), Notes on Freedom of Information Legislation in Different Countries, Commonwealth Human Rights Initiative, New Delhi.

Smiley, D.V. (1978), The Freedom of Information Issue: A Political Analysis. Research Publication prepared for the Commission on Freedom of Information and Individual Privacy, The Commission, Toronto.

Transparency International. (2003), "Global Corruption Report 2003: Special Focus on Access to Information", Transparency International, http://gcr.netscript.kunde .sserv.de/download, *Transparency,* Volume 3, No.l,

UNDP. (2004), Promoting Right to Information Legislation- Practice Guidance Note, UNDP Publication.

United Nations Development Programme (2004), "Right to Information: Practical Guidance Note", Bureau for Development Policy, Democratic Governance Group, Oslo Governance Centre (Oslo: UNDP).

Universal Declaration on Human Rights, http://www.un.org/Overview/rights.html

U.S. Department of Health, Education and Welfare (1979), Report of the Secretary's Advisory Committee on Automated Personal Data Systems: Records, Computers, and the Rights of Citizens 1973 (Official Records of the General Assembly, 209th meeting, p. 357).

U.S. Privacy Protection Study Commission: Personal Privacy in an Information Society (1977), Washington D.C.: Government Printing Office.

World Bank (2004), "Legislation on freedom of information: Trends and Standards", PEEM (Poverty Eradication and Economic Management) Notes Number 93, World Bank (2007), "Strengthening World Bank Group Engagement on Governance and Anti- Corruption" (Washington DC: The World Bank).

World Bank Institute and Inter American Investment Corporation (2007), "Companies and the Right to Access Public Information", Report of a Round table held on April 26, Buenos Aires, Argentina.

WORKING PAPERS

Access to Information in Developing Countries (1998) Working Paper by Robert Martin and Estelle Feldman, Transparency International

Baviskar, A. (2007), "Is knowledge power?: The Right to Information Campaign in India", Paper prepared for the project on Citizen Engagement and National Policy Change, Institute of Development Studies, Brighton.

Goetz, A.M. and R. Jenkins (2002), "Voice, Accountability and Human Development: The Emergence of a New Agenda", Occasional Paper, Background Paper for the Human Development Report 2002, Human Development Report Office, UNDP, New York

Kidambi, S. (2008), "Right to Know, Right to Live: Building a campaign for the right to information and Accountability", The Center for Victims of Torture, Minneapolis.

Luckham, R., Anne-Marie, Goetz. & Mary, Kaldor. (2000), "Democratic Institutions and Politics in Contexts of Inequality, Poverty and Conflict: A Conceptual Framework", Working Paper 104, Institute of Development Studies, Brighton.

Mazdoor Kisan Shakti Sangathan (2010), "Story of the MKSS: a process of peoples' political mobilisation for democratic rights", unpublished paper downloaded from the MKSS website.

Mishra, Neelabh. (2003), "People's Right to Information Movement: Lessons from Rajasthan", Discussion Paper Series - 4, Human Development Resource Centre, UNDP, New Delhi

Newell, P. & S. Bellour. (2002), "Mapping Accountability: Origins, Contexts and Implications for Development", IDS Working Paper 168, Institute of Development Studies, Brighton.

Puddephatt, A. (2009), "Exploring the Role of Civil Society in the Formulation and Adoption of Access to Information Laws: The Cases of Bulgaria, India, Mexico, South Africa, and the United Kingdom", Access to Information Working Paper Series, World Bank Institute, Washington, DC.

Rodan, G. (2004), "Neoliberalism and Transparency: Political Versus Economic Liberalism", Working Paper No. 112, Asia Research Centre, Murdoch University, Perth.

World Bank Research Working Paper (2003), Do More Transparent Governments Govern Better: better information flows means better governance, World Bank, Washington, DC, No- 3077.

CONFERENCE PAPERS

Alexander, J.M. (2003), "Inequality, Poverty and Affirmative Action: Contemporary Trends in India", Paper prepared for the WIDER conference on "Inequality, Poverty and Human Well-being", 30–31 May 2003, United Nations University, Helsinki, Finland.

Mander, Harsh and Abha Joshi (1999), "The Movement for Right to Information in India: People's Power for the Control of Corruption", Paper presented at the conference on Pan Commonwealth Advocacy, Harare.

Mazdoor Kisan Shakti Sangathan (2005), "The Problem", in "Speaking Truth to Power: A Symposium on People's Right to Information", *Seminar*, 551.

Yilmaz, Bulent . (1998), "The right to information: is it possible for developing countries?", Paper presented at Amsterdam, *64th IFLA General Conference,* Netherlands, August 16–21, 1998, www.ifla.org.

NEWSPAPER ARTICLES AND EDITORIALS

Article 19, Centre for Policy Alternatives, Commonwealth Human Rights Initiative and Human Rights Commission of Pakistan (2001), "Global Trends on the Right to Information: A Survey of South Asia", Article 19, CHRI, CPA and HRCP, London, Colombo, New Delhi and Lahore. 316 http://www.humanrights initiative.org/Basu, Moushumi. (2005), "Secrecy and Governance", *The Hindu, March* 30.

Bhaduri, Amit. (2005), "On Improving the Quality of democracy", *The Hindu,* March 22.

Central Information Commission (2006), *Annual Report 2005–06*, New Delhi: Ministry of Personnel, Public Grievances and Pensions. http://www.rti.gov.in , http://www.article19.org/

Chatteijee, Mohua.(2001),"Village books the conupt by asking why" Times *of India,* April 8.

Chauhan, Chetan. (2004), "Babus likes to keep their secrets from you" *Hindustan Times* February 25.

Editorials. (2005), "Accountability and the Right to Information", *The Hindu,* May 14.

Kumar, Siddhartha. (2002), "Little enthusiasm for Right to Information", *Statesman,* May 6.

RTI Cell, Secretariat Departments, Heads of Departments and Other PAs, 2019 http://www.homeodisha.gov.in/

Section 27 of the RTI Act (No.22 of 2005) Right to Information Rules 2005 published by Odisha Information Commission. http://www.orissasoochanacommission.nic .in/

Sharma, Kalpana. (2002), "Right to Information will check corruption" *The Hindu,* February 24.

The computerization and maintenance of all records remaining under administration control connected with Central Monitoring Mechanism of the Nodal Departments report, 2019, http://www.odisha.gov.in/

Transparency International. (2003), "Global Corruption Report 2003: Special Focus on Access to Information", Transparency International, http:/ I gcr.netscript.kunde .sserv .de/ download *Transparency,* Volume 3, No.l, http://www.transparency.org/

Various Clauses of Right to Information Rules 2005 published by Odisha Information Commission, Government Press, Cuttack , http://www.rtiindia.info/

Venugopal, Ayswaria. (2001), "Babus query: Is there a Right to Information Act" *The Indian* Express, December 30.

Index

About the Author

Dr. Bibhuti Bhusan Nayak is a political scientist and former ICSSR Doctoral Fellow at Department of Public Administration, Utkal University, Odisha, India. He completed his MA from Utkal University, MPhil from Sambalpur University, and PhD from Utkal University, Odisha, India, in 2021. He is a Fellow of Royal Asiatic Society, Great Britain and Ireland. He is currently working as a visiting faculty in the Department of Governance and Public Affairs, XIM University, Bhubaneswar, Odisha. He also teaches at the PG Department of Public Administration, Utkal University, Odisha, India, from 2016 to 2018. He has been involved in teaching for the last six years and attended several national and international conferences. He has contributed many articles in national and international journals and also contributed many book chapters for edited books. He is associated with many national as well as international organizations. He is a Life Member of World Association for Sustainable Development (WASAD), UK; Life Member of Global Association for Humanities and Social Science Research (GAHSSR), Malaysia; and Life Member of Association for Development of Teaching Education and Learning (ADTEL), Malaysia. His research interest consists of four closely interrelated and mutually guiding programs: (1) Right to Information and Digital Divide, (2) Development Administration in Odisha, (3) Class Dimension of Information Society in India, and (4) Transparency and Accountability in Governance in Odisha. The regional focus of his research is on the impacts of crisis and Right to Information Act on social, cultural, and economic transition of rural communities, gender relations, and citizenship in South Asia, India, and Odisha.

www.ingramcontent.com/pod-product-compliance
Ingram Content Group UK Ltd.
Pitfield, Milton Keynes, MK11 3LW, UK
UKHW040857081026
15587UKWH00016B/752

9 781666 925647